the *Wisdom* *of* Daughters

Two Decades
of the Voice
of Christian
Feminism

D1372134

edite[...] [...]dhaas

Press, Inc.

Published by Innisfree Press, Inc.
136 Roumfort Road
Philadelphia, PA 19119-1632
Visit our website at www.InnisfreePress.com.

Cover art and book design by Kari Sandhaas.

Material in this work was previously published in *Daughters of Sarah* magazine.
Every attempt has been made to locate each of the original authors and artists from the twenty-one-year span of this publication to give acknowledgment and update biographical data. Innisfree Press welcomes any additional information about any author so that appropriate credit may be given in future editions.

Library of Congress Cataloging-in-Publication Data
The wisdom of daughters: two decades of the voice of Christian feminism /
edited by Reta Halteman Finger and Kari Sandhaas.
p. cm.
Includes bibliographical references and index.
ISBN 1-880913-47-X
1. Christian women—Religious life. 2. Feminism—Religious aspects—Christianity.
I. Finger, Reta Halteman, date. II. Sandhaas, Kari, date.
BV4527.W565 2001
270'.082—dc21
2001039404

Where not specifically cited, all biblical references are from the *New Revised Standard Version (NRSV)*. Copyright © 1989 by the Division of Christian Education of the National Council of the Churches of Christ in the U.S.A. Used by permission. All rights reserved. Other biblical references, when known, are cited within the articles.

Abbreviations used for Bible translations:
JB—Jerusalem Bible
KJV—King James Version
LB—Living Bible
NJB—New Jerusalem Bible
NLT—New Living Translation
NRSV—New Revised Standard Version
REB—Revised English Bible
RSV—Revised Standard Version

This book is dedicated to all of *Daughters of Sarah's* readers and contributors who made the magazine's twenty-one years of existence possible. We honor your efforts to bring the gospel of equality and justice to all women, Christian and non-Christian alike.

Acknowledgments

The authors extend their gratitude and fond appreciation to Juanita Wright Potter to whom this book's original conception and inspiration is owed. We are indebted to her for ongoing assistance with production and editing details, including sleuthing efforts to locate over one hundred original *Daughters'* authors. We also thank Annette Bourland Huizenga, Sue Horner, and Juanita for writing three of the chapter introductions as well as for their invaluable advice and support. Thanks also goes to Cathleen Hockman-Wert, a *Daughters of Sarah* reader, who assembled a comprehensive list of *Daughters'* articles and poetry, which was immensely helpful in our initial planning stages.

We wish to acknowledge the faculty services at Messiah College in Grantham, Pennsylvania, for OCR scanning of the articles from the original magazines; and Marcia Broucek, Innisfree Press publisher, for her editorial advice and guidance.

Most of all, we wish to recognize and honor the many, many women who dared to integrate their feminism with their faith. It was their hard work, dedication, passion, and creativity that breathed life into *Daughters of Sarah* and sustained it, through their work as volunteers, staff, editorial board members, officers, executive board members, and advisors. While this list may not be exhaustive, below are the names of those who worked with *Daughters* for six months or more during the twenty-one years, from 1975 to 1996, of the magazine's and collective's existence:

Mary Lou Aderman	Jan Erickson-Pearson	Isolde Stella Koenig	Kathleen Peterson
Mattie Roberts Allen	Cathi Falsani	Ilene Kopanke	Lainie Peterson
Andria Anderson	Helen Claire Ferguson	Carla Lang	Mary Jo Pfander
Elizabeth Anderson	Kristina Fielding	Irene Lee	Deborah Piper
Gwen Bagaas	Dawn Fullerton	Leslie Lewis	Marta Poling-Goldene
Sharon Baker-Johnson	Dulcie Gannett	Wanda Lollar	Juanita Wright Potter
Jeanne Baly	Carolyn Gifford	Jan Lugibihl	Nikki Rinderer
Barbara Baxter	Janie Halteman	Patricia Hughes Mangis	Gretchen Ritola
Diane Benson	Nancie Hamlett-Leisen	Barbara Marvin	Marlys Rudeen
Linda Bieze	Nancy Hardesty	Frances Mason	Kari Sandhaas
Bonnie Borgeson	Helen Harmelink	Jean McElhaney	Marilyn Sandin
Lori Boyce	Cindy Hawkinson	Debra Mellinger	Jane Stoller Schoff
Karen Bradley	S. Sue Horner	Mary Miller-Vikander	Penny Shell
Ann Bretz	Nancy McCann Hostetter	Janelle Mock	Lucile Sider
Pat Broughton	Karen Howe	Evelyn Montgomery	Judy Smith
Carol Brown	Sherron Hughes-Tremper	Mona Mord	Nancy R. Smith
Naomi Burnett	Annette Bourland Huizenga	Wendy Morris	Alice Strain
Lorrie Carlsona	Lori Hunsaker	Juanita Natolino	Beverly Swan
Barb Cederberg	Julie Hurlbut	Grace Nelson	Dawn Swartz
Carol Christian	Laura Johnston	Sue Nelson	Kris Tomasik
Marilyn Dahlberg	Gwen Jolliff	LoraBeth Norton	Anna Trimiew
Barb Daly	Beth Junker	Sheryl Lee Olsen	Sandra Volentine
Mary Dean	Marty Kerr	Doreen Olson	Sue Wente
Carol Deshich	Kay King	Beth Oswald	A. K. Willard
Claudia DeVries	Corinne Klassen	Cindy Pearson	Linda Williams
Marianne Dietrich	Janet Kling	Joan Pearson	Sherrie Zimbelman

Table of Contents

Editors' Introductions:

A Joyful Collective:
The Making of a Christian Feminist Magazine
Introduction by Reta Halteman Finger, editor

Reta Halteman Finger joined *Daughters of Sarah's* staff in 1976 and was editor of the magazine from 1979 to 1994.

I pushed my way through a feverish haze to my first *Daughters of Sarah* meeting in September, 1976. Having just moved cross-country to Chicago with two pre-schoolers, I was a perfect host to Midwestern viruses. But I knew I wanted and needed to meet the courageous women who had started their own newsletter to explore the questions that feminism raised about Christianity. I had no idea what a turning point that warm day would be for me. *Daughters of Sarah* would become a central focus of my life for the next eighteen years.

Only a few years earlier I had discovered the emerging feminist perspective and realized immediately that it addressed some of the deep needs of my soul. I voraciously read both secular and religious feminist materials and wrote a couple of articles for my denomination's magazine. So when I met Lucile Sider at the first conference of the Evangelical Women's Caucus and told her our family was soon moving to Chicago, she had invited me to join the *Daughters of Sarah*. I was honored and excited to be part of a venture that brought together my interests in feminism, writing, and the Bible.

In 1974, eight women at North Park Seminary in Chicago had begun meeting regularly to study together what the Bible really says to and about women. Lucile Sider Groh, first editor of *Daughters of Sarah*, describes what happened:

> Most feminists in the early seventies declared the church a key oppressor of women. We were not convinced. We searched scripture and history and were surprised by both. Leonard Swidler's monograph, *Jesus Was a Feminist,* was food for our souls. Some of the early writings of Virginia Mollenkott, Letha Scanzoni, and Nancy Hardesty convinced us we were being faithful to scripture. Later that first year, we were delighted when Nancy Hardesty herself joined our group.

> Just as surprising was our discovery of women leaders in our own evangelical tradition. Catherine Booth, Phoebe Palmer, and others felt like friends and protectors. We quoted them often when facing hostile audiences. Their cleverest repartees we knew by heart, for who could deride our grandmothers?
>
> With a year of study behind us, we were exhilarated...and wanted to spread the word. So in September 1974 we collected thirty dollars to pay postage and copying, and two months later we sent two hundred copies of our first issue to friends and acquaintances.
>
> The response delighted us. We received subscription money and praise. We found women all over the country struggling with the same question. They joined us and wanted to hear more. Personally, we experienced a new sense of power. We as women could...bring about change. We were not destined to publish in magazines controlled by men. We could produce and manage our own.
>
> —*Daughters of Sarah,* November/December 1984

By the time I moved to Chicago and joined this animated group of women, they had eleven hundred subscriptions and needed extra office help. I volunteered and also began working as book review editor, and later as copy editor. When Lucile moved on to graduate school in 1979, I became editor.

As our circulation expanded, so did our vision. Many women who participated in our monthly discussions and many subscribers were from mainline as well as evangelical churches. We realized that Roman Catholics, Lutherans, Methodists, Baptists, Pentecostals, Seventh Day Adventists, Mennonites, and Presbyterians, among others, had a long way to go toward accepting women into the full ministries of their churches.

None of us had any experience or training in publishing a magazine, but with a deep commitment to our mission, we learned on the job. In the early years, each issue of *Daughters of Sarah* featured three major articles: one on biblical exegesis, one on women's history, and a third on a social or relational topic such as inclusive language, housework, or gender politics. But in 1978 we devoted a whole year to power issues from many different perspectives: biblical, historical, and social. In 1982 we explored the broad topic of sexuality. After that, nearly every issue centered around one particular theme.

Two major theoretical principles guided our editorial committee. First, no topic was off limits if it related to Christian feminism. What mattered was how we dealt with it. Thus we tackled not only topics such as women in ministry or democracy within the family, but we dared to offend some of our readers by tangling with controversial issues such as the emergence of goddess worship, homosexuality, sexism in the Old Testament, or global prostitution.

Second, we were committed to a range of Christian feminist positions within a particular theme. As our membership and readership expanded, we moved beyond strictly evangelical language and theology, learning to appreciate feminist perspectives within other church traditions. New books on feminist biblical interpretation and theology prodded and shaped our thinking. Nevertheless, diverse as we were, there were limits to what we could accept on both conservative and liberal poles. Controversies within our editorial meetings would arise, particularly concerning such multifaceted topics as abortion, the Re-Imagining Conference, or Jesus' crucifixion (Was it divine child abuse?).

As editorial coordinator and perpetual student and lover of the Bible, I was most interested in biblical interpretive methods and how they were changing over time. At first our efforts focused on positive affirmations of women in the scriptures, as well as reinterpreting the difficult texts that seemed to limit women's roles in the church. Later, as we read Letty Russell, Phyllis Trible, Rosemary Radford Reuther, and Elisabeth Schüssler Fiorenza (among others), we were able to more critically evaluate our sacred texts and face the patriarchal attitudes stated or implied in some of them. The writings of Jewish feminists also gave us a better sense of how Jesus fit into his own Palestinian context.

The articles and poetry selected for this book are only a sampling of the hundreds published by *Daughters of Sarah* over the two decades of the magazine's existence. They have brought many of us both joy and insight along our journey. Some of them are among the very best we have ever published. But our choices for this volume were painful and often arbitrary, for we could as easily have compiled another list of titles just as compelling as these. Some of the articles were chosen more for their historical value in highlighting the development of Christian feminism, but most remain quite applicable to people's lives in the twenty-first century.

The Daughters of Sarah were compelled to stop publication of their magazine in 1996 for financial reasons. Yet the real issues ran much deeper, for we had moved too far from an organic pattern where many dedicated volunteers worked together, to an organizational structure of individuals sitting in isolated positions. The little newsletter of the seventies that developed into the magazine of the eighties and early nineties had been created with very little money but with so much passion, commitment, and sacrifice on the part of hundreds of women. During the first years, everyone who came to the monthly meetings automatically became part of the editorial board that decided the content of the next issue. And every other month the Daughters would gather in the basement of Lucile Sider's home to collate, staple, code, and mail the new issue.

For years the collective center held, as we practiced non-hierarchical mutual submission to each other, learning to appreciate strengths in others that we did not have ourselves. But the collective was much larger even than the Chicago group, for it included all the writers and readers. We received many unsolicited manuscripts, many small (and a few larger) donations, and letters of encouragement—all of which reminded us of the larger community of women and men who had caught the spirit of biblical equality and were giving and receiving its joyful benefits.

In the most unexpected places I met women who said, "You may not know me, but I know you from *Daughters of Sarah."* When I was hired at Messiah College in 1995, I met several past subscribers, one of whom, a very successful scholar and professor of literature, said our magazine inspired her to push against her conservative background and go to graduate school. One of our most faithful Chicago members, Juanita Wright Potter, tells of meeting a woman in New Mexico just last fall "who immediately talked with me as if I were a long lost best friend when she found out I had been connected to *Daughters of Sarah*. She had written a couple of articles; she still feels connected, even though it has been fifteen to twenty years!" All of us who ever worked on the magazine have had similar experiences.

Today in many Christian circles, feminism is viewed either as passé or as a dirty word. Yet many gains have been made, and the very fact that women's roles are debated in conservative contexts testifies to the impact of feminism throughout the culture and the church at large. But these gains cannot be taken for granted, or they will slowly and imperceptibly be lost. Christian feminism must continue to challenge, prod, and disciple.

Snatches of some of the letters we received from subscribers after our announcement of closing hint at the continuing hunger and thirst for thoughtful Christian feminist reflection. And maybe, just maybe, *The Wisdom of Daughters* will inspire some women, somewhere, to resurrect a magazine for Christian feminists.

> I do not know of another publication that can fill the hole you will leave. But I must thank you for what I expect was a lot of struggle and hard work to keep *Daughters of Sarah* alive for twenty years. —*Annette Andrews*

This wonderful magazine has meant so much to me. I have felt such a bond of love with other women of all races, sexualities, creeds, hungers, beliefs, and sacrifices. It was a forerunner of honest communication, reaching the innermost spirit of the heart. —*Esther Leatherwood*

I will greatly miss your magazine. It always brought a different slant on current issues, and I thoroughly enjoyed each issue. Now I am delighted that I have kept every issue that has come into this house! Never mind the clutter! —*Martha Dougherty*

Daughters of Sarah was one of the few publications I receive that I always read cover to cover. The scholarship of the articles, combined with the passion of the various authors always gave me something to think about, as well as something to laugh or weep about. It's been a privilege to be part of your mission, and I feel closer to God as a result of sharing *Daughters* with you over the years. —*Lorraine E. Fox*

There is no way to thank you for your twenty years of rich, timely ministry. I have saved and savored every issue. I will miss your publication more than I can say. —*Josephe Marie Flynn, S.S.N.D.*

I celebrate all the creative, growth-enhancing, Spirit-filled issues you have produced. You have served a most needed role in helping many to seek wholeness in our lives in current issues of faith and community. —*Lois Fike Sherman*

I didn't like getting that letter about the ending of *Daughters of Sarah*. Many of us were well graced by its presence, its witness, its company. I teach a course on the Bible at Ohio University. *Daughters of Sarah* always constituted important ancillary readings for my students. They and I shall miss mightily the new issues, but the old ones will continue till time and use wears them out. —*Bill Kuhrz*

How sad. When you cease to publish, a beautiful and distinctive voice will no longer be heard. Since I discovered *Daughters of Sarah* I have never been bored. —*The Rev. Elaine M. Silverstrim*

———◆———

Hearing to Speech

Introduction by Kari Sandhaas, editor

Kari Sandhaas was *Daughters of Sarah's* art director, illustrator, and editorial board member from 1987 to 1994.

> "In an introduction to Faust, I remembered the writer/editor quoting Goethe as saying 'In the beginning was not the Word. In the beginning was the Act.' I blurted aloud, 'Ah' No! In the beginning was not the Word. In the beginning was the hearing. Suddenly the whole patriarchal interpretation of word and preaching reversed themselves for me."
>
> —Nelle Morton, *The Journey Is Home*; from her essay "Beloved Image," first written in 1977.

I have sifted these words of feminist theologian Nelle Morton time and again since I first read them in 1989, listening closely to their layers of meaning and "hearing" other women's words and experiences resonate within them. If there is any one lesson that the women's movement brought into crystal clarity, it is this lesson of "hearing to speech"—to empower one another by listening deeply and openly. From consciousness-raising groups to radical therapy sessions, to Bible studies and prayer groups, different groups of people have named this lesson in differing ways. But one thing seems certain: the first steps toward liberation of any oppressed group is that of an uncensored listening and identifying who we are and learning, often re-learning, to articulate that identity in a language that empowers us and liberates us from our oppression. Hearing, in this sense, can sift and recognize the differences and commonalities of our experiences, break through political and social structures, translate outdated meanings, and create a whole new way of being and interpreting the world.

The experience of the *Daughters of Sarah* was no different. In the various circles of membership, from Sunday night discussion groups to editorial board meetings to the extended circles of readers, we put into practice this very simple, yet practical tool of listening and speaking. As editorial board member Juanita Wright Potter wrote for the magazine's fifteenth anniversary: "*Daughters of Sarah* is a significant part of my church. With these women I'm learning to find my own voice, to listen to my own thoughts and dare to express them."

Eventually, we realized that women's experiences were both similar and very different. Tensions arise when differing opinions collide. But the wisdom of listening and the commitment to creating a magazine that provided an authentic forum for Christian feminist voices fueled us through many conflicts. Indeed, it guided us to openly engage conflicting opinions, even when such differences seemed widely irreconcilable. *Daughters'* reader Diann Doncaster wrote to us, "Thank you for the pleasure and inspiration I get from reading *Daughters of Sarah.* I don't always agree with everything, and sometimes squirm uncomfortably. Life really felt much safer before I began questioning my inferior place in creation. Growing hurts, but is less painful when others share the experiences. You have often helped." As I read her words, images of spiritual midwifery come to mind.

The editorial board was the locus of my own engagement with *Daughters of Sarah.* It was there we agreed to disagree, and yet we often found consensus. In my eight year tenure with the magazine, I learned to listen well with an open mind and heart to those who held opposing viewpoints. In this way *Daughters of Sarah* was, for me, a rare and valuable opportunity to put a passionate belief in equality and inclusivity to the test.

And listen, I did. I heard women awakening to their own strengths, talents, and dignity. As illustrator and art director, I sifted each article for images to honor, support, and elicit the meaning of each author's words. Word and image paired themselves together—reinforcing one another, that the author's words could be heard and remembered, etched in each reader's memory. As a Roman Catholic steeped in ritual, I experienced each issue's publication as a sacrament. A labor of love, like bread that is kneaded, baked, and shared, these articles, poems, and illustrations became an experience of community and the presence of grace in our midst.

None of us were professionals, the magazine was not slick or perfect. It was bumpy and uneven, with a home-spun quality years after it was solidified into a consistent bimonthly and then quarterly format. Looking back, I suspect this made it more accessible. Anyone could contribute. And hundreds did—in large and small ways: by word or image, by organizing and updating subscriber records, responding to letters, stuffing envelopes, searching for funds, proofreading, paste-up, and the myriad other tasks involved with keeping the magazine and the community alive and healthy.

Reta Finger and I are excited to offer this book to new and old readers alike—a sampling of insights gleaned from two decades of Christian feminists "hearing to speech."

— ◆ —

Why Am I a Feminist?

by Juanita Wright Potter

Daughters of Sarah, March/April 1985. Juanita Wright Potter lives and reads in Chicago. She served on *Daughters of Sarah's* editorial board from 1984 to 1992 as well as the executive board.

Why am I a feminist?
Because I am a woman
and because I enjoy being a woman
    as a result of the hard work of feminists before me.
Feminists of the past enabled me
    to get a good education,
    to vote,
    to have a voice in the assembly halls of my community,
        my state, my nation,
    to be able to work and earn my living,
    to no longer be considered as property,
    to know women who are scientists and artists,
        lawyers and doctors, diplomats and professors.
My grandmothers couldn't.

Why am I a feminist?
Because I join hands and work with women and men today who
dream of the day when women will be able
    to be paid equal pay for equal work,
    to be included in the Constitution of the United States
        (not just Amendment XIX),
    to be given an equal voice in our churches, our schools,
        and our homes,
    to no longer be expected to do all the serving,
        and only the serving,
    to be allowed to follow God's call,
        even when that call is to speak, to teach, to lead.

Why am I a feminist?

Because I join with women and men of the past, of today, and of
the future who dream of the day when all people will be able
to live lives free from poverty
free from violence
free from hatred
free from despair and fear
to know what it is like to live
with peace and compassion
instead of war and domination.
with love and joy
instead of anger and dismay.

I have a full, happy life.

But the majority of people in the world do not.

I am a Christian feminist because I want to keep passing on
the rich, bountiful gifts that have been given to me
by God and by those who have faithfully lived out the
Good News.

I am a Christian feminist because the organized church
has carelessly thrust women
into a soul-bending, spirit-crushing, ungodly mold
that makes it nigh impossible
to dream the dreams and see the visions
that God has for us all.

I dream and work for the day
when saying that I'm a Christian
will say it all.

But until then,
I am a Christian feminist.

—◆—

The following logo and statements of purpose and identity eventually appeared in the front of each issue of Daughters of Sarah *magazine:*

The Magazine for Christian Feminists

THE PURPOSE OF *Daughters of Sarah* is to educate and sustain Christians to change and transform church and society on issues of mutuality, justice, and equality through publication of a provocative and personal Christian feminist magazine. Given that Christian feminists hold a wide range of viewpoints, we find it necessary to *agree to disagree* that we may create a true forum on faith and feminism. We invite you to enter this conversation, both as reader and as writer or artist, that the diversity of all our voices may be heard.

Who We Are

We are Christians.
We are also feminists.
Some say we cannot be both,
but for us
Christianity and feminism
are inseparable.

DAUGHTERS OF SARAH
    is our attempt
    to share the discoveries,
    struggles and growth
    of Christian feminist women.
We are committed to Scripture
    and we seek to find in it
    meaning for our lives.
We are rooted in a historical tradition
    of women who have served God
    in innumerable ways,
    and we seek guidance
    from their example.
We are convinced that Christianity
    is relevant in all areas
    of women's lives today.
We seek ways to act out our faith.

Why Sarah?

Sarah was a strong woman,
    equally called by God
    to a new land of promise.
We are Daughters of Sarah,
    not of the flesh,
    but of the promise,
    as Scripture says,
    co-heirs of God's grace and life.

Chapter 1

Women in Scripture

Feminist approaches to the Bible have varied over time and across religious backgrounds. The beginning of Christian feminism's resurgence in the 1960s and 70s primarily saw a search for women in the Bible. Who were they? What did they do? How were they treated, especially by Jesus and Paul? But Christian feminists also asked broader questions, asking how passages might be translated and interpreted more accurately or inclusively. Feminists also challenged inconsistent applications, such as the insistence that women be silent in the church (from 1 Corinthians 14) while Paul took for granted in 1 Corinthians 11 that women would be publicly praying and prophesying.

Phyllis Trible's work in the Old Testament and Elisabeth Schüssler Fiorenza's ground-breaking methodology of New Testament feminist biblical interpretation opened up new avenues for research and reflection. The Daughters joined other feminists in attacking patriarchal ideologies within the Bible, such as when the rape of Tamar in 2 Samuel 13 is seen more as an affront to the male members of her family than to her own self. We learned to read critically and between the lines, searching for the submerged presence of biblical women and bringing them into the foreground through the use of gender-inclusive language and proper exegesis.

Most of the material in this section shines a spotlight on biblical women, both their strength and wisdom as well as the injustices they endured within patriarchy. Other, more analytical or theological articles are scattered throughout this book.

—Introduction by Annette Bourland Huizenga, managing editor of *Daughters of Sarah* (as well as other supporting roles) from 1980 to 1989. Annette was a pastor at LaSalle Street Church in Chicago from 1989 to 1999, and is currently a doctoral student in Biblical Studies at the Divinity School of the University of Chicago.

— ◆ —

The following two poems were printed in *Daughters of Sarah*, July/August 1991. At that time Judith L. Roth was a freelance writer and editor. She also had been a youth minister and an editor for Gospel Light Publications.

From Eve's Journal (1)

by Judith L. Roth

It's the strangest thing

I could have sworn
   during the GARDEN SCANDAL
that Adam was right next to me keeping
his little mouth shut
   (amazing how much that mouth
   has G R O W N since then)

but the way he tells it now—

he was out watering the back forty
he never saw no serpent
he never knew that fruit was from
   THE TREE

he only ate cuz I looked so foxy
(he never knew what foxy was)
he was really in control

   until I tricked him

Really

It's the strangest thing

From Eve's Journal (2)

by Judith L. Roth

I'm getting just a bit nervous

Baby #1 was a boy
   I thought—well, that's the way
   things are going to be now
   just have to get used to it

Baby #2 was a boy
   I thought—just a minute
   maybe they get first dibs
   but girls should at least get second choice

   I picked out a feminine name
   for the next one
   ready to sway the odds

Baby #3 was a boy
   I said—Heck, I'll name him
   Seth, anyway
   serves him right

   Thought—was I such a goof
   there's only going to be
   one of me?

Hey, God, when he said, "Mother of all Living"
   I didn't think he meant it literally
   This poor body can only take so much....

Illustrations by Kari Sandhaas, published in *Daughters of Sarah*, July/August 1991.

Why Sarah?

by Nancy Hardesty and Letha Dawson Scanzoni

Daughters of Sarah, March 1975. Nancy Hardesty and Letha Dawson Scanzoni were both integral to the beginnings of *Daughters of Sarah* as well as the Evangelical and Ecumenical Women's Caucus. They co-wrote the tradition-breaking *All We're Meant To Be: Biblical Feminism for Today*, first published in 1974. Nancy is Professor of Religion at Clemson University. Letha is a professional writer specializing in religion and sociology.

Invariably members of the editorial committee for *Daughters of Sarah* are asked, "Is it the 'Sarah' who called Abraham lord?"

The questioners are familiar with 1 Peter 3:5-6 where wives of non-Christian husbands are encouraged to win them by Christ-like living rather than by preaching. Wives in that situation are reminded of Sarah who supposedly "obeyed Abraham, calling him lord."

From what we know of Sarah in the Old Testament, it is difficult to say where the writer got this idea, but the usual cross reference for this verse is listed as Genesis 18:12, where Sarah had just overheard God tell Abraham that they were to have a child. Knowing that her husband was nearly one hundred and she ninety, and, as *The Jerusalem Bible* puts it frankly, she "had ceased to have her monthly periods," Sarah laughed to herself thinking, "Now that I am past the age of child-bearing, and my husband is an old man, is pleasure to come my way again?" What pleasure she had in mind is not recorded, but the Lord read her mind and chided her for laughing.

Sarah is not here recorded as addressing Abraham as *lord* but as simply thinking about him. In most major translations other than the King James, the word "husband" rather than "lord" appears in the verse. The author of 1 Peter was perhaps looking at the Septuagint which rendered the Hebrew word whose root is *adon* into the Greek *kyrios*. The Greek word is the one usually translated "Lord" in the New Testament and applied to Jesus as God. It was a word used in other contemporary religions to designate their gods, and it was used in the imperial cult to speak of the emperor.

Likewise, in Hebrew and other Semitic languages, *adon* was used of temporal as well as supernatural rulers. It is a plural form in the Bible and refers to God as full of life and power. In a patriarchal tribal culture where wives were considered almost part of one's property, Sarah thought of her husband in the same terms as everyone else in her culture did.

Did she obey him? Some point to Genesis 12:10-20 and 20:1-18 where Abraham told the Egyptian Pharaoh and Abimelech the king of Gerar that Sarah was his sister. In both cases the men took her into their harems until God intervened. Some today argue that this means that a wife must submit to her husband's will even to the point of possible immorality (from which, it is hoped, God will save her).

Yet in terms of the narratives which we have, we often find Sarah, rather than Abraham, calling the shots in their relationship. It was she who suggested that he take Hagar and have a child by her (Genesis 16:2 *JB*). And so "Abram agreed to do what Sarah had said." (This arrangement was common in both Hurrian and Babylonian cultures and was considered a proper legal and moral way to beget an heir.)

However, once Ishmael was born, Sarah resented Hagar's understandable pride. Again Abraham acceded to Sarah's wishes: "Your slave-girl is at your disposal. Treat her as you think fit" (*JB*).

Thirteen years later, Sarah and Abraham finally had their own son. Again Sarah wanted to get rid of Hagar and Ishmael. This time Abraham was not quite so willing until God specifically commanded: "Grant Sarah all she asks of you, for it is through Isacc that your name will be carried on" (Genesis 21:12 *JB*).

Abraham was "husband" to many women and fathered many children. Genesis 25:1-6 tells us that he later married Keturah by whom he had six sons and that he also had sons by many concubines.

Abraham himself had laughed at God's promise and suggested that Ishmael was the child of promise. But God was adamant: "No, but Sarah your wife shall bear you a son whom you are to call Isaac.... I will establish my covenant with Isaac, whom Sarah will bear to you" (Genesis 17:19, 21 *JB*). Paul makes the same distinction in Romans 4:19 and 9:9, though perhaps he gives Abraham a bit too much credit.

The author of Hebrews 11 is a bit more careful. He (or she) gives Abraham credit for having faith enough to leave his homeland to follow God and to offer Isaac as a sacrifice at God's command. But Sarah gets credit for having the faith that God would make good the Promise.

We are the daughters of Sarah who judged as faithful God who had given her a promise. We are not, as Paul says, the children of the flesh, but of the Promise. All Jews, and spiritually all Christians, are not simply the children of Abraham, but specifically the children of Sarah.

We are the daughters of the Promise. May our faith be as Sarah's.

— ◆ —

Sarah

by Kathleen M. Henry

Daughters of Sarah, July/August 1991. At that time Kathleen M. Henry lived in Jamaica Plain, Massachusetts. She was and still is liturgist and Artistic Director of CREDO Liturgical Dance Company.

There once was Sarah
    her tomb-womb sunken
    the river, dry
Who laughed, no, giggled
(lightly, not hysterically)
When God said, "You shall bear."

Oh

She dried her eyes, then,
    when
Her laughter passed, and,
Catching a tear trickling
down
a
wrinkle
She planted it inside her being,
Ripe.
She believed she could change.
(Some things don't change,
some things won't.
Women do.)

—— ♦ ——

Lot Is My Father
(Genesis 19:1-11)

by Judith Roth

Daughters of Sarah, March/April 1990. At that time Judith Roth lived in Ventura, California, and was an assistant editor at Gospel Light Publications.

I was promised to a man
    (I don't remember now if he was beautiful)
but I was still pure
    an unused vessel

That night, when the men surrounded our house
    demanding to use our guests
Our father bargained with them
    and offered us instead

    (My man was out there, too...
    what did he think of this offering?
    Would he have used me
        with the others
    and then turned away forever?)

They went for my father instead
    (which seems fair)
but he was saved by his guests

Now I ask you
    If women are so weak
    why won't someone protect them?

    If women are so weak
    what would you call men...
        who give them up so easily?

—◆—

A Tent Full of Bedouin Women

by Rosemarie Anderson

Daughters of Sarah, Winter 1993. At that time Rosemarie Anderson was an Episcopal priest and Associate Professor of Psychology at the Institute of Transpersonal Psychology, Palo Alto, California.

Many times after a newsworthy event, I have read the morning paper and wondered who wrote the story and what were her or his political motives. Nowadays I do the same for biblical stories. What viewpoint dominates the narrative? What political motives were involved? How can I reconstruct—not just deconstruct—this story based on my own experience and knowledge of women's culture?

Take the story of Tamar and Judah in Genesis 38. As late twentieth-century feminists, we must tell the story as best we can from Tamar's point of view instead of the narrator's. We must retell it in ways that reflect our knowledge of the anthropology of women's culture, especially women's culture in the tribal societies of ancient Palestine.

Tamar the Canaanite was a tribal woman, a Bedouin in modern terms; and she lived in a society filled with nomadic peoples and contending tribal leaders. Judah was one such leader and Tamar's marriage to his son must have elevated the status of her entire tribe, who were likely all interrelated.

But the tribe's good fortune doesn't hold. The text tells us that after Judah's oldest son, Er, Tamar's first husband, dies childless, Judah gives Tamar his second son, Onan, to raise up offspring for Er. (In levirate marriage, the first baby legally belongs to the dead brother.) Onan is not interested in producing a son that would not be considered his, so he practices the oldest form of birth control, spilling his seed on the ground. For his selfish efforts, Yahweh gets rid of Onan as well. Judah, afraid he'll lose his third son, sends Tamar back to her tribe to wait until the third son grows up.

The text says nothing about Tamar's suspicions of being cast into eternal limbo, or her family's loss of face at having a daughter returned to them with her virginity gone and no husband and child to show for it. Instead, the narrative records the death of Judah's wife, making him an eligible widower, and after his time of mourning, sends him to shear sheep near to the territory where Tamar's family lives. Knowing this, Tamar assumes the role of a prostitute, seduces Judah, keeps his signet and staff to prove Judah's identity, and conceives twin sons.

Naively, Genesis 38 suggests that Tamar acted alone in her efforts to gain her rights. Anthropology tells us, however, that people in a small tribal Bedouin village almost never act alone. Tribal villagers, especially women, act in groups. Individual acts are part of an orchestration of village life that is almost unimaginable to Americans or Europeans today. We must assume that all those who had a stake in Tamar's rightful return to the house of Judah were motivated to preserve their power and status.

Is it possible that Tamar, unaided, shed her widow's garb in a Bedouin household full of women and children and the constant comings and goings of an extended family? Is it possible that Tamar, unaided, proceeded through her small village clothed as a harlot? Did no one but Judah and Hirah the Adullamite notice her at the crossroads (38:12-15)? And where did Tamar—inexperienced in harlotry—take her client Judah?

My speculation assumes the collaboration of many. Tamar's extended family, perhaps her entire village, had experienced humiliation by Judah having sent Tamar back to her home. The whole village—or at least all the women—must have aided and abetted Tamar's deception of Judah. Later, when Judah's friend Hirah the Adullamite returned with a kid in payment so Judah could redeem his signet and staff, he asked the townspeople where she was. "No prostitute has been here," they replied. Did all the people lie? Perhaps yes, perhaps no. Knowing what we do about Bedouin society, we cannot answer that question. Rather, we should ask another: what did the villagers have to gain from Tamar's actions?

Asking new questions of this text demands that we not play by the old rules of scholarship, so often used against the already disempowered. In this case, feminist theory—insisting on retelling the story from a female perspective—combines with anthropological insights into women's behavior in a tribal culture. The reader can now imagine a small sub-culture comprised of a number of Bedouin women who take it upon themselves to cleverly manipulate the patriarchal rules of levirate marriage and patrilineal descent to get what they want—the restoration of the dignity of their village and tribe. When it becomes clear that the story is not about one unusual woman acting alone, but about a group of ordinary women, such an interpretation can help undercut the patriarchal construct of the token woman who doesn't behave like typical women. In the story of Tamar and Judah, feminist theory and anthropology unearth a women's culture necessary to the story's outcome, but which was entirely hidden in the text and in its traditional interpretations.

— ◆ —

Wise Up, O Men of God*

by Pat Adams Furlong

Daughters of Sarah, Winter 1992. At that time Pat Adams Furlong was a writer and poet living in Knoxville, Tennessee.

While bathing, I think of Bathsheba
by lamplight, how she tends her body,
caresses supple curves, gentle angles,
takes her moonbath demurely within her private courtyard,
not knowing a royal voyeur longs to summon her to his bed.

King of the Mountain observes her luminous body
from his palace on the city's heights.
He is home for a season, still seeking tasty booty,
too much time on his hands.

I've grown weary of church talk, how Bathsheba tempted David.
Don't these patriarchs know that David was king, that any
woman had to come to his court when commanded?
I'm weary of bad press, of Eve's blame, too—
her simple sharing of an apple as any good wife would do.

---

*This poem's title is derived from the hymn, "Rise Up, O Men of God."

——◆——

The Last Days of Jephthah's Daughter

by J'Laine Robnolt

Daughters of Sarah, Summer 1992. At that time J'Laine Robnolt was a well-published poet from Fayetteville, Arkansas. She also co-directed the Arkansas Writers in the Schools Program and was a volunteer advocate for Rape Crisis.

Once on the mountain
I was already dead. My friends plaited laurel
in my hair, oiled my limbs, and kissed each beautiful
scrape. They caught me in the thicket of their arms—
folds of their loose hair stuck to my wet cheeks,
their skin softer than anything I had known.
They did not know, my would-be women,
how their bodies confused my dreams of men,
the calloused hands and nose hair, that mysterious dark.
My girls had not felt their fathers' tears
slip across the delicate bones of their feet
as my father had wept until the dust ran to mud beneath my toes,
and I stood in silence, focusing on heat slicks in the distance.
The two sounds I remember—
the flap of hair ribbons in the sudden gust;
the rasp of his chin on my ankles.

Once on the mountain,
I saw the ten-fold of all things:
knifed shadows slicing the stems of day lilies,
the scars dug deep in the beetle-trekked leaf,
sun motes measuring air between the sky
and me. I had survived the enormous silence
when the world had stopped, a quaint desert tableau
of man knelt to statue. But I died then to everything,
to the cruelties in every beauty. I am telling you,
on the mountain I was dead. I died
two months before Jephthah took to altar
one pure thing. He gave a wild look
to a bramble as we passed. And I tell you,
there was no ram.

—◆—

Who is Huldah, What Is She?

by Emily Sampson

Daughters of Sarah, July/August 1985. At that time Emily Sampson was a lecturer in the Hebrew Scriptures for the Episcopal Diocese of San Diego. She received her Ph.D. in religion from Claremont Graduate University in 1992 and currently teaches at Cuyamaca College in El Cajon, California. She has written a book on Julia Smith, the only woman to translate the entire Bible from Hebrew and Greek, forthcoming from UT Press.

Have you ever gone to one of those parties where everyone talks but nobody listens? Have you ever wanted to throw something outrageous into the conversation such as, "I strangled my husband before coming here," just to see what would happen? I've invented my own version of this game that I play when I'm surrounded by clerics. I usually draw my material from the Hebrew Scriptures which is a rich source for improbable comments such as, "What do you think of the story of the golden hemmorhoids?" (There really is such a story in the New English Bible.) I also like to ask them about a little known woman named Huldah. But that's a more serious matter....

In the second book of Kings, chapter 22, we find the city of Jerusalem in the midst of a religious revival. The year is 621 B.C.E. and good King Josiah, a thorough-going Yahwist, has ordered that the temple be refurbished. In the midst of repairs a jar is found which contains a scroll (a situation duplicated millenia later with the Dead Sea scrolls found at Qumran). Reading the scroll, its finders say (freely translated), "Oh boy, no wonder we're in trouble, this is the law of God and we haven't been keeping it." Immediately the skeptics challenge them saying, "Hey, wait a minute, how do we know whether or not this is really God's law?" The scroll is taken to Huldah the prophetess, who is to determine whether or not it is authentic. She declares that it is and says (still translating freely), "Not only is this the law of God but ignorance of the law is no excuse. The kingdom is going to fall but, since Josiah is such a good man and has tried so hard to bring the people back to pure worship, this won't happen until after his death."

Now the first thing that strikes me about this story is that nobody bats an eyelash at taking the scroll to a woman for authentication. Her authority seems to be undisputed; there isn't even a hint of asking for a second opinion. When I first began working on my graduate degree in religion, professors, all male, often commented on the low status of women in Semitic society. This story makes me want to ask, "How come

Huldah had such clout if the women of the Bible were always such unlearned, down-trodden creatures?" Her authority is all the more striking if you examine the cast of characters more carefully. It is the high priest, Hilkiah, who first discovers the document. He takes it to Shaphan, a sort of prime minister, and they go together to the king. By the time that their rather Chicken-Licken, Ducky-Lucky procession gets to Huldah, it contains five of the most highly placed men of the kingdom. Huldah is no slouch in the social credentials category herself. Tradition makes her a relative of the prophet Jeremiah, her husband's family has court connections, and they live in an affluent heart of the city.

One day I happened to mention this story to a male Episcopal priest who was visiting. He not only was unaware of Huldah but dismissed her completely saying, "But that's such an unimportant story!" Back in those days I was more docile and I accepted his judgment without comment. But Huldah would not leave me, and I thought and re-thought about her story.

Scholars feel that the document that was brought to Huldah contained the core of the writing we know as the book of Deuteronomy. Every time a Jew declares, "Hear O Israel, the Lord our God, the Lord is One," she quotes Deuteronomy. Every time a Christian reads, "Thou shalt love the Lord, thy God, with all thy heart, with all thy soul, and with all thy strength," she may be thinking of Jesus, but Jesus was quoting Deuteronomy. The history of Israel from the days of Joshua to the return from Babylonian exile was recorded by scribes so infused with the theology of this book that they are known as Deuteronomic historians. Not important? From one point of view Huldah's authentication could be considered foundational!

Some scholars argue that the finding of the scroll was a put-up job. In my opinion that makes Huldah's decision even more important, not less. When you're trying to convince the public, you'd hardly cite an authority that they would be likely to reject! Jewish tradition says that the scroll was brought to Huldah rather than Jeremiah because her femininity gave her a gentler heart and she was less likely to excoriate the people. Whatever the reason, it should also be noted that this story is repeated in 2 Chronicles 34, which underlines the strength of the tradition.

Now that there are more women active in the field of biblical scholarship, stories of women in the Bible are being examined from a new perspective, and previously held assumptions about their role in society are being questioned. Huldah is a case in point. I give her to you as a role model. Let her take her rightful place with the other strong women of the Bible. She's waited in obscurity far too long.

That Yvette!

by Mary Cartledge-Hayes

Daughters of Sarah, November/December 1990. At that time Mary Cartledge-Hayes was a freelance writer from Spartanburg, South Carolina, who enjoyed melding the secular and sacred in women's lives. She was a frequent contributor to *Daughters of Sarah*. Now a United Methodist minister, her spiritual autobiography will be published by Crown Publishing in 2002.

Sit down and eat some of these pinto beans and let me tell you what that Yvette's gone and done this time.

No, she can't tell you herself. I sent her to her room, and I'm not letting her out except to go to the bathroom. I ain't ever going to let her out if she doesn't start telling me the truth.

Yes, thanks, I could use a cup of coffee to settle my nerves.

All right! I'll say it! The girl's pregnant. Oh, Lord, don't start crying yet. That ain't even the worst of it. She's lost her mind, too.

The father? If you ask me it's Anthony from the other end of the trailer park. He's been sniffing around here since New Year's Day. He's a mechanic down at the Ford place, and they tell me he's a good worker, but you couldn't prove it by me. All I know is he's got way too much energy left when he gets here in the evenings.

Yvette? She says he never laid a hand on her. I threatened to take a belt to her, and she didn't change her story....

Oh, Lord, you all right now? I never should have said it straight out like that when I knew you were getting ready to take a swig of coffee. I almost choked my own self when she told me.

I know, I know, she's crazy as a coot. And do you think she's ashamed? Not that girl. She's not crying, she's not pouting, she's not doing a thing I can see but sitting in that room listening.

She says she's trying to hear the angel. Said she already heard it once, and she doesn't want to miss it if it comes again.

"What'd it say?" I asked her.

"That God wants me to name the baby Immanuel," she told me.

Like that Emmanuel Lewis on TV? I asked her.

"No, Mama. The Immanuel that's Hebrew for 'God with us.'"

"Yvette, honey," I told her, "you don't know no Hebrew."

She just looked at me.

"You're going to break your daddy's heart," I told her. "What do you think he's going to say when I tell him you're pregnant, and you with no husband and only sixteen years old?"

"He'll be happy later on, when the baby gets grown." Then she started in on this long story about how this never would have happened if Mary'd said yes when she had the chance. I asked if that was Anthony's old girlfriend. She said no, that Mary was the first one God asked to carry this baby, and when Mary said no it took God awhile to get around to trying again.

I told her I'd wash her mouth out with soap if she kept talking that way, making God out to sound like a nineteen-year-old trying to get a girl to accept a cubic zirconia engagement ring, like God would give somebody a choice in a matter like this. No, siree, I told her, if God wanted something done he wouldn't ask, he'd tell. He'd never put up with this dibbling and dabbling and letting a girl make her own decision.

I know it's crazy. God's going to trust a holy baby to a kid who can't even remember to pick her clothes up off the floor of her room?

I know, I know, you've got to go. I didn't mean to keep you so long. I'm just so wrought up I don't know what to do. Imagine me being a grandma at my age and that girl acting like it's the most natural thing in the world. I tell you it just ain't right.

——◆——

Illustration on facing page by Zana, Jewels Graphics, published in *Daughters of Sarah*, November/December 1990.

What Child IS This?

by Mary Cartledge-Hayes

Daughters of Sarah, November/December 1984. At that time Mary Cartledge-Hayes was from Spartanburg, South Carolina and an active member of Trinity United Methodist Church. This short story evolved from research she did in preparing to teach a Sunday School class on women in the church. She now holds an M.Div. from Duke University and an M.F.A. in creative nonfiction from Goucher College.

When the angel Gabriel came to Mary, she quailed at sight of him. "Be not afraid," spoke the angel. "I am come from the Lord to deliver great tidings. Unto you will be born a child to bring light into the darkness. Generations will rise up and call your babe blessed: its name will live forevermore."

Mary was greatly troubled but placed her faith in the Lord. She and the angel spoke at length and then retired, the one to return to God, the other to find Joseph, her affianced.

Joseph heard the story told by Mary and was filled with wonder. He, a poor man, to share in the miracle of the birth of a savior.... With firm steps, he led Mary to the house of her parents.

"The Lord has spoken. Mary carries a child who will bring peace on earth."

The wedding feast was held with much rejoicing.

At length the time came for Mary to be delivered. She and Joseph journeyed to Bethlehem and found shelter there. In the night sky appeared a wondrous star, leading shepherds and wise men to the stable where the baby lay.

The first shepherd looked into the face of Joseph and was sorely afraid.

"What child is this whose birth causes the angels to proclaim from on high?"

Joseph spat upon the ground; a great trembling wracked his shoulders.

"Is this not Mary, your wife, gone to childbed? Does not the light of the world wait here, in the manger, for us?"

Joseph spat once more and dragged a hand through the beard upon his face. "No child of mine lies here," spoke he, "nor wife of mine." He strode forth and disappeared into the night.

The shepherds and wise men came together, asking, "What manner of man is this,

who can leave his wife, who can turn his back on the Lord and on our salvation?"

Greatly troubled, they approached Mary. Her face was still damp from childbirth: her eyes shone with the radiance of God's love.

The babe, wrapped in swaddling clothes, lay close at hand in a manger. Wise men and shepherds knelt in adoration. They placed gifts before the holy child. At last one wise man rose and offered his hand in thanksgiving to the mother. "Verily, I say unto you, this is the Son of God. Praise to him, and to you, who have entered into this miracle."

Mary brushed a tendril from her forehead with a weary hand and smiled. "All praise to God...but my child is not the son of God."

Consternation flew across their faces like clouds before the moon. "But the angel on high spoke to the shepherds; the star has led us here to you. Doubt you, woman, the messages of your God?"

"I doubt not," spoke Mary. "God is here with us, incarnate, but my child is not the son of God. She is the daughter of God, sent to cleanse us of our sins and lead us to the life everlasting."

In silence, the men withdrew to consider these words. Then they gathered their entourages and rode into the night, their mouths sealed against this blasphemy. The final shepherd to leave, with many a cautious glance over his shoulder, hurled a torch into the stable. The straw, long dry, kindled quickly.

The blazing star hung low over the stable; flames rose to embrace it. The beacon shone long into the night.

Then the world sank into darkness....

After many generations, God, in great wisdom, sent another child to the weary earth. This one's name would be Jesus. He, at least, would be permitted to speak.

———◆———

Going Back for Mary: A Protestant's Journey

by Sue Monk Kidd

Daughters of Sarah, Fall 1991. At that time Sue Monk Kidd wrote and spoke on spirituality, was author of the bestselling book, *God's Joyful Surprise*, and was a contributing editor of *Guideposts* magazine. This article was first published in *Anima*, No. 15.

In the Southern Baptist tradition which I inherited, Mary was not a paramount figure. If the Christmas story had not been read once a year in the Baptist churches I attended, it would have been easy to forget that Jesus had a mother.

Given the indifference toward her in my religious environment, it might be surprising that I had an experience with Mary at all. I encountered her at age twelve in what remains a vivid memory in my childhood. I was spending the night at the home of a Catholic family, and on the mantel in the guest bedroom was a porcelain statue of Mary. Standing upon a crescent moon, she was a mystery that called up an inexplicable rush of feeling. I experienced what I can only now name as the magnetic pull of the Eternal Feminine. In spontaneous adoration, I reached out and touched her, whispering the only words for her I knew: "Hail, Mary."

Later I questioned my veneration of the virgin. I felt as though I had eaten a forbidden fruit. I would not taste it again for a long while. It never occurred to me that my moment with Mary was a pull to the feminine side of the Divine, the side which gestates, nourishes, regenerates, and centers us in being and relatedness.

Mary has represented the archetypal pattern of the Eternal Feminine in varying degrees throughout church history. She has worn such titles as Mother of God, Compassionate Intercessor, Queen of Heaven, Lady all-holy, and Sovereign Mistress of the World.

Illustration by Kari Sandhaas, published in *Daughters of Sarah*, Fall 1991.

After the Reformation, Protestant churches stripped away such titles. An air of indifference grew up around Mary, and her image underwent a drastic revision. The emphasis was no longer on Mary's blessedness, but on her lowliness. The phrase, "Mary was just a woman," became a Baptist litany that prefaced most conversations about her. We imaged her as a humble, submissive virgin, the lowliest of handmaidens.

The Repressed Feminine

Historically and spiritually the feminine has been dormant and repressed within my own and similar Protestant traditions. Its alienation is multi-faceted, but the exile of Mary as a feminine archetype has played a significant part. Certainly it affected my own spiritual formation as I struggled to connect my womanhood and my Christianity.

I want to mention four ways in which the lack of a feminine figure of devotion and spirituality affected my Southern Baptist environment in general and me in particular.

First of all, the absence of a strong feminine archetype conspired with repressive forces which attempted to keep women stereotypically submissive. I was taught that in both church and home men held authority over women. My task was to submit. I tried, both as a good daughter of the church and later as a young wife. At times I felt like a coat rack upon which the church hung its projections of what a good Christian woman should be. I bent and folded my soul, trying to adapt to the patriarchy. Yet inside I kept asking, who am I that I cannot choose and initiate without masculine permission?

Diminishing the feminine in our gods renders a woman "hand-less," severed from the power to "handle" her own life. I once saw a drawing of the Madonna sketched in detail except for one thing. She had no hands. The omission struck me as symbolic. The wounded Mary seemed to depict the impotence of the feminine archetype. The picture spoke to me of the Baptist Mary.

One version of the fairy tale of the miller's daughter has been used by analyst Robert Johnson, as well as others, to illustrate the loss of the feminine. In the tale the miller promises to give the devil a pair of feminine hands in exchange for a water wheel that will bring the miller success. When the father asks his daughter for her hands, the good, docile daughter sacrifices them to him. She gives up her ability to "handle" herself and her life and becomes "the handless maiden."

The church has its share of handless maidens who have amputated their true selves and sacrificed them at the demand of a patriarchal religion. The question is whether handless maidenhood within the church, a wounded and diminished feminine, can be traced back to a wounded and diminished feminine archetype, to a handless madonna.

Handless women need a feminine archetype that mirrors the fullness of what it is to be authentically female. The ancient definition of the virgin as "one unto herself" was not part of the Baptist Mary. Yet the woman who is whole is balanced in both her masculine and feminine selves and handles her own life out of that balanced consciousness.

Secondly, the loss of the feminine had a strong impact upon the image of God and the kind of language that functioned in the church. Because there were so few sacred images of Mary that could mediate the divine feminine, we failed to develop a feminine side of God. God was boxed into Father and Son images. If we had allowed Mary to be a symbol pointing to God our Mother, if we had let her be a metaphor of Sophia-Wisdom, or a feminine personification of the Holy Spirit, perhaps we might have been less inclined to create a purely masculine God.

Because God, the Bible, the church, and many of the hymns were so thoroughly masculine, I gradually began to feel excluded from divine realities. God was always portrayed as the God of Abraham, never of Sarah. Without the feminine, our language subtly communicated to me that women were nonentities in the church, that we counted only as we related to men.

One of the few sermons I remember from my childhood was preached on Adam and Eve, the idea being that since Eve was created second and drawn out of a man's side, woman came to completion through man. It was a devastating notion to me as a girl. The formative years of my religious experience left me wondering whether I was an afterthought, an appendage that could find completion only through the masculine "rib."

Thirdly, our myopic vision of Mary also contributed to a repression of matter and sexuality. Where we impoverish the feminine, we impoverish the earth and the body. We split apart body and soul, spirit and flesh.

This dual image was cast on Mary. When she did gain our attention, it was as an untainted ideal of virginal purity from which the earthly had been excised and buried. She might have been lowly, but she was pure—a paragon of virtue whom we never seemed to picture as bulging with her pregnancy or nursing Jesus in the night. Even her impregnation conjured up images of a shaft of light spilling around her from heaven.

As C. G. Jung pointed out, what we will not deal with consciously will brew in the unconscious and turn on us in negative ways. With the dark, sensual aspects of Mary closeted away, they grew in the shadows and came to be projected onto women in the form of Eve-as-temptress, a creature to be condemned and controlled.

Finally, the absence of a feminine archetype made an impact upon the shape of Protestant spirituality. We tended to relate to God in linear ways, through theologizing propositions, intellect, and dogma. My overarching metaphor of God was as a stern, loving Father who had an agenda of shoulds and oughts.

I sought God through a blaze of religious dogma, through climbing the corporate church ladder, and chasing after religious achievements. My spirituality seemed imposed from without, rather than grown organically from within my own soul. I longed to know the ground of my own experience, the deep feminine ground of being and becoming.

Recovering the Feminine

In my early thirties, struggling with the patriarchy, I began to experience a religious burnout. While visiting a small Catholic oratory, I found myself in the church beside a statue of the Virgin Mary. Twenty years had passed since I was twelve and last stood before her. I pondered her this time without ambivalence. By now I had experienced the imbalance of a church and a spirituality that was almost entirely masculine-oriented. I was starting to feel like Celie in Alice Walker's *The Color Purple* (Harcourt Brace, 1982), who said, "When I found out that I thought God was white and a man, I lost interest."

That night I had the following dream: I am riding on a train filled with people. I notice through the window that we are approaching a slum area that has been quarantined. I see a rundown house and on the porch a weeping black woman. I turn to the other passengers. "Look! Do you see her?" I cry. But no one looks. The woman fixes her tearful eyes on me and I see a terrible loneliness etched in them. Suddenly I have the most amazing awareness. This black woman in the quarantined slum is Mary, the mother of Jesus. I beat on the train window and call to her, "I will come back for you!"

I found Mary again. I found her living impoverished and quarantined in my own soul. This was the beginning of balancing my spiritual journey with a feminine consciousness. I began my journey of "going back for Mary," a journey in which a woman descends deep into her soul....

The journey to become whole necessitated finding and embracing both masculine and feminine, while moving through the pain and risk of divorcing myself from the projections of the patriarchy. Restoring the amputated feminine was a work of reclaiming my feminine hands.

Recovering the feminine through Mary opened me to a new vision of the fullness of God and to a growing sense of inclusion in divine mysteries. I discovered God my mother, as well as God my father.

Healing also came as I began to unite the split of body and soul. Resurrection of the feminine archetype always does a reconciling work. Envisioning Mary as a complete feminine image, seeing her not just as pure, heavenly Virgin, but as the powerful, dark, earth mother and Black Madonna affirmed the joyous song God sings through my body and creation.

Mary birthed Christ through her flesh. In doing so she portrayed the marriage of matter and spirit. In Mary we are called to birth the divine life, the transcendent which is neither male nor female, but simply is. But we do so in a pile of stable straw, earthed in creatureliness.

Finally, Mary offered me an archetypal pattern for a more feminine spirituality. Her feminine principle taught me to be, to sink into the abyss, to open, to dance, to let go, to wait and live the questions. She became a paradigm of the spiritual seasons of the feminine life, especially in her incarnation journey. Her initial words to the angel, "Let it be," taught me how to provide the womb, the dark stillness and receptivity necessary for the birth of my own inner Christ and a consciousness of compassion.

The impregnated Mary offered me a model of courage as she faced the patriarchy of Judaism. It was her moment of crisis, her enormous risk. In her rejection of their judgments upon her, she became a threshold for every handless woman (and man) who undertakes this same passage.

In the next phase of Mary's incarnation journey, she visited Elizabeth. In this act Mary invited me to seek the support of others. Bonding with women friends became a vibrant spiritual experience that caused my new life to quicken and leap inside me just as Elizabeth's leapt in her in Mary's presence.

The long season of Mary's waiting for the divine birth taught me the contemplative posture of being, how to ripen the God-life and tap the transformative energies of love.

While no longer a Baptist, I remain in the Protestant world struggling to dance the balance of masculine and feminine and flow from my own center. An icon of the Black Madonna sits on my desk. She is there to remind me of deep secrets, that I am both mother and father birthing the divine child. I open my arms to her. In my dreams she no longer weeps.

—— ◆ ——

The Other Disciples

by Richard and Catherine Kroeger

Daughters of Sarah, September 1977. At that time Richard Kroeger was a Presbyterian pastor (PCUSA), also teaching at Bethel College; and Catherine was a graduate student at the University of Minnesota.

Every Sunday school child is aware of the twelve disciples whom Jesus called, but few know of a second cohesive and identifiable group of disciples whom Jesus taught and prepared to proclaim the good news of his life, death, and resurrection. The first mention of this second group occurs in Luke 8:1-3:

> *Now after this he made his way through towns and villages preaching and pro-claiming the Good News of the kingdom of God. With him went the twelve, as well as certain women who had been cured of evil spirits and ailments: Mary sur-named the Magdalene, from whom seven demons had gone out, Joanna the wife of Herod's steward Chuza, Susanna, and several others who provided for them out of their own resources. (JB)*

The two groups are placed in juxtaposition, each sharing in the ministry. As was done earlier with the male apostles, the names are given and the experiences which led them to Jesus. These were persons of special need; and indeed it was this need which liberated them to follow Christ. The Jewish woman of that day simply would not have been permitted to leave her home to follow an itinerant preacher. The rejects of society, those healed of appalling spiritual and physical infirmities, comprised the group of female followers. Christian tradition holds that it was from this initial group that the order of widows was founded (see 1 Timothy 5:9-10). The Greek word for "widow" implies any woman bereft or needy in any way. These organized widows maintained a vigorous ministry during the first three centuries of the Church.

For Jesus to have sent these women out alone on a public preaching and healing mission would have been impossible. Talmudic scholars were told never to speak to a woman in public, not even their wives. Nor were they permitted to discuss the things of God with a woman, as this was an enticement to sin. Jesus fully appreciated that conversion must take place before such attitudes could be changed, and so he first sent out Jewish men to teach and preach. But Jesus himself taught both his male and female disciples a very different way of doing God's will.

"Better give the Torah to be burned than to teach it to your daughter," said some rabbis of the day. But Jesus received Mary of Bethany as a "learner," much to her sister's distaste. Jesus replied that she had chosen the better part and that it should not be taken away from her.

In the gospel of John, the male disciples were dismayed to find Jesus seated as a public well engaged in discussion with a woman, but they dared not ask him why (4:27). As a matter of fact, this is the longest private conversation of Jesus that we find recorded (4:7-26). At its close, he sent this woman back to the people of her town to proclaim his Messiahship. As the townsfolk start over the fields to hear for themselves, Jesus points out to his disciples that they are soon to reap where another (a woman) has sowed (4:36-39).

Jesus obviously used women as part of his evangelistic team. On another occasion, he required the hemorrhaging woman to give public testimony of her healing (Mark 5:25-34). At the end of his ministry, Jesus explained to the women as well as to the men the significance of the coming events. The angel at the empty tomb reminded the women: "He spoke to you while he was yet in Galilee, saying, the Son of Man must be delivered into the hands of sinful men, and be crucified and on the third day rise again" (Luke 24:6 *KJV*).

It was important that the women understand, for they would be the major witnesses of Jesus' death, burial, and resurrection, just as one had been the major witness of the Incarnation. Those who had been instructed in Galilee followed him to the cross:

There were some women watching from a distance. Among them were Mary of Magdala, Mary who was the mother of James the younger and Joseph, and Salome. These used to follow him and look after him when he was in Galilee. And there were many other women there who had come up to Jerusalem with him (Mark 15:40-41 *JB*).

Again we see an identifiable group who are named. They are mentioned also in Matthew 27:55-56 and John 19:25. Jewish law required two or three witnesses to establish a fact. Women were there, able to document the final events of Jesus' life.

Certain biblical critics have suggested that the tomb was empty on Easter morning because the women became confused and went to the wrong tomb. But Mark is clear:

"Mary of Magdala and Mary the mother of Joseph were watching and took note of where he was laid" (15:47). Matthew adds that Joseph of Arimathea was burying Jesus, "Mary Magdalene and the other Mary were there, sitting opposite the tomb" (27:61).

In John's record, Mary Magdalene found the stone rolled away from the tomb and ran to tell Peter and John. Although the men ran to the tomb to confirm her news, Jesus did not appear to Mary until after they had left.

After Jesus' ascension, the disciples gathered in the upper room in Jerusalem. Both groups were present and are mentioned together (Acts 1:13-14). They participated in the selection of Matthias to replace Judas, and they shared in the experience of Pentecost. Both women and men were filled with the Holy Spirit and both women and men spoke in tongues (Acts 2:1-4; 17–18).

Jesus told his disciples to be witnesses of him to others. Without the witness of either the men or the women, the testimony would have been incomplete. Both groups had shared in his ministry, and both must be a part of the leadership in his church.

— ◆ —

The Good Samaritan Woman

by Peggy Weaver

Daughters of Sarah, July/August 1990. At that time Peggy Weaver was a teacher working in the Division for Global Mission, Evangelical Lutheran Church in America, in Chicago.

Yesterday I heard a sermon which angered me. Everyone else seemed touched by it. Even the priest cried as he spoke of two men who had been mentors in his life. It was not the individual stories that bothered me. It was the concept being presented: give everything of yourself. Give it until the very end, until you have nothing left. And then your reward will come.

How readily women hear that message! How easily we believe these words. Give all. Don't question. Don't be angry. Don't doubt that your reward will be on some distant horizon.

Perhaps the lesson the priest spoke of is needed by those who are not familiar with commitment, with toughing it out until the end. But there is another lesson to learn, and we women especially need to hear a new message. Most of us do not need more instruction in holding on until the end. We need instruction and mentors to teach us how to let go.

The Parable of the Good Samaritan came to my mind, but with a new lesson, one particularly for women.

> *...a Samaritan, as she journeyed, came to where he was, and when she saw him, she had compassion, and went to him and bound up his wounds, pouring oil and wine, then she set him on her own beast and brought him to an inn, and took care of him. And the next day she took out two denarii and gave them to the innkeeper, saying, "Take care of him; and whatever more you spend, I will repay you when I come back."* (adapted from Luke 10:33-35 *KJV*)

She left. She left! The woman tended to his wounds, brought him to a safe place, took care of him, and paid his way. And then she left.

It sounds almost sinful when we replace the "he" with "she." You mean she didn't stay long enough to be sure that he had a job or a home? What kind of woman would leave so quickly? Yet the parable tells us that the woman had compassion when she saw the man. The lesson is that she also had compassion for herself. She knew her limits. She did what she could at the time, and then she went on her way. The Samaritan woman did not leave the man totally alone; she arranged to return when she came back through town, to pay any extra costs. She trusted that the man would know when he was healed and would leave of his own accord. She knew how much she could give; she knew how much to trust others to provide.

Jesus said, "Go and do likewise."

Amen!

— ♦ —

The Bent-Over Woman

by David G. Owen

Daughters of Sarah, May/June 1982. At that time David G. Owen was a United Methodist minister working at Gallahue Mental Health Center in Indianapolis, Indiana, as well as a part-time teacher of Old Testament and world religions at Indiana Central University. This sermon is reprinted from *The Church Woman*, 1979.

Is it your impression as well as mine that the story of the Bent-Over Woman (Luke 13:10-21) has long been neglected in the church? Somehow it never made it to the Top Ten or even to the Favorite Forty along with the Good Samaritan, the Prodigal Son, Blind Bartimaeus, the man with the withered hand, the Woman at the Well, and little Zacchaeus up in a sycamore tree.

The Gospel episode begins when Jesus is teaching in the synagogue on a sabbath day and sees a woman who is bent over and unable to straighten up. At first, that made me think of times when I sit in a draft or something and get a crick in the back of my neck. But, no, that's not what is being talked about here, because this woman has been bent over for eighteen years! Can you imagine being bent over for eighteen long years?

What was the burden that was weighing her down? That would seem a pertinent question, but the Bible doesn't say. Luke left it open to our imaginations. If you really want to know, ask a bent-over woman. I tried that recently. Their answers were illuminating.

"Her children!" one woman answered sharply, and her tone of voice suggested that all was not well at home.

"Don't forget her husband," another piped up. "She's probably permanently bent over from picking up his dirty socks for thirty years!"

"Maybe she was tired of working like a slave for a minimum wage," said a third. "Or maybe," said a disgruntled housewife, "she was tired of working like a slave for no wages at all."

"Maybe she had a doctorate in economics," suggested another bent-over woman, "and found that nobody was listening to her when she talked about inflation or tax structures, but instead paid attention to some pompous man—even if he hadn't read a serious book on the subject for years."

"It may have been that her spine was curved from always looking down from atop her pedestal," said a woman who was tired of being her husband's eternally elevated, perpetually unruffled Barbie doll. "Or perhaps every time she held her head up and tried to be somebody, the people around her—both male and female—did all that they could to deflate and diminish her again."

"Or maybe," said one female minister, "she wanted to be a disciple, but found that all the positions just happened to be filled by men."

Of course, we don't know specifically what weighed this woman down. Yet there is something extremely important that we are told about her condition. For Luke says that it was a "spirit of infirmity" that had bent her down all those years. Her difficulty was not physical. It was primarily *her spirit* that was infirm.

"Spirit" and "infirm" are interesting words because they have a variety of meanings. To be "infirm," for instance, means to be "weak," "feeble," or "deteriorated"; while "spirit" can mean "disposition" or "temper," or "life force," or even "vivaciousness." To say that the Bent-Over Woman was suffering an "infirm spirit," then, means that "her life force had been weakened"; that she had been "feeble of temper" (does that mean that she couldn't even become angry anymore?); or that her vivaciousness had deteriorated. For eighteen years, she had been walking around with most of the vivaciousness drained out of her. For eighteen years she had been *depressed!*

It is one thing to be a bent-over woman because life has momentarily laid a heavy load on you, but it is a far more insidious and devastating thing to believe in your heart that you were *meant to be* a Bent-Over Woman. That your crooked, weary spine has its origins in the eternal order of things. That the life is *supposed* to be drained out of you. That you were *never intended* to stand tall! When you believe in your own heart what the oppressor is saying and thinking about you, then your primary problem is no longer your oppressor, but it is internal.

The reason that it is so important does not relate to the diagnosis but the cure. For if the Bent-Over Woman's problem is really *spiritual*, that means her world will not be changed until something *inside* her is changed. That means that she will never be able to straighten herself until she decides that she has been a Bent-Over Woman long enough!

While Jesus was teaching in the synagogue on the sabbath day he saw the Bent-Over Woman, and he called her to him and said, "Woman, you are freed from your infirmity!" Do you see what Jesus is doing? *He is giving her permission to stand up!* He is telling her that it would be okay if she stood up. "You don't have to be stooped down anymore, sister," he says to her. "God won't strike you dead if you stand up!" And, miracle of miracles, that must have been the word she needed, because when Jesus walked over to her and put his hands upon her, immediately she straightened up. That's what the Bible calls a miracle—when you tell a woman who has been utterly depressed for eighteen years that she doesn't have to be bent-over anymore, and she straightens right up! And when she was straightened, she began at once to praise God in the midst of that congregation. I can almost hear her shouting: "Praise God! Thank you, Jesus! Hallelujah, Lord! Thank you, Jesus!"

At that point the leader of the synagogue, seeing that a formerly bent-over woman was straightened up—seeing that a person who had been weighed down for eighteen years and suddenly *in his own synagogue* had her *vivaciousness revived*—himself became so thankful and so enthusiastic that he, too, began to sing and dance and shout, saying: "Praise God! Hallelujah! Thank you Jesus!" Is that the way the story went? No, that's not the way the story went.

Instead of rejoicing, the synagogue leader began to grumble and grump. He began to construct some elaborate arguments about the synagogue not being the place or the sabbath not being the day. He said, "After all, we are here to be religious and to glorify God! We're not here to help Bent-Over Women stand up! What would happen if more and more of them began to stand up?" He said, "This isn't a matter for the church. This is a matter for business, or industry, or the private sector!" And Jesus, seeing his fearful fussing, just looked at him and said, "Since it was the Devil himself who bent her over, what better place than the church and what better day than the sabbath to have her stand up?" The synagogue leader didn't like that because he didn't know how to deal with women who were standing up, but the common people heard Jesus gladly and together began to rejoice that the Bent-Over Woman had finally heard the liberating Word of God and straightened up.

That's not quite the end of the story. As Luke tells it, Jesus then said, *"Therefore."* Jesus said, *"Therefore,* let me tell you what the kingdom of God is like."

This is not the sudden insertion of a new teaching. What Jesus is about to say is connected to the story by "therefore," and is a way of summarizing what the story means. "The kingdom of God is like a mustard seed that falls into the ground and takes root." Or "The kingdom of God is like a lump of yeast within the loaf that eventually causes the whole loaf to rise." Or "The kingdom of God is like telling a bent-over woman that she is free to stand up, for lo, every now and then a bent-over woman actually hears the Word and does stand up! And when *one* bent-over woman stands up, that's like yeast in the loaf, and causes another and another and still another bent-over woman to stand up—until *all* the bent-over women are standing up."

"What is the kingdom of God like?" It's like more and more bent-over women standing up. How can we know if the kingdom of God is actually coming? Why not look around and see if there are formerly bent-over women standing up?

The message of this story seems to be in two parts—or is it two directions?

"Brother, if ever you see a bent-over woman beginning to unbend and to straighten herself, at the very least you had better give her a little standing room, because that isn't just another woman standing up. That's your *sister* rising to her full stature—and that's God's *kingdom* cranking up!"

"And, sister, if for whatever reason you are still bent over and weighed down, and you think that that's the way it was intended to be or must always be, then know that you have been given divine permission to straighten yourself fully and to stand up. And know, too, that since it is Satan who wants you to be a slave, only the Devil himself would say that *now* is not the time or that *this* is not the place. If your spirit is bent-over, you are free to rise up!"

Let it be so, brothers and sisters! Again and again and again, let it be so!

—◆—

Illustration by Anna Trimiew, published in
Daughters of Sarah, 1979.

A Story on the Nature of Prayer (Luke 18:1-8)

by Roberta Nobleman

Daughters of Sarah, January/February 1986. Roberta Nobleman is an actress, storyteller, and teacher.

S he had tried to explain it to him hundreds of times. The problem was, of course, words. He simply didn't listen—shut out the sound of her voice and went on his own sweet way.

So what to do when you're right at the bottom of the ladder, female, a widow, with no man to support you in a world run by men? Big men dressed up in impressive costumes with awesome titles: Your Honor, Your Grace, Your Excellency.

And just getting to them—the endless lines, the secretaries that protected the manager's office, the judge's chamber. All the most important men seemed to be inaccessible and overprotected, but most of all, uncaring. He just didn't give a damn!

But, she thought, my cause is just. I have to reach him somehow. So she tossed and turned all night, pondering it deeply in her heart. "Maybe your cause isn't just after all," said Demon No. 1.

"Maybe you should just give up and stay home and be a good girl," said Demon No. 2.

Said Demon No. 3 (she always turned up around three in the morning, and her fantasy knew no bounds): "How about the judge's head, on a platter, with french fries, and a nice fat pickle?"

Came the light of dawn, as the sun rose over Mount Zion, a still small voice inside her (she called her Gabriel) said, "Don't be afraid, Roberta. Don't give up now. Judgment belongs to God alone, and with her all things are possible.

"Now sweetie, this calls for action, so listen carefully." And the angel whispered a long, long whisper in her ear. And the widow began to smile, and titter, and giggle like a little girl, because the plan was so simple and yet, so, well, miraculous.

"How can this be happening to me?" she thought to herself. So, when she finally made her way to see the Big Man himself she remembered the angel's voice: "This calls for action."

And act she did, with tears and sobbing and falling on the ground, and practically fainting and begging and pleading with her hands outstretched and hair tumbling in her eyes. She had even considered rending her garments—but when you're poor, you just can't afford to go that far. Oh, it was amazing to see! Salome herself could not have done better!

Thought the Great Man: "This woman is so great a nuisance, she has quite worn me out with her persistence! I shall have to see her righted." And he finally began working on the papers she needed.

As she said to her sister the next day: "You see. Prayer changes things!"

———— ◆ ————

"Sin No More"

Subversive Bible Study in a Christian Base Community of Women

by Gay Redmond, CSJ

Daughters of Sarah, Winter 1993. At that time Gay Redmond was a Sister of St. Joseph of Medaille.

"**B**ut was she guilty? Why didn't she say something to defend herself?" "Can you imagine being dragged in front of a crowd to be accused like that!" "Maybe she's like us."

The lively voices in the next room told me the women were ready to begin our Bible study of John 8 on Jesus and the woman accused of adultery. Approaching the door, I thought back to my arrival in Honduras a year ago. I would never have guessed then that today I would be leading a Bible study for young women in crisis.

After completing a Master's degree in Spanish, I spent two summers helping in an orphanage in Honduras called Aldeas S.O.S. This orphanage cares for more than a thousand children whose parents have died or who could no longer care for all their children. Many families of this Central American country daily must choose to buy beans or rice, but cannot afford both. The director of this orphanage invited me to stay as a full-time staff member. My religious order, the Sisters of St. Joseph of Medaille, readily agreed to this new endeavor. My first assignment was to assist the young women of the orphanage to move from the only home they had ever known to economic and emotional independence.

However, I soon found myself drawn to another stage in the cycle—the home the orphanage ran for pregnant women. Some Hondurans refer to these women as "unwed mothers," but most label them as prostitutes, and therefore bad. But the real demon is poverty. These young women, many hardly more than children themselves, feel forced to sell their bodies to provide basic existence for themselves and for their own children. The home provides a place for the women to stay during pregnancy.

The plight of these impoverished women quickly taught me about the vicious side of Honduran society. For many, the only source of income is to prostitute themselves to men. Some of the johns are enjoying a weekend military pass or seeking a nightly pleasure, some are just teenage boys trying to prove their "manhood." In other cases, families, desperate for money, have sold a teenage daughter to houses of prostitution. The female is usually not viewed as a wage earner in Honduran society, and hence is an economic liability.

Unfortunately, few of these women know how to avoid pregnancy. Yet culture dictates that a child born out of wedlock is a "non-person"; only the father's surname gives legitimacy. Nor is a woman with such children considered by this male-dominated society as acceptable for marriage. In some respects she becomes a "non-woman."

This project, called Hogar Esperanza (Home of Hope), provides food, shelter, and child-care classes as well as basic literacy classes, since many of the women cannot read. However, the women realize that societal bias makes it almost impossible to leave their present status.

Twelve of the women took the initiative to request help to begin a Bible study group. The administrator asked me to assist the women and promised to provide a Bible for each participant. Since some of the women cannot yet read, the passage scheduled for study is read aloud a few days ahead of time to any who want to hear it. In this way, everyone could be prepared to share at the meeting.

It has taken a long time for these women to be able to share their feelings and ideas. Yet this communal experience has helped the women reinterpret scripture in a way that empowers and liberates them in their own life situation. It has certainly taught me a lot too.

Today the passage for discussion, John 8:2-11, seemed especially important to the community. And everyone was quite anxious to begin. The title I had used for this episode was "The Jewish Woman in the Temple." Immediately the women questioned the title, for they all knew this woman as the Adulteress. I suggested we wait until the end of the discussion to talk about the title.

At first the discussion reflected what many had probably heard in sermons: that Jesus forgives all sins, including that of adultery. Some thought that Jesus, along with the scribes and Pharisees, believed that the woman was guilty. The difference between Jesus and the accusers was that Jesus was willing to forgive sinful acts, especially those of women. This led some to express their feelings of guilt for their life style, and relief that forgiveness is possible.

But Angelina, who sat nursing her first child, said she didn't feel guilty about what she had to do in order to survive. She had no choice about her life. She had no educational opportunities. Her job as live-in maid for a wealthy family had included being on call for the two teenage boys when they wanted to have sex. She became pregnant, so the family dismissed her.

Juana, eighteen and pregnant with her third child, spoke. "Why didn't the Jewish woman speak out and defend herself?"

Marcela, a woman in her late forties, had a quick response. She had been a street vendor until coming to the home to recuperate from being gang raped. Now, due to the concern and care she showed for all the women at the home, she was asked to stay to help orient the newly arrived. "Juana, when you're mistreated, how often do you speak up? You know no one will listen to people like us. Besides, if those religious leaders thought she was guilty, everyone else in the crowd would have thought so too."

"Sure. The crowd just accepted the word of those scribes and Pharisees," added Carla, a woman in her late twenties. "Everyone was ready to condemn this woman by throwing stones at her. But Jesus stopped them. Remember, he wrote on the ground twice."

"I wondered what Jesus wrote?" mused Angelina. "I'm glad I wasn't there, because I couldn't have read whatever it was. But I bet the crowd was mostly men. They were the ones who were educated, just like today. Anyway, they sure got scared after Jesus told them that the one with no sin could throw the first stone. That woman must have been terrified too. She probably expected to be killed."

"But the crowd just wanted to accuse her," commented Cristina, fighting for concentration while holding her four-month-old twins on her lap. "I bet they just wanted to label someone else a sinner rather than look at themselves."

"I feel sorry for that poor woman. She had to stand in front of men pointing a finger at her. And if any women were in the crowd, they didn't help her. It looks like she was treated very badly by her own people." Marina was a newcomer at the home and had been desperately trying to find work to feed eight younger siblings. Prostitution was her last resort. But when she got pregnant, her mother only saw another mouth to feed, so she threw her out of the house. Even her four teenage sisters did not speak up on her behalf. Her brothers just laughed.

At this point, Elvia, a frail, thirty-five-year-old woman who looked sixty, spoke. She began so quietly that we all strained to hear her. "The woman in the temple should not be called an adulteress. She is a Jewish woman. And she had a lot of courage to accept Jesus' invitation not to sin any more. I think that meant that she wasn't going to accept any more labels and false judgment others would make about her.

"This Jewish woman has given me new eyes to see myself as a Honduran woman in the same situation. We are all Honduran women, and we want to care for our children and for each other. We don't want to imitate the stone throwers. We want to be treated the way Jesus treated the Jewish woman and have the courage to follow Jesus as the Jewish woman did."

Elvia finished. No one spoke and a reflective silence broken only by baby noises filled the room. The expression on the face of each woman showed the gift of Elvia's words. She had answered the question about the title, "The Jewish Woman in the Temple."

Meeting with these outcast women week after week was like watching the re-enactment of the story Jesus told of the woman who hid leaven in mounds of bread dough until all of it was leavened. It is from such base communities of poor and victimized women that the power of the gospel can be experienced by all women who gather together to celebrate the good news of liberation.

— ◆ —

Anachronisms

by Maren C. Tirabassi

Daughters of Sarah, Winter 1995. At that time Maren C. Tirabassi lived in Portsmouth, New Hampshire and was a freelance writer, workshop facilitator, and pastor.

ark-tender
woman of the flood
dove-keeper
watcher of rainbow, I
want to give you...
al-anon.

weak-eyed sister
love-distant, rich
in son and mandrake,
reading your broken
daughter's
heart,
I want to give you...
bifocals.

midwives of egypt,
abolitionist-willing
to save both girls
and boys,
risking death for
birth,
I want to give you...
medical degrees.

fringe-clutching bleeder
with the hollow eyes
of too-much diagnosis,
dog-under-the-table mother
with your chin high
and your little girl's hand
tight-tight,
lamp-lighter, house-sweeper,
parable-incarnate

wife of a fisher turned
traveller,
I want to give you...

son-grieving weeping widow,
judge-hounding knocking widow,
coin-giving laughing widow,
hair-loose, heart-sob
footwasher-lover,
I want to give you...

bent-over patient woman,
story-in-the-dust trapped
woman,
innkeeper woman,
seed-sower woman,
net-mender woman,
five-loaf, two-fish,
lunch-maker woman,
palm-waver woman,
I want to give you...

cleaning woman in the
upper room, going home
with one precious
passover crust in
your pocket,
and several not-mary women
with spice on your hands
at a dawn-open tomb,

I want to give you...
names.

Chapter 2

God as She

"**I**f God is male then male is God," penned Mary Daly, one of the first contemporary feminist theologians. These words succinctly exposed the foundational hierarchical assumption undergirding many sexist doctrines and laws—the maleness of God. But Christian feminism offers not only a reciprocal feminine vision, but also a broader one. Christian feminism reimages God as Father, Mother, Sister, Brother, and lover; as life-giving Wind, passionate Fire, and cleansing Rain; as Mystery and Presence; and a myriad of other exquisite forms—no longer conceived in purely masculine images and concepts.

Christian feminism recognizes God in the mundane experiences of everyday life—such as the old woman shelling peas that we read about in Martha Popson's poem, "The Lap of God," reprinted in this chapter. It elicits new insights from the common stories and parables, as Roberta Nobleman tells us in her article "Once Upon a Time." It rescues the nearly forgotten traditions, such as Wisdom and Shekinah. And it sifts the fragments of ancient texts and cultures, as one would pan for gold, hungry for answers to the mystery of Divine Presence in times past and present.

—◆—

The Lap of God

by Martha Popson

Daughters of Sarah, November/December 1987, 15th anniversary issue. Martha Popson lives in Knoxville, Iowa.

She was shelling peas,
apron-covered knees
spread wide to catch
each pea/each pod

I, shaky, needy
wandered near

Her ancient swollen hands
pushed back the hair
that hid my face

She set down the pan
and, patting her knee,
said:

oh, child
come on up here
and let me have a look at you

Her voice was safe and so was I
sitting in the lap of God.

— ◆ —

Once Upon a Time: Storytelling with Jesus

by Roberta Nobleman

Daughters of Sarah, July/August 1989 issue on women's art. Roberta Nobleman, from Dumont, New Jersey, is a British-born actor, teacher, and storyteller well known for her one-woman plays.

In Haiti and in other poor countries of the Caribbean, storytelling is a fine art, as it was among the slaves of the South in our own country. I imagine it was the same in Jesus' time. The greater the oppression, the greater the need for story—either to divert attention from the pangs of hunger or pain, or to pass idle hours while unemployed, or as relief from backbreaking work like picking cotton. I'm quite sure slaves had more stories to share and greater skills in the art than slave owners!

Stories also amuse children who should be in school. Word spreads around the village like wildfire: "The storyteller is here!" And the people gather in the marketplace or the "piazza" or the "house in Capernaum" to listen.

Who made up the audience when Jesus told stories? The Pharisees or scribes were more interested in systematic theology and debate than little tales of mustard seeds and lost coins. Perhaps a large percentage of Jesus' audience—besides those infamous taxgatherers and "sinners"—were women and children. Perhaps when the children grew up they remembered and repeated the stories to the Gospel writers.

Now what of the modern storyteller who attempts to bring these stories to life for twentieth-century listeners? We know how dreary they often appear when dished out Sunday by Sunday from behind the huge lectern in church. Let me tell you a little of what goes on when I, as a woman actor, storyteller, and pilgrim, explore one of Jesus' stories and act it out for listening audiences.

First I ask myself: Whose version of the story are we hearing? Take a look at the encounter between Jesus and the Samaritan woman at the well. Who told that story first, Jesus or the woman? It's a decision, as storyteller, that I have to make. Or to whom did Jesus confide the story of his temptations in the wilderness? Why? When?

If it's one of Jesus' own parables, like the Good Shepherd, I ask myself: Where is the shepherd? When does he discover he's lost one of his sheep? What is he doing? How does he know that one is missing? How is he feeling—tired, angry, overworked, worried? What sort of person is this "good" shepherd? How can I show his "goodness"?

And what about gender? The telling of stories was at least traditionally viewed as a male province. What crumbs can I as a female storyteller pick up from off the rich man's table? If heroines are in short supply, must I constantly identify with the hero?

One of the amazing graces I have discovered through acting out these Gospel stories is that God our Mother is a lot more active in the life of Her son than we realize. Jesus may call Her "Father," but what he is actually talking about time and time again is Mother God! Take the story of the Prodigal Son who returns home to a father who hugs and kisses him tenderly, fetches a robe for him—the best one—puts a ring on his finger and slippers on his feet. If that's not a Jewish Mother, or anyone's good loving mom, then I dunno! Or take the nocturnal encounter of Nicodemus and Jesus. The discussion is all about motherly stuff, like birthing.

It is God our Mother who speaks through Her son Jesus, especially in suffering. Women who have known the pain and terror of difficult labors will understand Jesus' loneliness in the Garden of Gethsemane. I remember thinking to myself in about the twenty-third hour of labor with my first child, "I don't think I want to go through with this. Cancel the agreement—I don't want this baby!"

But God our Mother whispers that She is with us and it is worth it, just as She did for Her son in the garden. And look at Jesus' words to the weeping women as he ascends Calvary. "Daughters of Jerusalem, do not weep for me; weep for yourselves and for your children...." Is that God our Father speaking? No, it's the Mother. Fourteenth-century mystic Dame Julian says that one of the things that Jesus is doing on the cross is birthing us all, in agony, nakedness, blood, sweat, water, and tears.

So one of the advantages of being a woman telling Jesus' story is that I bring experiences that shed a different light on the Gospel—a female truth. Yes, the story was probably reported and written down mostly by men, but the feminine half of the story—repressed, ignored, or denied—cannot help but ooze through the cracks. How refreshing it would be to hear that "The Last Temptation of Mary" was making big news in the media! Or that the latest hit on Broadway was a play called, "I Was the Man Not Taken in Adultery!" Or how about, "Silent No More! The True Story of What Women Were Talking about in the Church at Corinth!"

Through acting I have come to know a warm, real, humorous, tender being called Jesus. He is also the Christ who images God our Mother and Father with a grace and truth untarnished even by two thousand years of patriarchal church history.

It's a difficult, narrow path—and a lonely one. My style of storytelling and the issues of justice I feel called to reveal through stories are not easy or popular tales. My play, "Solo Flight," on the life of the "irregularly-ordained" Rev. Jeannette Piccard is not what every Roman Catholic seminary is calling for. Protestant churches are not breaking down doors to attend my workshops on incest and sexual abuse. And just imagine what a time the Vatican would have with priestly celibacy if we all knew about St. Peter's wife! ("You've been what?" asks this veritable Jewish fishwife. "Walking on the water? Then how come you're so wet?")

I won't soon forget one rude Episcopalian priest, for example, at a cathedral in a diocese that refuses to ordain women. Before I performed my one-woman play, Julian, he had sniffed upon hearing about it, "Oh, Julian of Norwich. Who is he?" He then made a big fuss about me performing at the High Altar, so I was relegated to a side chapel of St. Somebody-or-Other, and he sat through the whole play stony-faced, arms folded—until I reached the part where Julian speaks of God as Mother. With a great male snort, he got up and retreated to the sacristy, where he must have busied himself laying out his vestments for Holy Eucharist the next morning.

Afterward he made an unpleasant comment to me about "hoping I would be good enough to quickly clean up the mess around his altar," and left. Obedient to my betters, I rushed to comply, but before I left the sacristy where I changed clothes, I hung an old red silk bra over his white chasuble. It was never returned!

Sometimes storytelling can be gratifying. At St. Meinrad Seminary in Indiana, I gave "Solo Flight" and told the seminarians Jeannette Piccard's joke about how when you know in your heart and mind that something is right, you just have to have the ovaries to go ahead and do it. "Having the right equipment is terribly important for the priesthood, they tell us," she comments wryly. When the play was over I asked the audience to tell me how they felt. One young man struggled for a minute and said, "I feel—I feel—this is my story too."

Then there was the dear old Roman Catholic Sister of Charity who clasped my hands after my performance of Julian and said, "Thank you, Dame Julian, for writing that lovely book, Revelations of Divine Love!" How could I possibly disillusion her?

Until justice for women in the church rolls down like water, I will keep telling stories as Jesus did. Jesus tells me that the Christ once was a widow with a just cause who, in spite of rejection by the judges of her day, persisted. Finally the judge said, "This woman is so great a nuisance she has quite worn me out! I will see her righted!" And then (and this is the part Luke forgot to mention) "all the other women in the town rejoiced, and killed the fatted calf, and there was music and dancing!"

— ♦ —

A Prayer to God Our Mother

by Kathy Coffey

Daughters of Sarah, November/December 1990 issue on feminist liturgy, worship, and Bible study. At that time, Kathy Coffey was a mother of four, a teacher at the University of Colorado at Denver and Regis College. She now gives retreats based on her book, *Hidden Women of the Gospels* (Crossroads Publishing).

God our Mother,
pulsing in our breath
cleanse and clothe us,
find in our faces
the features of God.

We mirror you, Mother:
fragrant as rain
essential as earth
to our flowering.

God our Mother
of the large embrace—
never the small, cramped gesture.
God who spoils us with beauty,
God who keeps the porch light burning
and the dinner warm.

God who loved us first,
from nothingness,
only a flicker of fifth month movement,
a heartbeat on a stethoscope clouded
with static, a fuzzy ultra-sound.
Beloved before we ever won the
spelling bee
(or even if we never did.)

God delighting in the naked newborn,
despite inefficient plumbing
and nocturnal waking habits.

God of the midnight feeding,
rumpled hair, blurred vision,
robe clutched tight,
yet she comes in reassurance.
Crying soothed by warm milk—
and she will come again at three,
when the howling splinters
her dreams and she is groggy.
In soundless rhythm,
she'll repeat the feeding
and create the cosmic dance.

God delighting in our slightest grace:
"how original—to make a drum
from an oatmeal box!"

God swift to retrieve us;
in split seconds the arms
catch the tumbling child.
No matter how crazy the leap,
how foolhardy the risk,
God cushioning the fall.

God of the long view, who calms:
"It's all right; I'm here,"
despite monsters in closets,
creepy noises, and nightmares.
Face bending over the bad dream,
circle of light, dispelling fear.

God who cherishes our good,
whose breath catches in the throat
at the thought of our harm, who holds
the shaky hand through shots and
stitches, dental fillings, flu.
Who watches, sleepless,
by the tortured beds
of our personal hells.

God who loved us last:
without any irony, calling
a 46-year-old business executive
in pinstriped suit and wingtip shoes,
with a car phone and 15 employees,
"my baby."

God faithful as Argentinian
mothers of the disappeared
silent presence, calling to account
even those most brutal, most corrupt,
most far from care. Hoping always
for the exiled child's return.

God like the Aran Islands mother,
knitting each son a unique pattern,
(intricate as the Book of Kells).
So if he were lost at sea,
the sweater would wash ashore, then
she would know: "Ay, Sean, or

Patrick, or Colm"—and keen.
How skillfully we are knit: how
lightly we wear the wool of your care.

God in the aging mother
who mentally leaves the nursing home
to live more happily when the children
were small, hungry, needing her,
bumping into her, nestling into
pajamas and bedtime books.
She returns to that time,
knowing it the best,
fleeing the senility, the wheel chair,
seeking their young faces again.

God, like mothers,
quick to see our loveliness:
formed from God's sinew
nurtured with God's breath
harbored under God's bone
warmed beneath God's wing.

God of our origin and end,
guide us back to our beginnings
when we realize that
we've never left your womb.
Coming into God, we
enter the embrace we've
yearned for, but rarely expressed.

"She looks like her mother!"
people say, never suspecting
how in motherhood
we discover God, and in God

find motherhood.

CAUTION!
Inclusive Language May Change Your Life!

by Joe LaMadeleine

Daughters of Sarah, Summer 1992. At that time Joe LaMadeleine, from Waterbury, Connecticut, was a priest ordained with the LaSalette Missionaries.

As a Catholic priest in Spiritual Direction, over the years I have discovered an important insight. We are created in God's image, and as we seek to paint our own portraits through self-understanding, our image of God plays an important role. A judgmental person will probably have as a predominant image a judgmental God. Someone very strong and always in control will probably image God as strong and always in control of everything. One whose God looks like Saint Francis of Assisi will likely be a humble person always looking out for the underdog.

Spiritual Direction is essentially helping someone reflect on and articulate her or his predominant image of God. The key is that the more we consciously try to articulate the image of God, the more it changes and becomes larger than any name or combinations of names we can give. And amazingly, the more our image of God changes, the more we change along with it. As our God becomes less judgmental, we become less judgmental. As our God becomes more accepting, we become more accepting. This kind of Spiritual Direction—formal or informal—plays an important part in both our spiritual growth and our personal growth.

The greatest contribution to my spiritual growth over the past few years has come from using inclusive language. I must confess I began using it for a paternalistic reason. I had many feminist friends who enlightened me about their feelings of exclusion at traditional Catholic liturgies. The male imagery left them feeling Catholic religion was for men only.

So in my attempts to be a good priest, I decided that if Christ were here talking, he would not use language that would make people feel excluded, even if he himself did not feel it was exclusive. As he did in his parables, he would use language people could relate to. So I decided that, even though it wasn't an issue for me, I would use inclusive language because it was an issue for others.

It did not take me long to master this language, and it made me feel pretty good about myself. I felt I was being sensitive as I believed God would be sensitive. After all, if you are a man and your predominant image of God is male, then your striving to be like God is much easier than if you are a woman and your predominant image of God is male. I figured I would keep my personal image of God for my private prayer life and use more inclusive imagery for public services.

Over the years, however, this constant use of inclusive language has impacted my spirituality and personhood. As a teenager, I remember that whenever I was really desperate, I would find myself praying to Mary instead of God because I felt that as a woman she would be more compassionate than God the Father. Now that my image of God has both male and female attributes, I find God more approachable. Just as important, I find it easier to accept my own male and female attributes as good and holy.

Inclusive language has also changed my image of the Trinity. Traditionally, the Trinity is presented as very male and very hierarchical. A male Father is actually in control of everything while the Son and Spirit are just gofers who keep everything working. Acting out of that image as a priest, I found myself taking on the role of God the Father, who naturally had to be in control of everything. I had to be strong and make sure the rest of the community carried out their duties correctly.

But inclusive language calls the Trinity "the God who created us, the God who redeemed us, and the God who continues to work through us to make us holy." This image freed me from male-dominated imagery of the Trinity and all the baggage that went along with it. Feminist theology has also helped me see Trinity as a community of persons—three beings sharing decisions and responsibilities and operating out of a consensus model.

This has had a direct effect on my priesthood and personhood. My need to be in control has greatly diminished and my desire to work with a community has greatly increased. My priesthood now puts me in the midst of a community rather than at its head, and my life has become better because of it.

I am still committed to using inclusive language, but no longer do I use it as a ministry to women. When I reflect on how it has changed my own spirituality, I now know that women have ministered to me much more than I ever did to them. By introducing me to inclusive language, they freed my image of God all chained up in maleness to a God who goes beyond images. I now understand more about the God who said to Moses, "Tell them 'I AM WHO I AM' sent you." This for me is a holy experience.

———◆———

Shekinah—The Glory of God

by Kristin Johnson Ingram

Daughters of Sarah, Spring 1994 issue on interreligious dialogue. Kristin Johnson Ingram is the author of over fifteen hundred articles and ten books. At that time her most recent book was *Who Killed Stutz Bearcat*. She lived in Springfield, Oregon.

The beginning of my adventure with Shekinah[1]—God's fiery female face—was remarkable. But scary. I love Jesus, and I didn't want to leave him; yet after years of adventure with a very masculine savior, I was beguiled by the Spirit I glimpsed as not only a feminine name but as a female presence.

"Hear O Israel, the Lord your God is One God" began to have a different meaning for me: God is One but the Spirit of God, the Presence, the fullness of God was suddenly revealed to me as female, and the personality of Shekinah emerged as different from the other two Persons in the Trinity.

Theologians have tried to convince me that in the Trinity, the Father and the Son love each other so completely that their love becomes the Third Person, the Holy Spirit.... Come, now: could two male Persons give birth to Shekinah, who is female?

My own sense of gender was at stake: as a woman, I needed to know the other side of God. I'd met the Bridegroom; now I yearned to know the Bride, one I imagined to be quiet and reassuring.

I will know Her, I had told myself for years. I will surely know God the Mother when She comes to me. I knew she would be kind, calm, and meek, would be like the portrayals in movies of the Virgin Mary—wise-faced, full of sweetness, a quiet and gentle spirit. Sagacious words would fall from her lips like petals, her hands would steady me, she would be clothed in righteousness and adorned with charitable works. *She will be nothing like me*, I said, *but she will make me better.*

I sometimes prayed to her, calling her Lady and Sister; I waited for her beside quiet pools and in the fernlight depths of the woods. I listened for her in the voices of flutes and harps, sought a vision of her in moments of peace.

---

[1] *Shekinah* (she-KI-nah or SHEK-i-nah) is a transliteration of a Hebrew word not found in the Bible but used in many of the Jewish writings to speak of God's presence. The term has feminine gender and means "that which dwells." It is implied throughout the Bible whenever it refers to God's nearness either in a person, object, or God's glory. It is often used in combination with glory to speak of the presence of God's shekinah glory.

And so it was without my expectation that Shekinah roared into my life like a hurricane, like unchanneled electricity, like a torch suddenly thrust into the black darkness, like cosmic fanfare. She came unpredictably and unpredictable, full of demand and violent love, yanking me up and plunging me into the fire.

She came as Wind, she came as passionate intuition, she came as blinding light and breath-sucking presence. Shekinah came not as a handmaiden but as a queen, not whispering but crying out like a hoyden in the streets, bringing no consolation but urgency of motion. She sails out of heaven on powerful wings, she dives out of heaven in flashing tongues of fire, she blazes from heaven onto altars like a supernova. She moved over the face of the waters at Creation and caught the blood of the crucified Christ in her chalice. She is glory, she is light, she is clothed with the sun and stands on the moon, she wears a crown of twelve stars on her head.

She takes other names: she is Shabbat, she is Presence: and she is Spirit, the Hebrew *Ruach*. In the beginning, Breath or Spirit or Wind rippled over the face of the womb of creation, brooded over and within the womb, stirred the waters to break and gush out and let God give birth to everything.

She moved over the face of the waters, roughing them up as she blew over them, sending her own divine Breath into the deep, sending down all the primal Causes through whatever was here when there was nothing. She is the Life-Giver, the Paraclete, the wildest force known to God. She is God and she is God's breath; she is the Spirit of God, she is the wind that blows suns and Magellanic clouds and gravity and particles from Kingdom Come and back again. And she is God.

She travels at warp speed and beyond: she is in the mouth of blessed Miriam on the far shore of the Yam Suph, drives Miriam to grab her tambourine and lead the dance of rejoicing. Shekinah vaults to glorious Deborah, and gives her an army and a song; she races into the mouth of angry Huldah as she warns the men of Judah that they have forsaken God and God's book; she speaks through Isaiah's prophetess wife, she comes forth in the host of heaven to say she will go forth and delude the priests of Ahab. And Shekinah swirls over a young Galilean girl and lines her womb to prepare it for a salvific miracle.

She is not content with the past, but wants your present life. She hovers over a woman kneading the Communion bread who wants to be a priest, and rushes on to dance on the teeth of a Colorado teenager who is determined to speak in tongues.

When Shekinah comes into your life she ruins it. You may be perfectly happy until you forget yourself for a moment and pray; and then there she is, on your threshold or sliding down your chimney or peering in your windows. The Breath of God is also the wrath of God that can both woo you back to life and start a nuclear winter of the soul. Her name also means something like "a region of the sky," which I presume means that she not only creates but somehow participates in her own creation.

"That's it!" you yell; "that's far enough. This is heading toward pantheism."

"Actually, pan-en-theism,"[2] Shekinah says. "I am in nothing I make, but all I create is in me. Allow me to set you on fire, and then you'll understand."

Don't run. Don't run away from the fire. And don't just get warm: burn. Shekinah sets a universe aflame and drives it with her fiery breath until you are fire all over, until fire heats your bones and surges out of your fingertips and consumes your soul. Spirit will cool you as well as heat you, too. God's Wind shimmers over the deep of your mind and heart until the surface tension is broken, until ripple after ripple become wave after wave, and the waves break on fresh, untrod rock and the rock breaks into sand and the cool sand begins to heat up again like a throbbing womb. The Breath of God holds you in her hands and breathes into your interstices until life pours into you and through you and over you until you are bathed in Creation.

God the Spirit is not only holy but determined to make you holy too. She urges you to eat, yes, just a little of this bread, and here, drink some of this wine, just to wash it down, just so you'll grow strong, just so you'll be fit for the Kingdom of Heaven.

"Act like God," you yell at raucous, fecund Shekinah. She reminds you that she is acting like God, is as a matter of fact being God, whose whole, full Name rings Creation like a bell and who roars through your bones like a mighty, rushing wind. Because she is ageless, so are you in her presence: she doesn't care if you are fifteen or sixty-seven. Because she is tireless, so are you when you're full of her, writing or sculpting or singing or rocking children into the night. Because she blesses Earth, she will drive you to making bread or shearing lambs, to preaching or painting, to using your hands to bless when you are in her presence. She will swallow you alive and make you more yourself than you dreamed you could be.

A man planning to be a Catholic priest comes to see me regularly for spiritual counsel. "Do you know God as Shekinah, as Mother?" I ask him one day. He blanches; he cringes.

"I'm afraid," he says finally. "She will consume me."

Yesss . . . !

---

[2] pan-en-the-ism—the doctrine that God includes the world as a part though not the whole of God's being (Webster's Dictionary).

Is Your God Right-Handed?

by Steve Love

Daughters of Sarah, January/February 1989. Steve Love was a student at Moody Bible Institute in Chicago, Illinois, and Calvin Seminary, in Grand Rapids, Michigan where he "stirred up trouble" with his writings concerning the position of women in the church. Steve wrote this article in 1975 while attending Moody; it was his first published article.

The Bible states that God always uses his right hand to do anything of importance (Rev. 2:1). To be blessed of God is to be on his right hand, and to be cursed is to be on his left (Matt. 25:33-34). It is with the right hand that God expresses might and power (Exod. 15:6). With this basic understanding, it is possible to say that the right hand is predominant in the mind of God. In fact, Jesus was probably right-handed, because anything to the contrary of this characteristic is usually stated (Judg. 3:15). To say that in Christ there is neither right nor left is to imply that God has the mind of a child (Jon. 4:11).

The people of God exemplify this truth as well. To express great blessing on a person one must use his right hand (Gen. 48:14). In our Christian communities we must accept another into our fellowship with our right hand (Gal. 2:9). It is obvious that there is intrinsic worth in the right hand and intrinsic foolishness in the left (Eccles. 10:2). Finally, with all this, do we need more proof to believe that to be God-like is to be right-handed?

Ridiculous, isn't it? This is solely an anthropomorphism used by a people who respected the right hand above the left. Certainly, if the Hebrew nation had been just the opposite in this matter, Jesus would have been left-handed.

By the way, is your God male?

— ◆ —

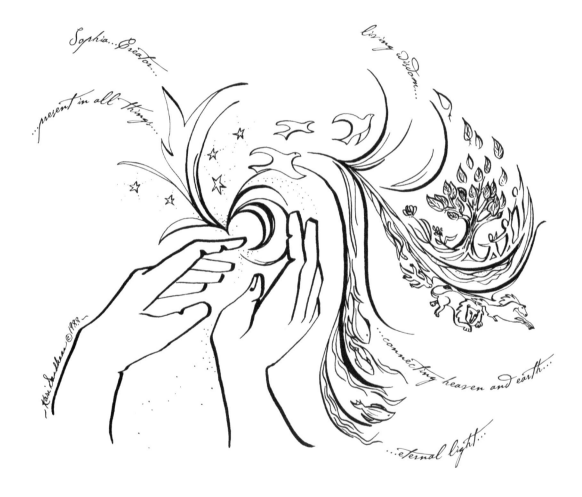

Sophia illustration by Kari Sandhaas, published in *Daughters of Sarah*, November/December 1988.

Jesus and Sophia

by Susan Cole and Hal Taussig

Daughters of Sarah, November/December 1988 issue on christology. At that time, Susan Cole (then Cady) was pastor of Emmanuel United Methodist Church in Philadelphia, Pennsylvania. She presently pastors Arch Street UMC in Philadelphia, Pennsylvania. Hal Taussig was a United Methodist clergyman in Philadelphia, Pennsylvania and was teaching at Albright College, St Joseph's University. He is still a United Methodist clergyman and now teaches at Union Theological Seminary and Chestnut Hill College. All translations used in this article are either from *The Jerusalem Bible* or *The New Jerusalem Bible.*

Christian feminists have begun to ask the question, "Can a male savior save women?" This question has been especially pointed, since Jesus' maleness has been used to keep women from full participation in the church.

How important it is, then, to discover that Jesus and Wisdom/Sophia, the divine female in the Bible, are very closely related. In fact, the closer biblical scholarship has looked, the clearer it is that Jesus draws much of his character from Wisdom/Sophia.

Who is this one called Wisdom, or Sophia, in our Bible? (We will use Sophia, her name in Greek, from now on to recall better her gender and personhood.) We need to explore who she is in the Old Testament, her relationship to Jesus in the New Testament, and the implication of this relationship for women.

Sophia in the Old Testament

Most people, if they have heard of Sophia at all, assume that she must be at most a marginal figure in the Old Testament. This is, however, far from the case. There are more passages about her than all other figures except God, David, Moses, and Job.

In many passages Sophia is Creator. For instance, in Proverbs 8:23-25 and 29b-31 we read how she speaks of herself:

From everlasting I was firmly set...
The deep was not, when I was born,
There were no springs to gush with water
Before the mountains were there,
  before the hills, I came to birth....
When he [God] laid down the foundations of the earth,
I was by his side, a master craftsman,
delighting him day after day,

ever at play in his presence,
at play everywhere in his world....

In the Wisdom of Solomon (a book included in the Bible accepted by Episcopalians and Roman Catholics, but in the Apocrypha for most Protestants) her creativity is not limited to the beginning, but continues in the present:

In her company all good things came to me... All these delighted me, since Wisdom brings them, though I did not then realize that she was their mother (7:11-12).

Other passages describing Sophia as Creator are found in Ecclesiasticus 1:7, 24:3-5; Proverbs 3:18, 8:22, 8:26-28; Wisdom 7:25-27, 8:1-4, 9:1-4, 9-10.

Closely related to Sophia's role in creation is her presence in all things. Wisdom of Solomon 7:22-30 has this picture of her:

For within her is a spirit intelligent, holy, unique, manifold, subtle, mobile, inci-sive, unsullied, lucid, invulnerable... friendly to human beings, steadfast, depend-able... all-surveying, penetrating all things, pure and most subtle spirits. For Wisdom is quicker to move than any motion; she is so pure, she pervades and per-meates all things.... She is a reflection of the eternal light, untarnished mirror of God's active power, and image of his goodness.... She is indeed more splendid than the sun...compared with light, she takes first place.

Other passages about her presence in all things are Wisdom 6:12-13; 7:27, 8:1, and Ecclesiasticus 24:7,12.

Sophia as Creator and her presence in all things help us understand two other close-ly related roles in the Scriptures: living wisdom and teacher. She is portrayed as living wisdom in many passages. For instance, in Proverbs 4:1-2, 5-6 we read:

Listen, my children, to a father's instruction;
pay attention, and learn what understanding is...
Do not forsake my teaching....
Acquire Wisdom, acquire understanding,
Never forget her, never deviate from my words...
love her, she will watch over you.

Other passages that show her as living wisdom are Wisdom 6:12-19; Ecclesiasticus 1:1-6, 51:13-26; and Proverbs 3:13-18.

Because Sophia is understanding itself, she is the perfect teacher. In Proverbs 8:1, 3-5, 8, 15-16, 18, she announces herself as such:

Is not Wisdom calling?...
by the gates, at the entrance to the city...
she cries out, "I am calling to you, all people,
my words are addressed to all humanity...

fools, come to your senses.
All the words of my mouth are upright,
nothing false there, nothing crooked...
By me monarchs rule... by me rulers govern...
With me are riches and honor, lasting wealth and saving justice.

Other passages portraying her as teacher are Proverbs 1:20-33, 9:1-5, and Wisdom 9:9-12.

As Creator, Wisdom, and teacher in all things, Sophia regularly plays a connecting and mediating role. For instance, in Ecclesiasticus 24, she connects heaven with earth:

I came forth from the mouth of the Most High,
and I covered the earth like a mist...
I have made the circuit of the heavens...
I looked to see in whose territory I might pitch camp.
Then the Creator of all things instructed me,
"Pitch your tent in Jacob.
I have taken root in a privileged people..." (24:3-4, 7-8, 12).

These preceding Sophia passages are only a small portion of the fascinating texts about her in the Old Testament. There are passages in which she directs Israel's history (Wisdom 10), she is Yahweh's beloved and consort (Wisdom 8:3-4), she is the Law itself (Eccles. 24:23-27), she is a glorious tree (Prov. 3:18, Eccles. 24:12-22), and more.

Furthermore, it must be clearly stated that she is far more than a mere personification in these texts. She walks, talks, protects, enters into relationship, creates, and teaches. Part of the neglect of Sophia/Wisdom has occurred by calling her a mere personification of a concept. Clearly the depth and breadth of her characterization goes beyond this to describe what is a real divine person for the biblical writers.

Jesus as Sophia's Child

Recent detailed analysis of the way some New Testament texts were written has revealed a layer of pre-New Testament documents which portray Jesus as Sophia's child. Such an understanding is based in passages like Ecclesiasticus 4:11 *(Wisdom brings up her own children and cares for those who seek her)* and Wisdom of Solomon 7:27 *(passing into holy souls, she makes them into God's friends and prophets)*. These texts picture Sophia as the mother of those sages who take her seriously.

In early layers of the New Testament we find just such an image of Jesus—as one who is a friend of God and seeker of Sophia, and therefore a child of Sophia. For instance, Jesus speaks of John the Baptist and himself, and concludes, *Wisdom is jus-*

tified by all her children (Luke 7:35). And in Luke 11:49 we hear in the mouth of Jesus, *And that is why the Wisdom of God said, "I will send them prophets...."* Other passages that show Jesus as Sophia's child are Luke 10:16; non-biblical, very ancient Syriac Odes of Solomon; and the Gospel of the Hebrews.

Jesus as Sophia

For those who know the Sophia of the Old Testament, what Paul is saying about Jesus in I Corinthians 2:6,7 is clear: *It is of the mysterious Wisdom of God that we talk, the Wisdom that was hidden, which God predestined to be for our glory before the ages began.*

Paul is asserting that Jesus and Sophia are the same person.

This may seem strange and unusual, but it is actually a rather commonplace association for first-century Christianity. For instance, the first three verses of the Gospel of John read as follows: *In the Beginning was the Word: the Word was with God and the Word was God. He was with God in the beginning. Through him all things came into being, not one thing came into being except through him.*

Since the "Word" of God in the Old Testament is never described in terms anything like these, it is clear that the Gospel of John has taken the character of Sophia and applied it to Jesus, the Word Incarnate. Both Sophia and Jesus are at the beginning, both are close to God, and both are the means by which all things come into being. Colossians 1:15-20 does exactly the same thing in its description of Christ as "the image of the unseen God" and "the first born of all creation."

Matthew's Gospel has a similar and more thorough-going affirmation of Jesus as Sophia. For instance, the passage in Luke 11:49 (already cited as a text from the early layer of tradition) says, *The Wisdom of God said, "I will send them prophets and apostles, some they will slaughter and persecute..."* is changed by Matthew to read *I (Jesus) am sending you prophets and wise men and scribes; some you will slaughter and crucify....* (23:34). In Matthew 11:26-28 Jesus speaks as if he is the Sophia described in Ecclesiasticus 6:28-31, and Matthew 11:19 refers to Jesus' miracles as *Wisdom's deeds.*

There are other texts which directly identify Jesus as Sophia like those in Paul and Matthew (I Cor. 1:23, 25; Luke 10:21; Matt. 23:27-39; Luke 13:34). There are many more characterizations of Jesus with Sophia's traits like those in John and Colossians (John 1:14; 5:19-22; 8:23, 24; 10:37, 38; 12:44-48; Eph. 3:9-11; James 3:13-17).

But even though Sophia and Jesus are clearly identified with one another in these texts, there is a strange reticence to follow through on this association. It is clear that most of the New Testament authors know of a strong first-century current that says

Jesus and Sophia are the same person. It is equally clear that these same authors are inhibited by this association.

Two major theories have developed to explain this muted approach to the identification of Jesus with Sophia. One, articulated clearly in Joan Chamberlain Engelsman's *The Feminine Dimension of the Divine*, is that patriarchal spirituality reasserted itself and inhibited early Christian "Jesus is Sophia" impulses. The other, first suggested in Hans Jonas' *The Gnostic Religion*, is that gnostic Christians' enthusiasms for the Jesus-Sophia connection was so strong that New Testament authors sought to avoid any misunderstanding that Jesus as Sophia might evoke.

We tend to think that both patriarchy and gnosticism combined to inhibit the articulation of Jesus and Sophia's relationship in the New Testament.

Implications of the Sophia-Jesus Connection

The connections the New Testament makes between Jesus and Sophia are so dramatic that the question with which we began this article must be revised. Based on the early tradition of Jesus as Sophia's prophet, the question could be, "Can a male who is a prophet of the divine female Sophia save women?" Or, based on the identification of Jesus with Sophia, it could be, "Can a savior who is both male and female save women?" Or, "Can Sophia who entered Jesus and enters holy souls still save women?"

These shifts in the question delineate the profound shifts in Christology which the acknowledgement of Sophia's presence and influence in the Christian scriptures and tradition necessitates. More than a change in Christology is involved; Sophia changes the theological and spiritual landscape for all who recognize her presence. The most basic change that Sophia brings is the ability of women to identify with her. She is female, as are they. Identification with Sophia brings affirmation of women's experience, of women's bodies, of women's power.

Given how much Sophia is a part of the New Testament pictures of Jesus and given her impact on women's identity, how shall we now think of Jesus and Sophia? Shall we think of Jesus as Sophia's prophet? As one of her many messengers? As one who replaced Sophia in Scripture and tradition, and who now should be replaced by her? As an equal partner with Sophia?

These questions in response to the discovery of Sophia in the New Testament open up an exciting new vista for feminists who value the Christian tradition.

——◆——

Sophia's "Henchpersons"

by Reta Halteman Finger

Daughters of Sarah, January/February 1991 issue on women and aging.

Many Christian feminist women ask how Jesus as a male can be an adequate role model and savior for women. But I have fewer problems with Jesus' maleness than I do with his comparative youth. If Jesus was killed in his early or mid-thirties, how can he in his human nature understand what it is like for me to be approaching fifty—and to know that I may live another thirty-five or forty years?

If God became human in Jesus to show the rest of us how to live fully human in this world, how are we supposed to handle the second half of our lives without Jesus as a role model? Does it mean we should have been as radical as he in challenging evil and, like the modern martyr Martin Luther King, Jr., have been cut down in the prime of life? I raise that as a serious question.

On the other hand, if Jesus had managed to survive another twenty or thirty years, would his fearless confrontation of hierarchy and domination have mellowed over time? Would his radical criteria for life in God's called-out community (à la the Sermon on the Mount) have been tempered by years of living with the foibles of his all-too-human disciples? Would the devil eventually have worn down his resistance to temptation? Or would aging and increasing intimacy with his divine Abba have deepened and strengthened him even more?

Someday I would like to participate in a discussion with other middle-aged or older Christian feminist women and explore without flinching how Jesus can or cannot be a role model for us in our age and gender.

If we cannot look to Jesus directly as a role model for an older woman, to whom can we look? Old women have not been held in particularly high esteem in the church. Mary, the primary female role model in Christendom, is inevitably characterized as a young, beautiful virgin, a condition no woman (including Mary) can maintain indefinitely.

I first discovered the honoring of older women in Wicca, the Old Religion, where various stages of a woman's life are represented by the Maiden, the Matron, and the Crone. The positive connotation of a crone as a valued old woman capable of wise leadership was new to me. I instinctively felt that Wicca had grasped an aspect of

Good News that a more male-oriented Christian church had overlooked or repressed.

But Wicca is not my tradition nor the ground of my salvation; I am a Christian feminist. So it was with joy that I began reading about the biblical Sophia (Wisdom), first in essays by Elizabeth Schüssler Fiorenza and more recently in books such as *Wisdom's Feast* by Susan Cole, Marian Ronan, and Hal Taussig (Harper & Row, 1989). Just this past summer at the conference of the Evangelical Women's Caucus, composer Ken Medema focused an entire concert on Sophia and her (as he called them) "henchpersons."

Illustration by Kari Sandhaas,
in *Daughters of Sarah*,
November/December 1990.

It has only been eight or ten years since I've been formally introduced to Sophia as the female personification of Yahweh. Only since then have I imaged her as an older woman walking the streets or seated in a rocking chair—waiting for me to come to her. Yet in meeting her more explicitly as Lady Wisdom, I realized I had known her for many years in the persons of older women who had become my mentors when I was young.

Of the many older women whom I loved and whose wisdom fed my spirit over the years, I think of three who met me at critical times of spiritual development. The first was my grandmother, Elizabeth Bean Guntz, who loved me unconditionally from my birth and delighted in each of my childish accomplishments. Rooted in the here-and-now with cows to milk, peas to shell, and a flock of grandchildren to buy Christmas presents for, Grammy seemed centered in a mysterious Spirit I could not then name. Death seemed to hold no fear for her, only a joyous homegoing.

It was typical of her lifelong caring that, just before my twenty-third birthday, as she left home for what she knew was her last trip to the hospital, she reminded my aunt to "make sure you give Reta those bird pictures I got her for her birthday. They're in my lower dresser drawer." During the generation that has since passed, Sophia has often come to me in the form of my Grammy—and I am a little girl and I crawl into her lap.

As a young teenager, I taught Vacation Bible School in the mountains of Pennsylvania. For two weeks each summer I stayed in the home of Thelma Felton, a widow with three small children. Still young herself, but nearly twice as old as I at the time, I saw the grace of Wisdom upon her and I heard her pray as I had heard no woman pray before. She loved me, and she fed me from the springs of her deep faith. Now in her sixties, Thelma's smile is the same, and when we visit, we pick up where we left off. Once in a halfwaking moment I had a vision of what this diminutive, polio-crippled woman would look like in the New Creation—and I fell at her feet in wonder.

As my college years were ending in the 1960s, I was asked to work as dean of girls in the dormitory of the Mennonite high school on the same campus. A middle-aged woman, Miriam Barge, was leaving that position to become a college administrator.

My education had given me little formal preparation for living with high school girls, and Bargie—as she had been affectionately called by her charges—became, very literally, my mentor. Pouring out my own life day and night with these youngsters, I would fly to her for emotional replenishment and for wisdom, and she never let me down. The uncounted hours spent talking, praying and laughing, the delight we both felt being together, literally grew me up emotionally and spiritually. Often now when I see Lady Wisdom, I see Bargie in her chair and I kneel beside her and put my arms around her neck and am strengthened.

In many respects, I now am what I am because of the ways Sophia and her hench-persons have cared for me year after year. But today many of us are middle aged or older. We do not have many older women to depend on as mentors. We *are* the mentors, the grandmothers, the role models for younger women. (As Dave Barry put it in his book, *Dave Barry Turns Forty* (Fawcett Books, 1991), "We are no longer the Hope of the Future. We are the Hope of the Right Now.") And we have an opportunity to be Sophia's henchpersons. It's scary, but frankly, I find this incremental growth in wisdom great compensation for bifocals and salt-and-pepper hair.

As we mentor, love, and serve as role models for others, it is comforting to know that we are still children compared to Sophia, the Ancient of Days, present with God at the world's creation. There is still a lap for us to crawl into, arms that fit around us. What more comforting words can we find than those of Sophia God found in Isaiah 46:3-4:

Listen to me, O house of Jacob [and Rachel], all the remnant of the house of Israel [and Leah], who have been borne by me from your birth, carried from the womb; even to your old age I am [s]he, even when you turn gray I will carry you. I have made, and I will bear; I will carry and will save. (NRSV)

— ◆ —

Recognizing the Goddess

by Anne Ramirez

Daughters of Sarah, Spring 1994 issue on interreligious dialogue. Anne Ramirez, of Springfield, Pennsylvania, was a long time contributor to *Daughters of Sarah*. At that time she was writing a book on Christ-like women in literature which later became her Ph.D. dissertation. She is now a temporary full-time instructor at Neumann College.

We hear much about "the Goddess" in contemporary culture. Radical post-Christian feminists and conservative Christians agree, ironically, that she has no place in the Judeo-Christian tradition. Yet I have come to believe "the Goddess" is part of the biblical God. If men and women are both made in God's image and are called to represent Christ to one another, then God must include maleness and femaleness. I do not say this lightly. As a Christian feminist it matters to me that I am not revising so much as rediscovering part of my heritage—part of the treasure hidden in a field of which Jesus spoke.

From the years my children watched Sesame Street, I recall a sequence in which a little boy marvels that he is seen differently by the various people who know him. He is a son, a grandson, a neighbor, a paper boy, a student. All these descriptions are true even though he is a single individual, and some of his acquaintances will never have occasion to see him in some of his roles. So it is with God. People in fact have experienced God through many different images, some of which are female.

To see God as both male and female is not to imply there must be two deities, unless one believes gender is the most important distinction between human beings—a notion hardly supportable from the New Testament. Of course, it does not follow that any and all possible perceptions of God are equally accurate. I believe Jesus came to dwell among us in response to all human seeking for God. If one looks to Christ as the standard for discerning the divine nature, one will reject certain perceptions. For instance, one will not believe God to be racist, power-hungry, or cruel. However, biblical references to God as female have been carefully documented by such scholars as Virginia Mollenkott in *The Divine Feminine* (Crossroad, 1983) and Leonard Swidler in *Biblical Affirmations of Woman* (Westminster, 1979).

Swidler concludes that cultural influences led the early Christian church away from three significant characteristics of its founder Jesus: an emphasis on service rather than authority, an affirmation of the material blessings of this life, and an egalitarian attitude toward women. The repression of these three closely related ideals forced certain spiritual needs and forms of expression underground. Positive images of women reappeared in popular devotion to Mary and a host of female saints, as well as in so-called secular literature.

Protestantism has traditionally discouraged such female-affirming elements of our Christian heritage, regarding them as pagan because many pre-Christian religions overtly portrayed the feminine dimension of the divine. This reasoning is quite illogical, considering that most non-Christian religions also portray male deities, but one never hears this fact used as an argument against male metaphors for God. Therefore, the mere fact that a particular image or experience is part of pre-Christian religion cannot in itself invalidate it as part of the Christian faith.

On the other hand, there is a widespread belief among feminists that "the Great Goddess" was once the object of adoration by a more or less utopian human society, only to be displaced by the more recent, hopelessly patriarchal, religions of Judaism, Christianity, and Islam. Tikva Frymer-Kensky, *In the Wake of the Goddesses* (Fawcett Columbine, 1992), expresses exasperation at this common misunderstanding of the field to which she has devoted her scholarly life. We have no record of ancient religions that believed in a single Great Goddess; rather, we know that other cultures surrounding the early Israelites were polytheistic, worshipping many powerful gods and goddesses simultaneously. A similar observation has been made by Celtic scholars concerning the polytheism of the ancient Northern Europeans. As the three great monotheistic religions developed, they dealt with the resulting questions about gender and sexuality in different ways, often unsatisfactorily from a feminist perspective.

It is true that by the early Christian era the Roman Empire had brought together such a multitude of belief systems that educated Hellenes began to suggest there might be only one Great Goddess known by many names. In *The Golden Ass*, the second-century writer Apuleis (best known for his story of Cupid and Psyche within this same work) gave eloquent expression to this possibility. His character Lucius has a splendid vision of the Goddess, who claims the Egyptian title of Isis as her true name. This passage is crucial to the argument of Robert Graves' influential volume *The White Goddess: A Historical Grammar of Poetic Myth*, originally written in 1948 well before recent feminists began interpreting the Goddess more literally.

What seems to have happened is that the Great Goddess was a relatively late image, apparently developing alongside a monotheistic Christianity which had become dominated by masculine imagery. Had the Church retained the inclusive attitude of its founder Jesus, perhaps people would have felt no need to create a separate Goddess religion. Robert Graves, Joseph Campbell, and many other modern thinkers see all female portrayals of divinity as aspects of one Great Goddess, no matter how varied the values and customs of the cultures from which these portrayals arise.

Similarly, modern witchcraft deliberately selects and combines various symbols, rituals, and myths in a belief system that can never be proved to have existed in the same form in the distant past. In theory, one might also choose to say that all masculine images of God in every land are manifestations of a single God. Whether consciously or unconsciously, we all select which of all the beliefs we have encountered shall govern our lives.

As a Christian, however, I feel it necessary to be very aware of what images and beliefs I choose to accept. Surely it is an insult to all cultures and religions—not just to the Judeo-Christian tradition—to carry syncretism to the extreme of saying that all female and/or all portrayals of God can be melded into one. In Apuleis' Cupid and Psyche story, Venus may be seen as the White Goddess figure, but I much prefer Psyche, the human and paradoxically Christ-like bride who suffers hardships and ventures into the world of the dead for the sake of her beloved husband. Which is a true image of divinity, Venus or Psyche?

I am enriched by numerous myths and folktales from other cultures, providing they illuminate the realities of experience in ways that seem consistent with the truths of my Christian faith. But it does not follow that I accept all such stories indiscriminately. Nor do I blindly accept pronouncements about God from professing Christians if they appear inconsistent with my understandings of Christianity. The little boy of

Sesame Street may be many things, but it does not follow that he must also be a dragon, a leaf, or a bicycle.

I find it reassuring to realize the diversity among different branches of the early Christian Church. As many feminist scholars have observed, the winners of history are not necessarily in the right. Perhaps I would be seriously attracted to post-Christian goddess cults if I had not been blessed through my study of literature with bits and pieces of tradition which I now recognize as Celtic Christianity. The rural Christians of northern Europe developed a world view very different from that of the Roman Church, shaped by dualistic theologians like St. Augustine. Among the Celts, wise women served as healers, midwives, and religious leaders. During the Christian era, abbesses such as St. Brigid of Kildare and Hilda of Whitby governed large religious communities that included both male and female monastics.

Celtic Christian literature celebrates relationships with God, with one another, and with the natural world, invoking God's blessing upon the light of the morning fire, the planting of seeds, and the singing of blackbirds. This sense of the "blessed creation" and the holiness of daily life is deeply refreshing in an age filled with barriers separating the secular from the sacred. Through such books as Robert Van de Weyer's *Celtic Fire* (Doubleday, 1990) and Esther de Waal's *Every Earthly Blessing* (Servant Publications ed., 1992), I feel I have found my spiritual home, where all our limited metaphors for God are transcended in a profound peace.

At the heart of the Catholic college where I teach is a small chapel. The front of the sanctuary is dominated by a tall crucifix, illuminated by a well-placed skylight. Only upon turning to leave does one see the statue of Mary standing in a recess in the back wall, with her Child on her arm and a spray of flowers precariously tucked in her other hand. As a good Protestant I firmly believe that Mary the mother of Jesus was a human woman like myself. But as a Christian I also believe she symbolizes the feminine face of God. If preoccupied, one might enter the chapel, pray, and turn to leave without ever noticing Our Lady, yet she stands there all the same.

Lack of attention does not affect the reality of her presence or the love in her eyes. She reminds me that the One who called the worlds into being has always existed and always will, whether or not we choose to imagine an exclusively male or exclusively female deity. That which is both God and Goddess is also the light of the world, the water of life, the yeast in the dough, and the rushing wind of the Spirit.

— ◆ —

The Invincible Woman of Revelation 12

by Virginia Ramey Mollenkott

Daughters of Sarah, July 1977 issue (language updated January 2001). Virginia Ramey Mollenkott is author of *The Divine Feminine: Biblical Imagery of God as Female* (Crossroad, 1983), and eleven other books.

By the church of my youth I was taught that in the Bible, powerful females were always symbols of evil. Perhaps the most massive refutation of that put-down occurs in the twelfth chapter of Revelation, which describes a huge portent visible in the sky—a woman clothed with the sun, standing on the moon, crowned with twelve stars. Verses 1-6 depict her first victory over the seven-headed dragon that hoped to eat her offspring: she gives birth to the universal king who is immediately snatched up to the throne of God, and then makes good her escape into the desert.

Verses 7-11 describe a second defeat of the dragon, this time by Michael and the angels of heaven. Verses 13-17 describe a third defeat of the dragon, which by now has been identified as Satan. The woman is once again the object of the dragon's hatred, but as it spews out a river to sweep her away, the earth swallows the river. In its frustrated rage the dragon gives up on the woman and turns to making war against the rest of her children.

Who is this magnificent, non-violent, invincible woman? The answer is suggested to us through her offspring. She is the mother of "a male child, who will rule all the nations with a rod of iron" (v 5). Psalm 2:9 prophesies the coming of a Messiah with a rod of iron, and Revelation 19:15 says that someone named the Word of God will rule the nations with a rod of iron. So the baby is the Christ.

Yet Revelation 2:26-27 extends the meaning somewhat by telling us that everyone who overcomes evil and does God's will to the end will be granted authority over the nations and will rule them with a rod of iron. So the baby symbolizes not only Jesus but also the whole church body of which the Christ is the head. The snatching of the child up to the very throne of God symbolizes the powerlessness of Satan to prevail over Jesus and the entire Body of Christ.[1]

In the many-faceted way of symbolism, not only is the church triumphant included in the symbol of the infant ruler, but it is also depicted as "the rest of her children" identified as "those who keep God's commandments and hold to the testimony of

Jesus" (v 17). Thus we must conclude that this woman who gives birth to Christ and all the faithful is a figure of heroic and even cosmic dimensions, especially since she appears "in heaven."

She comes with a supernatural aura as the symbol of ultimate goodness paired off in a single combat of non-violent resistance against the violent force of ultimate evil. She is clothed with the sun. Traditionally the sun is a symbol of permanence. In patriarchal myth it is a symbol of the son and heir of the god of heaven; and the Old Testament closely associates the sun with the Messiah, the sun of righteousness (Mal. 4:2; Ps. 19:4-5; 72:17; Isa. 60:1-3). So the woman is simultaneously clothed in the Messiah (and thus identified with the godhead) and bringing forth the Messiah. And she is standing on the moon—traditionally the symbol of the constantly changing human condition, which by being beneath her feet both supports her and yet is subject to her.

Since the sun is usually a masculine symbol and the moon a feminine one, the woman encompasses all genders. Her inclusiveness is further emphasized by her crown of twelve stars. Stars are symbols of the spirit (especially in its struggle against the forces of darkness), and twelve is a number symbolizing cosmic order and salvation (the twelve signs of the Zodiac, twelve tribes of Israel, twelve disciples of Christ). Once she has delivered her child, she flees into the wilderness, traditionally regarded as the place most conducive to divine revelations. The wilderness or desert is, after all, the domain of the sun.

That the woman is symbolic of ultimate goodness is reinforced by the parallel confrontation of Michael with Satan in verses 7-12. Clearly, Michael symbolizes Christ's power by triumphing over Satan and Satan's cohorts. Milton's *Paradise Lost* makes the war in heaven a magnificent symbol of the uneven battle between ultimate good and evil. Through the centuries interpreters have never had any trouble recognizing the powerful symbology of warfare; but little has been said about the equally powerful depiction of Satan's defeat through the feminine symbology of giving birth. Nor has much attention been focused on the fact that Revelation 12 both begins and ends with the defeat of Satan via nonviolent feminine symbols, whereas the much-touted masculine symbols are used only in the middle passage.

After the dragon has been thrown down to earth, it springs into pursuit of the woman. But she is once again closely aligned with God, for she is given the wings of a great eagle, traditionally the bird of Divine Majesty and psychologically a symbol of the Mother/Father. She flies back to the wilderness, the domain of the sun. Satan (still depicted as a dragon or serpent) tries to drown her by vomiting a river. Moisture is symbolic both of physical birth and of moral corruption, while a river symbolizes fertility and the ravages of time. But the earth, almost universally regarded as female, comes to the woman's aid by soaking up the river, and the serpent is frustrated once again.

Since evil cannot defeat the woman, the serpent goes off in search of her children. But because her children are those who "keep the commandments and hold to the testimony of Jesus," we know that evil will never be able to prevail against them either. We are reminded of that earlier woman, crestfallen before the Judge, who heard even in the hour of humanity's disgrace that there would be enmity between her seed and the serpent's seed, but that it would be her seed that would inflict the head-wound (Gen. 3:15).

Many commentaries tell us that the invincible woman of Revelation 12 is Israel. On one level, certainly the woman is the Hebrew nation out of which comes the Messiah.[2] The problem is that most commentaries fail to point out the larger dimensions of the woman as Israel. Galatians 6:16 speaks of Christ's followers as "Israel," while Psalm 73:1 and John 1:47 imply that anyone with a clean, guileless heart is entitled to the name of Israelite. On an even grander scale, Christians universally interpret Isaiah 49:3 as referring to none other than Jesus the Christ when it speaks of "God's servant Israel." The invincible woman of Revelation 12 symbolizes Israel in all three of these senses—the community of God's chosen people the Jews, the community of Christ's Body the Church, and the Jesus the Christ as the Sovereign One, victor over the forces of evil.

In the latter capacity, obviously, the woman serves as one of the many biblical indicators of a powerful "feminine component" in the nature of God and God's people. Those of us who are disturbed by the violence can rejoice at the presence of a non-violent feminine symbology in the Bible. In an all-too-violent world, we can perhaps begin to de-emphasize Christian soldiership and begin to lay more stress on defeating evil by giving birth to goodness, by close cooperation with the earth, and by flying on eagles' wings to the domain of the sun.

---

[1] On biblical symbolism, see "Symbol, Symbolism" in *The Interpreter's Dictionary of the Bible* (Nashville: Abingdon, 1962), IV, 472-6. On symbolism in general, see J.E. Cirlot, *A Dictionary of Symbols* (New York: Philosophical Library, 1962); and Maria Leach, et. al., *Standard Dictionary of Folklore, Mythology and Legend* (New York: Funk and Wagnalls, 1972). On the genetic implications of the Virgin Birth, which show that Jesus is not an exclusively male savior, see Virginia Mollenkott, *Omnigender: A Transreligious Approach* (Cleveland: The Pilgrim Press, 2001), 105-6.

[2] For other parallels between Israel's experience and the woman's, see Harry Whittaker, *Revelation: A Biblical Approach* (Cornwall, England: Wardens of Cornwall Ltd., 1973), 162.

——— ◆ ———

Psalms

by Molly McDaniel

Daughters of Sarah, Spring 1993 issue on women in ministry. At that time Molly McDaniel wrote, gardened, and enjoyed her husband and bulldogs in rural Maryland.

O God of mystery and presence
your mercy overflows my soul like
cello and oboe resonate deep

you lullaby soothing my frantic tomorrow
you celebrate singing the newborn and reborn
your voice is all starts and moon
your voice is all sky and water

you write, O God, with words of size and sound upon my heart
an alphabet of grace and truth;
you call my name amidst the clamour, silence me to solitude and surrender,
your words are texture taste and rhyme.

You lavish sight with purple and white
fill my veins with red and blue
cast your spectrum shadow of light on all I see and imagine.
Your colours, O God, are movement and dance
your colours are depth and play
your size, O God, is mystery, infinity, eternity, present, today.

O God, my God,
your mercy arouses my senses.
I celebrate singing your mystery and presence.

Rainmaking God, my soul thirsts for a thunderstorm.
Violent violet violins scream across summer silence,
slice vaporous skies silly.
Western wind wraps whistling,
enraptures tango-tied birch & maple leaves loose,
soaks my soul's dry desert dust,
saturates my leaping limbs,

I dance the baptismal dance,
wild water music.

Chapter 3

Women (& Men) in Ministry

S hould women preach? Should women be ordained? Is it okay for women to teach men in church? As Christians became conscious of gender issues in the early 1970s, one of the first questions concerned women's role in ministry.

Though only a minority of Christians of either gender choose ordination, the question of equal access to ministry is a crucial one. When women care about the Church and sense the Holy Spirit calling them to share the Good News and nurture believers, the stained-glass ceiling used by the Church to limit women's authority quickly becomes oppressive. Restrictions against carrying out the Great Commission challenge the very nature of the gospel itself.

Since most scriptural restrictions to women's full participation in the ministries of the church depended upon a few New Testament references in 1 Corinthians and 1 Timothy, many articles in evangelical publications attempted to exegete these passages. *Daughters of Sarah* authors, however, also featured scores of ministering women in history and the contemporary church. They went on the offensive, highlighting the Apostle Paul's egalitarian relationships with his female co-workers, or humorously hedging about male ordination, or ridiculing nit-picking restrictions about what women could or could not do.

The following articles represent only a small selection of many highlighting women (and men) in the ministry of the Church.

— ◆ —

Peace Talk

by Irene Zimmerman

Daughters of Sarah, November/December 1989 issue on war and peace. At that time, Irene Zimmerman was a published poet and member of the School Sisters of St Francis, taking a sabbatical year for prayer, writing, and study.

> "Of course," you say,
> "the women have a role to play.
> How would we fare in Geneva
> without you wonderful hostesses
> and secretaries working behind the scenes?"
>
> Gentlemen, do not forget
> that at the highest summit
> of all time,
> a woman dialogued alone with God
> and wove the fabric
> of an everlasting peace.
>
> This is not to say
> in anger or naiveté:
> "We women are more able."
> but to say the Prince of Peace
> called everyone in to sit at the table.

—◆—

"I Am Among You As One Who Serves"

Jesus and Food in Luke's Gospel

by Jennifer Halteman Schrock

Daughters of Sarah, Fall 1993 issue on women and food. At that time Jennifer Halteman Schrock was a free-lance writer from Columbus, Ohio.

Nowhere has the relationship between Jesus and food been explored more thoroughly than in the Gospel of Luke. In Luke, it is sometimes said, Jesus is either going to dinner, coming from dinner, eating dinner, or telling stories about dinners. The odor of food wafts through every chapter.

In Luke's theology, the kingdom of God comes through table fellowship. It is through eating with outcasts that Jesus announces God's redeeming love; it is in the breaking of the bread that he is first recognized as risen Lord. The meals he shares with his disciples are in many ways acted parables of the Jewish understanding of the end time—a time when God would "prepare a feast of rich food for all peoples" (Isa. 25:6) and the righteous would eat and rejoice in the presence of God.

Luke's focus on food brings up an interesting question: How did all these meals magically appear on the table? And where do women—the primary preparers of food—stand in a gospel of good things to eat?

What is even more interesting is how difficult it is to find anyone who is wondering along these lines. A trek through ten or twelve standard commentaries reveals no hint of the gender dimensions which may be present beneath the surface of texts involving food.

It is surprising, therefore, to find that the author of Luke has actually taken pains to

Illustration by Kari Sandhaas, published in *Daughters of Sarah*, Fall 1993.

treat this topic. Luke includes at least four texts where women and meals intersect, three of which are unique to this Gospel. These texts present a positive yet nuanced picture of the women's work that brought food to the table. Luke recognizes women's service in traditionally female ways as an important part of Jesus' ministry but does not confine women to these roles only. As Luke's Gospel unfolds, its attention to women and table service also leads us to read Jesus' role as servant lord in a new way.

It does not take a hotel manager to see that a band like the one Jesus led wandering from town to town were dependent on the hospitality—and housekeeping—of others along the way. We briefly glimpse one of these households in Luke 4:38-39. Here, Jesus stays with Simon Peter and heals his mother-in-law who is suffering from a high fever. "Immediately she got up and began to serve them" (*NRSV*), the text says.

This two-verse snippet from Capernaum is not one of Luke's juicier healing stories, but it nevertheless has some interesting features. One is the first appearance of a word that will occur several more times in the Gospel of Luke: *diakoneo*. This word is generally translated "serve" and has given us the English word "deacon." The implied meaning here is that Peter's mother-in-law prepared and served a meal. Later, as it is used in other contexts, it is helpful to remember this homely scene as an example of the most basic meaning of the word.

The story of Peter's mother-in-law is also a small clue pointing us to a cadre of disciples whose contribution is generally overlooked: the scores of stay-at-home women who hosted Jesus, his fellow travelers and (as, is likely, judging from Luke 4:40-41) the sick and the crazed who followed him like flies.

The second woman whose table service is recorded in Luke turns up on the floor. She is the "sinner" in Luke 7:36-50 who interrupts a Pharisee's lunch to wash Jesus' feet, lavishly kissing, wiping, and anointing them. Today the story is a bit hard to identify with because we think of kissing men's feet as a sign of pathology. Jesus, however, takes this woman's ministrations as an expression of love. Even Simon, who does not welcome her in his home, objects to her character rather than her behavior.

The story makes sense only if we accept that washing feet was a normal, everyday role for a woman at a meal at the time. It was a job that routinely fell to the wife of the host. If we scan the gospels for other examples of this amenity, we find Mary in John 12:1-8 anointing Jesus' feet and wiping them with her hair at a dinner shortly before his death. Matthew and Mark both contain a similar act carried out by an unnamed woman (Matt. 26:6-18; Mk. 14:3-9). A woman is the washer in all of the feet-washing stories in the New Testament—except one. One wonders why more sermons on Jesus' embracing of the basin and towel at the Passover supper in John 13 don't happen to mention this.

Women, meals, and the word *diakoneo* reappear again in Luke 8:1-3. Mary Magdalene, Joanna, and Susanna, among others, travel with Jesus and provide for him (*diakoneo*) out of their resources. Like Peter's mother-in-law, their service seems to stem from the experience of being healed. Commentators do not agree on exactly what role these women played in Jesus' ministry, but whatever shape their discipleship took, it is likely, given the times and the presence of the word *diakoneo*, that it included preparing and serving food.

Here, Luke shows us a slightly different model of female discipleship: women who exercised traditional roles in a radical way. Table service was women's work, but leaving home to travel with a rabbi was not. This text doesn't tell us whether Mary, Joanna, and Susanna were also co-preachers at this point in Jesus' ministry, but all the same their presence as chefs and administrators is paired with the Twelve.

The third text where Luke makes us aware of the women who served and nourished Jesus is a close-up: the familiar story of Martha and Mary in Luke 10:38-42. Here for the first time, we see a woman move out of a service role. We also see the tension it creates. A conflict erupts between the two sisters when Mary is too busy sitting at Jesus' feet to help with the housework. Mary's audacity and Martha's annoyance are clarified by the fact that to sit at a rabbi's feet means to study with him. Mary is not a dreamy contemplative here so much as a woman usurping a male role. Likely there were a number of men sitting at Jesus' feet at the time as well, and Martha was going to have a crowd to feed when the lecture let out. Again, the verb *diakoneo* is part of the story; Martha complains that she is left alone to serve.

In the hands of another writer, Luke 10:38-42 might have looked very different. Luke could have focused on the men's conversation and we would never have known about the woman in the back row and the crisis in the kitchen. None of the other gospels tells us this story. Instead, Luke zeroes in on a woman's issue that is as alive today as it was two thousand years ago. Do women who adopt male roles and opportunities abandon their more traditional sisters and denigrate their contribution?

The story of Martha and Mary—and Jesus' affirmation of Mary's choice over her sister's—can of course be read in ways that are damaging and divisive to women. If we assume at the outset that of course Jesus would prefer a bright-eyed student to a well-cooked meal, it won't work. It must be remembered that everywhere else so far, *diakoneo* is a very positive word. Jesus' words to Martha, coming on the heels of the portrait of women's work that Luke has already given us, should be read as one of his truly shocking statements.

So shocking, in fact, that Luke spends the rest of his gospel answering Martha's charge: "I am left alone to serve." Never again in the Gospel of Luke does *diakoneo* appear as a word associated with women. Instead, it takes on a new life and turns up in teaching material as behavior Jesus adopts himself and expects of male disciples.

Diakoneo occurs in the parable of the watchful servants in Luke 12:37, in another parable comparing disciples' responsibilities to those of a servant in 17:8, and in a dispute about greatness that breaks out at the last supper in 22:26-27. In each of these texts, the sense of serving a meal is preserved, but the meaning of the word broadens to include men as well as women.

Of course Jesus' preaching about *diakoneo* could just be a fine metaphor that no one paid the slightest attention to. And that business about the basin and the towel in John 13 may have been merely a ritual and a token. But it seems there were men in Jesus' time who took his words literally and were willing to adopt service roles more typically occupied by women. Luke 22:10 gives us a clue. Here, Peter and John are sent to look for a man carrying a water jar who will direct them to a place willing to host their Passover meal. Why does Luke include this seemingly insignificant detail and how was it helpful to Peter and John? Women were the water carriers in those days, and a man with a water jar would indeed stand out on the street. It appears that a certain fluidity around gender roles was a mark the early Christian community used to recognize each other. (Perhaps today Jesus would tell us to look for the men doing dishes if we need help finding other disciples.)

In Luke, Jesus' ministry takes its shape not only from Moses, not only from the Hebrew prophets of old, not only from John the Baptist, but also from ministering women. And Luke, lucky for us, was insightful enough to document this in a way that honors tasks which are sometimes scorned. Table service is recognized as an indispensable part of table fellowship, and Martha is not left alone to serve.

Apparently Luke's vision and the gender flexibility he describes lived on for many years in at least some quarters of Christendom. According to medieval legend, even Martha got a break from the kitchen. Later in life, she went on a preaching tour to France where she was known not only for her cookery but also for slaying a dragon with a pot of holy water. This indeed is the crazy world of the Gospel.

——— ◆ ———

Should Men Be Ordained?
A Theological Challenge

by Gracia Fay Ellwood

Daughters of Sarah, January/February 1983. At that time Gracia Fay Ellwood lived in Pasadena, California, and was editor of the magazine *Mythlore*.

Spurred by the sight of various oppressed groups calling for liberation and equality, men are now demanding admission to the ordained ministries on an equal footing with women. While their claims are not totally without merit, I hope to show on the basis of Scripture and traditional Christian practice why their admission would not be appropriate at present.

Any Christian knows why men have not been ordained to the ministry. They belong to the Ruling Club. Men represent secular power; nearly all societies and governments have been and are presently patriarchal. Any Christian can observe that men run things—or if they don't, they get credit for it.

Which is exactly why a man makes a poor representative to a Christian sacramental or preaching ministry. The Scriptures proclaim an entirely different understanding of power. The theme of Exodus pervades both Old and New Testaments. Our God is one who hears the cries of the oppressed and leads them to freedom, while overlords are reduced to insignificance. Jesus incarnated this theme in his life and teachings, especially in regard to women. In his time, women were expected to be silent stay-at-homes. But he commissioned women to be the first apostles—that is, witnesses of his resurrection.

When a woman preaches, she is herself a living testimony to a God who turns Nobody into Somebody. God spoke, and out of nothing created persons, who could themselves speak. Jesus spoke to the non-persons, and those who were silent became bearers of Good News. Outside the church, women are still struggling with inferior jobs, low pay, trivialization, wastage of their talent. But within the church, women are proclaiming a God who put down the mighty from their thrones and exalted the humble and meek.

This is even more clearly seen in the administration of the sacraments. The woman who ministers at the font and at the Holy Table is a living symbol of the act of grace she is celebrating. Consider baptism, direct and powerful in its appeal, which draws upon ancient womb imagery. Noah's family was reborn from the ark and the flood-waters, into a newly reborn world. Jonah was reborn from the sea and the fish's belly, making possible a new birth for Nineveh. Both point toward Easter morning, when Jesus was reborn from death and from the earth. Thus the initiate comes forth from the baptismal waters, from the divine Womb, as a new person, ready to be nourished by the pure Milk of the Word.

The point is more than obvious. How can the sacrament of second birth be administered by one whose body cannot give first birth? This would sadly impoverish our imagery. The next thing would probably be an alteration of baptismal liturgies to represent the rebirth-giving God as exclusively masculine. Eventually the idea of being born again would become a meaningless puzzle.

Honesty compels me to admit that there is other symbolism implicit in the sacrament which may be compatible with a male ministry and a masculine deity. Among some Christian sects, baptism is performed by sprinkling a few drops of water on the initiate. There is an analogy to the fructification of the earth by rain, and to the male contribution in human procreation.

However, before we abandon the mode of immersion in a rush to the mode of sprinkling so that men will not feel left out, I must point out that this way of baptizing conveys little of the drama implicit in the reality underlying the symbols. I have attended such baptisms, and observed covert yawning and watch-glancing among those not immediately related to the initiates. Children and adults alike, deprived of a satisfying liturgical enactment of the great adventure of *regressus ad uterum Dei* and rebirth, are wont to seek expression of it in the scenarios of popular secular dramas, from Star Trek and Stars Wars to Superman. Such things have a valid place. They are largely harmless, no doubt, and often delightful, but they do not tend to a transformation of life.

Then consider the sacrament of Communion, in which the imagery of birth finds further development. The celebrant enacts the drama of Christ's self-emptying in death. Those present are aware, however dimly, that her body is one that (potentially or actually) gives life by sacrifice. In the pain and indignity and bloodletting of childbirth, a woman is in effect saying to her child, "This is my body...this is my blood, which is shed for you." What the celebrant is mirrors that which she presents. And the body that gives itself to bring another to birth also nourishes that new life, both in the rite and in the reality of physical motherhood. The newborn babes long for the drink of life, and receive it.

The association of woman and nurturing is deep and ancient, and it will be difficult for the masses of people to accept the disruption of its imagery as male hands attempt to offer the sacred food and drink. Of course, insofar as it is a matter of habit based on psychological patterns, it can be changed. Men do occasionally cook and serve food, as at our own church suppers. Planting and harvesting, exclusively female activities in many developing societies, have become male activities in our own. There is even no reason why a man cannot feed an infant with a bottle of animal's milk, appropriately doctored to resemble the real thing. But quite likely the food-giving man will never be as deeply resonating a symbol.

Having shown something of how deeply rooted in the nature of God the Church's tradition of a female ministry is, it may seem I have slammed the door once and for all in the face of young men aspiring to the ministry. I want to stop short of doing so. It would ill befit a woman, raised up by God from nonperson status to the Divine image, thus to imply: "You may think you have a calling by God to the ordained ministry. But I know God better than you do; I know my female being is more deeply akin to God's nature than your male being. God would never call you." Though the maternity of God is a major theme in Scripture and Christian thought, anchored in the pivotal reality of resurrection and rebirth, it is possible that God is also just as fully like a father. Occasional passages, undeveloped images may yet be explicated and drawn together to give undreamed-of insights, and deep self-affirmation to men. God loves men too.

There are Christians who assert that they could never speak of God as "He," since the term is not explicitly used in Scripture. They should bear in mind that neither does Scripture explicitly speak of God as Trinity. Yet the language of Trinity has long been second nature to us.

Perhaps it may be appropriate at times to use "He" for deity. We must not lay down to God the conditions under which we will agree to receive our life. If we trust in God, She will provide—far beyond anything eye has seen, ear has heard, or that has entered into the heart of woman....

Nevertheless, we need to proceed with great caution in considering males for the ordained Christian ministry. Subtly, unconsciously, we may absorb worldly standards of male dominance and thus forsake the very nature of the upside-down Gospel itself.

———◆———

Paul's Women Co-Workers in the Ministry of the Church

by David M. Scholer

Daughters of Sarah, July/August 1980. Dr. David M. Scholer then taught New Testament at Gordon-Conwell Seminary in South Hamilton, Massachusetts. He is now teaching New Testament at Fuller Theological Seminary in Pasadena, California.

The last chapter of Paul's letter to the Romans mentions twenty-nine persons, one by way of special commendation (16:1-2) and the others in a series of personal greetings (16:3-16). Often such lists of names in the Bible are overlooked or dismissed as of little interest or importance. Yet they provide personal and historical details which help in understanding the passage. This list in Romans 16 is significant for the information it provides on Paul's women co-workers in the ministry of the Church, for ten of the twenty-nine persons mentioned here are women. Apart from Priscilla, none are mentioned elsewhere in the New Testament. Although biblical scholars are giving increasing attention to this data about Paul and women, it is still not widely known or appreciated within the Church today.

"Working Very Hard" in Apostolic Ministry

Four of the women are greeted by name and can be grouped together: Mary (16:6), Tryphena, Tryphosa and Persis (16:12). All of these women are said to have worked very hard in the Lord (the words "in the Lord" do not appear in 16:6, but otherwise the designation is parallel). This has often been understood to refer to tasks which are menial and/or "women's work." However, the Greek verb translated "work very hard" *(kopiaô)* is used regularly by Paul to refer to the special work of the gospel ministry. Only twice does Paul use it in a common or secular sense, and in both of these instances it is used within a proverbial expression (Eph. 4:8, 2 Tim. 2:6). Paul frequently uses the term to describe his own apostolic ministry (1 Cor. 4:12; 15:10; Gal. 4:11; Phil. 2:16; Col. 2:29; 1 Tim. 4:10; see also Acts 20:35). Paul also uses the term to refer to the work of others in the ministry. In each case, they are leaders and persons of authority (1 Cor. 16:15-16; 1 Thess. 5:12; 1 Tim. 5:17). In each text in which Paul refers to the "very hard work" of others, his context also stresses the need of respect for and submission to such workers.

It is clear, then, that Paul uses the verb "work very hard" to refer to persons engaged in the authoritative work of ministry. Thus, Mary, Tryphena, Tryphosa, and Persis were four women who "worked very hard" in the Church's ministry. This is made even more clear by the inclusion of the phrase "in the Lord." In this connection, note also Euodia and Syntyche (Phil. 4:2-3), two women whom Paul describes as having "...struggled beside me in the work of the gospel" (4:3 NRSV).

Priscilla, Co-Head of a House Church

In Romans 16:3 Paul greets Priscilla and Aquila, a wife and husband "team" mentioned elsewhere in the New Testament (Acts 18:2; 18:18; 18:26; 1 Cor. 16:19; 2 Tim. 4:19). It is said that believers met in their home, that they traveled with Paul, and that they instructed Apollos, an important early teacher in the Church. In his greeting in Romans (16:3-4) Paul speaks of their deep personal commitment to him and of their recognition throughout all the Gentile churches. Though very unusual at that time, Priscilla is named first, as she is also in three of the five other references to her and Aquila in the New Testament (Acts 18:18; 18:26; 2 Tim. 4:19).

Paul designated Priscilla and her husband Aquila as persons "...who work with me in Christ Jesus" (Rom. 16:3 NRSV). Paul uses the term *synergos* (co-worker) regularly for other leaders in the gospel ministry, including Urbanus (Rom. 16:9), Timothy (Rom. 16:21), Titus (2 Cor. 8:23), Epaphroditus (Phil. 2:25), Clement (Phil. 4:3), Philemon (Philem. 1), Demas and Luke (Philem. 24) and several others (Col. 4:11). He also considers Apollos and himself "God's servants, working together" (1 Cor. 3:9). It is in this group of people who take leadership in the ministry of the gospel that Priscilla, without any distinction related to her sex, is included.

Phoebe, Deacon and Patron

Phoebe, commended by Paul (16:1-2), is assumed to have carried Paul's letter to Rome (Paul wrote Romans from Corinth; Cenchrea, Phoebe's city, was the eastern seaport of Corinth). Paul asks the Roman church "...to welcome her in the Lord as is fitting for the saints and help her in whatever she may require from you..." (16:2 NRSV). In this context of his concern for Phoebe and her reception at Rome, Paul describes Phoebe with two designations: *diakonos* (v. 1) and *prostatis* (v. 2). (The NRSV translates these words as "deacon" and "benefactor," while the less inclusive NIV uses "servant" and "a great help.")

Although the designation of Phoebe as *diakonos* has often been understood to be a reference to the office of deaconess (e.g., *RSV, Jerusalem Bible*, Phillips), this option is unlikely. There was no feminine term "deaconess" in first century A.D. Greek; later Christians coined the term for a developing office of women "deacons." Those passages in the New Testament which seem most likely to refer to the Church office of deacon (1 Tim. 3:8, 12; Phil. 1:1) mention the deacon in conjunction with the bishop. Although a woman "deacon" is a possibility (1 Tim. 3:11 may refer to such), it is very dubious that Phoebe should be called a "deacon." Paul's general use of the term *diakonos* makes another much more likely.

Apart from the "deacon" texts (1 Tim. 3:8,12; Phil. 1:1) and two texts which refer to a non-Christian person or action (Rom. 13:4; Gal. 2:17), Paul uses *diakonos* to refer to servants or ministers of the gospel. He makes general references to this connection (2 Cor. 3:6; 6:4; 11:15, 23) and designates certain persons as *diakonoi* (translated as servants/ministers by the *RSV, NRSV,* and *NIV*): Christ (Rom. 15:8); Apollos (1 Cor. 3:5); Epaphras (Col. 1:7); Timothy (1 Tim. 4:6); Tychicus (Eph. 6:21; Col. 4:7) and himself (1 Cor. 3:5; Eph. 3:7; Col. 1:23, 25).

Thus, to understand Phoebe's designation most accurately in Paul's context is to see her as a minister/servant of the church in Cenchrea. Earl E. Ellis, a prominent evangelical New Testament scholar, in a 1971 article on "Paul and His Co-Workers," had concluded that *diakonia* in Paul's letters refer to a special class of co-workers who were active in preaching and teaching.

Paul also calls Phoebe a *prostatis*. Translations of this term vary widely: good friend *(NEB, TEV);* looked after *(JB);* helper *(RSV);* great help *(NIV),* benefactor *(NRSV).* This is the only occurrence of the term in the New Testament. But it was a relatively strong term of leadership and was used in both pagan and Jewish religious circles. Its verbal form occurs in the New Testament *(proistemi),* only in Paul. Apart from two instances (Tit. 3:8,14), Paul uses the verb in connection with leadership in the Church (Rom. 12:8; 1 Thess. 5:12; 1 Tim. 3:4,5,12). Thus, it is probable that the use of the term *prostatis* for Phoebe is meant to indicate her position of leadership within the Church.

In the light of Paul's use of language, Phoebe appears clearly as a significant leader in the Church, a minister in the Cenchrean church, and part of Paul's circle of trusted coworkers in the gospel.

Apostle Junia, Female to Male and Back Again

The last woman to note among the ten in Romans 16:1-16 has very often been hard to find in most English translations. Her name is Junia (16:7), but in most translations the name has appeared as Junias, a male name (e.g., *NIV:* "Greet Andronicus and

Junias, my relatives who have been in prison with me. They are outstanding among the apostles, and they were in Christ before I was"). One possible explanation for the gender confusion is that in Greek both Junia and Junias would have exactly the same spelling *(Julian)* as the direct object of a verb.

However, the issue is not actually that simple or innocent. There is considerable evidence that Junia was a common Latin female name in the Roman Empire. There is, however, no evidence that Junias was used as a male name at this time. John Chrysostom (d. A.D. 407), one of the first Greek fathers to write extensive commentaries on Paul, and known for his "negative" view of women, understood that Junia was a woman. He marvelled that this woman should be called an apostle. In fact, according to scholar Bernadette Brooten, the first commentator to understand Junia as the male name Junias was Aegidius of Rome (A.D. 1245-1316). Ever since then Junias has been the common reading of the name in Romans 16:7.

The actual "problem" arose in connection with the clause describing Andronicus and Junia as "outstanding among the apostles." This would mean that the woman Junia is recognized as an apostle by Paul in Romans 16:7. Yet the weight of traditional attitudes towards women in the New Testament is so strong that an authoritative lexicon for New Testament Greek (Walter Bauer's first English edition) declared that the name must be the male Junias since the person is called an apostle!

It is true that Paul nowhere else explicitly names any other person than himself and members of the Twelve as apostle. However, his general use of the term apostle (e.g., 1 Cor. 4:9; 9:5-6; 12:28-29; 2 Cor. 11:5, 13; 12:11-12) implies that others bore that title in the early Church (see also Acts 14:4, 14).

Only a few translations (such as the *King James Version*) have recognized Junia as a woman apostle [later also: the *REB,* the *NRSV,* and the *NLT*].

Romans 16:1-16, then, allows us to see that Paul had several women co-workers in the Church's ministry. Mary, Tryphena, Tryphosa and Persis (as well as Euodia and Syntyche in Phil. 4:2-3) all shared in the hard labors of the gospel ministry. Priscilla also was a co-worker with Paul in the ministry. Phoebe was a minister of the Cenchrean church and a leader in the Church. Junia was, along with Andronicus, an outstanding apostle. When the issues of Paul's view of women in the Church are addressed in reference to such texts as 1 Corinthians 14:34-35 and I Timothy 2:8-15, these women co-workers in the ministry must be accounted for in the overall assessment of Paul's view.

— ◆ —

A Modest Proposal:
Men in Ecclesiastical Kitchens

by Christiana deGroot vanHouten

Daughters of Sarah, Fall 1993 issue on women and food. Dr. Christiana DeGroot (formerly deGroot VanHouten) was an associate professor of religion at Calvin College in Grand Rapids, Michigan. This article was reprinted with permission from *Partnership,* Autumn, 1992, the newsletter of the Committee for Women in the Christian Reformed Church.

It distresses many of us that drinking coffee after the morning worship service is no longer the dignified, orderly ritual it once was. We can no longer assume an experienced woman will be serving the coffee with just the right degree of cordiality. Sometimes we must put up with incompetent men who spill coffee into the saucer, or over-enthusiastic men who insist on greeting us by name. At other times, women are masterfully pouring the beverages, but an under-current of dissatisfaction among the men disrupts the beautiful harmony of the fellowship hall. The time has come to bring this issue to the fore. Who is properly to serve coffee after church?

Although Church Order 3½ spells out clearly that "All female members who meet the biblical requirements are eligible for the office of coffee cadette in the church," the practices of local congregations vary widely. They now include members from a wide variety of social, cultural, and ethnic backgrounds, and this variety has been reflected in differing practices in the kitchens, foyers, and fellowship halls.

On one side are the exclusivists, who allow only women in the kitchen. Only women fill the coffee pots, grind the beans, pour the cream, serve the coffee, wash the dishes and wipe up the counter. These congregations are following the example set by Jael, who served Sisera his milk (Judges 4:17-22). The exclusivists claim that although men and women are equal in status, and that men may also be gifted in serving coffee, it is to women that God has given this special role. Submission to scripture requires that we can do no other than keep the kitchen door closed to men. For this reason, when women are ordained as coffee cadettes, they are presented with the keys of the kitchen.

On the other side are the inclusivists who wish to delete the word 'female' from Article 3½ altogether. Outside the door of these church kitchens, the keys are hung so that anyone may have access. Inside the door, men can be seen preparing the coffee and cleaning up.

However, serving the coffee is delegated differently. Some congregations allow only women to serve all the coffee; others allow the men to serve the decaffeinated coffee but not the regular. Still others permit only women to pour the coffee, letting the men add cream and sugar. Some make distinctions based on the church function. Coffee after the Sunday morning worship service is served by women, but men are allowed to pour at the evening service, weddings and funerals, and other church gatherings.

The inclusivists' congregations claim that both men and women are gifted by the Holy Spirit to serve, and the church should not hinder the Spirit. The patience of these local churches is wearing thin, and they are asking that Synod open the office of coffee cadette to *all* qualified members, regardless of gender.

Can this denomination be saved? Or is there already too much coffee over the dam?

The Christian Reformed Church's Synod 1992 has given us an excellent example of how to bridge the coffee gap and submit the practices of my denomination to the Bible. First, taking resolution #4 as my model, I would recommend that the wording of Article 3½ be retained. "All female members who meet the biblical requirements are eligible for the office of coffee cadette in the church." Then, taking resolution #5 as my model, I would encourage the churches to use the gifts of men and women, acknowledging that both men and women have been gifted by the Holy Spirit.

"But how can both of these be done at the same time?" the gentle reader asks.

"Simple. Men are allowed to prepare the coffee, put sugar in bowls, cream in pitchers, pour the coffee, add cream and sugar, wash the dishes and wipe the counters under the supervision of the coffee cadettes."

"But doesn't that contradict Article 3½" the gentle reader asks.

"You haven't been listening carefully. Men are only allowed to pour the coffee. Ordained women serve the coffee."

"But to the person drinking the coffee, it doesn't make any difference if the coffee is poured or served," responds the gentle reader.

"You haven't been paying attention. It's the status of the coffee server that is at issue here, not the job being done. What we're doing is protecting the privileged position of the coffee cadettes. That will keep the exclusivists happy. But, we're also sharing the work. That will keep the inclusivists happy. What genius Synod 1992 had!"

"Excuse me," the less gentle reader responds. "It doesn't sound like genius to me. Who is going to be placated by this? Surely the inclusivists will realize that the men are being taken advantage of. They are doing everything a coffee server does without the benefits of training and the recognition of their call by ordination. The exclusivists will realize, surely, that this makes mockery of the office of coffee server."

"Now you have been paying attention too closely. The point was precisely to placate everyone. You weren't supposed to notice that the end result is hypocrisy, confusion, and the undermining of ordination. You were only to notice that both sides were listened to and acceded to. It's called a compromise."

———◆———

Shattering the Stained-Glass Ceiling

by Susie C. Stanley

Daughters of Sarah, Spring 1993. At that time Susie C. Stanley was an ordained minister in the Church of God (Anderson) and Professor of Church History and Women's Studies at Western Evangelical Seminary, Portland, Oregon.

Illustration by Angela McElwain, published in *Daughters of Sarah*, Spring 1993.

I sat on the stage of a small, conservative university, waiting for the preliminaries to conclude so I could begin my lecture at the Symposium on Gender. The students were noisy during the announcements but that did not diminish the calm I experienced. For one thing, the planning committee had warned me that the students were a rowdy bunch. Secondly, although I had initially felt some apprehension, I had been at peace for several weeks prior to the engagement. When I began speaking, relating my comments on gender stereotyping to the movie "A League of Their Own," students continued talking. Periodically I stopped until they stopped—a technique that served me well as an elementary school teacher but which worked only for a few minutes with this audience. I repeated my strategy several times until at one point the "audience participation" grew to a crescendo. From the podium, I could not distinguish any particular words; it was only after the chapel service and the lunch discussion period which followed that someone told me some students were booing.

Experts who research women's advancement in the work force introduced the term "glass ceiling" several years ago to explain the fact that, despite the inroads women were making in various professions, the top jobs in their chosen fields eluded them. They had climbed the corporate ladder until they reached an invisible barrier that prevents them from securing those jobs just barely beyond their reach. In most churches, a similar ceiling exists, more appropriately labeled a "stained-glass ceiling." (My thanks to Christie Smith Stevens for coining this phrase.)

While the negative response to my lecture at the gender symposium was a painful reminder of the continued resistance to dialogue on gender issues such as the stained-glass ceiling, it served a positive purpose by providing material for analysis. What caused some students to become so agitated that they actually booed my presentation? The discussion afterward provided several clues. The first comment came from a young man who read I Timothy 2:11-12 from his Bible: "Let a woman learn in silence with full submission. I permit no woman to teach or to have authority over a man" (*NRSV*). It is probably safe to say that every woman in ministry has confronted this verse at some point in her career. The student saw no need to develop his argument because, for him, the passage said it all.

Since the verses from I Timothy did not silence me, students attending the discussion period employed other arguments. For instance, I was accused of "male bashing." Needless to say, I never would have been invited to give the lecture if I was a "male-basher." By associating me with this negative label, disgruntled students sought to discount my efforts to challenge stereotypes by claiming that my approach was unchristian. (They might have been tempted to use stronger language, but the location of the symposium was a Christian liberal arts university.) The ultimate argument intended to shame me into silence was the accusation that I was a poor communicator; if I wanted to reach students, I had to learn to deal with the issue less "emotionally."

My experience at the university symposium bluntly reminded me of the strategies people employ to maintain the stained-glass ceiling. Generally, those who guard the ceiling are more subtle in their tactics. Prior to this symposium, I had advocated women's equal involvement with men in church, home, and society for sixteen years without encountering actual "booing."

I have to confess that the negative response to my presentation caused some anguish. I succumbed to the self-blame that victims of harassment, sexual or otherwise, often experience. I spent a sleepless night after the symposium, rehearsing every sentence of my speech over and over in my mind, trying to discover what I said to cause this reaction. The "blame the victim" tactic often succeeds. In this case, the students maintained that their behavior was my fault and tried to make me feel guilty. After subsequent discussions with colleagues and my students, I refused to internalize the false guilt they sought to impose on me. The university students' attempt to silence me by intimidation failed; instead, the experience generated the energy to write this article!

How is the stained-glass ceiling similar to the glass ceiling women experience in the secular work place? Both are invisible and artificial. Tradition and prejudice are twin pillars which help hold the glass ceiling in place. Stereotypes based on prejudice help shore it up. These factors support the stained-glass ceiling as well, with additional pillars of scriptural and theological justifications. Many contend that both ceilings are the creation of God. Nineteenth-century arguments, which continue to be recycled, incorporated the claim that God divinely ordained woman's place in the home. In the business world or church, however, the structures are false ceilings, humanly constructed.

Sexual harassment is another barrier preventing women from cracking the glass ceiling. Sexual harassment is defined as unwelcome sexual advances or requests for sexual favors in return for promotion. A broader interpretation of harassment includes actions or words that create a hostile or intimidating work environment. While both forms of harassment exist in the church, women most often experience a hostile environment that does not welcome or affirm their gifts. I could insert many horror stories here, culled from the testimonies of women clergy, but I will let my university experience serve as a representative example.

Like the glass ceiling, the stained-glass ceiling adjusts to various heights depending on the particular company or church. In some churches, women never cope with the stained-glass ceiling because a stained-glass door prevents them from assuming any professional position in the church. In December 1992 the stained-glass ceiling was raised (but probably not razed) in the Church of England. In my own church, since women have always been ordained, individuals continue to affirm women in ministry. Yet some are fabricating a stained-glass ceiling that would limit women to staff positions while preventing them from serving as senior pastors.

Title VII of the 1964 Civil Rights Act is in place to help crack the glass ceiling in the secular work place. Federal legislation mandates affirmative action to remove discrimination. Despite this legislation, many women decide the ceiling is made of cement or iron rather than glass and give up the struggle, leaving corporations to establish their own businesses. Because religious organizations are exempt from Title VII, women employed by the church have no legal recourse in their efforts to crack the stained-glass ceiling. Like women who have left the corporate arena, many women leave the institutional church and establish parachurch organizations, or leave the church altogether.

An extensive study recently conducted by the U.S. government documented the existence of the glass ceiling. Of the 4,491 executives included in the study, only 6.6

percent (296) were women. Former department of Labor Secretary Lynn Martin commented: "The glass ceiling…deprives our economy of new leaders, new sources of creativity—the would-be pioneers of the business world. If our end game is to compete successfully in today's global market, then we have to unleash the full potential of the American work force" ('Study Throws Light on Glass Ceiling,' *Oregonian*, 9 Aug. 1991). If the church's "end game" is to evangelize the world, we must use all the gifts that God has bestowed on both men and women.

So, how can we shatter the stained-glass ceiling? The following are a few suggestions:

1. Expose the ceiling for what it is—a humanly constructed barrier intended to prevent women from using their gifts in the church.

2. Clean up the environment in the church by reducing the hostile and intimidating atmosphere.

3. Make cracks in the ceiling from the other side. Church executives could implement affirmative action policies.

4. Appoint women as interim pastors. Congregations which have been reluctant to hire women have changed their minds after a woman has served as interim pastor.

Was Paul speaking about the stained-glass ceiling when he announced, "For now we see though a glass darkly?" Probably not. But his words inspire me to hope that God's love will continue to motivate others to join in the task of dismantling the stained-glass ceiling. When tempted to despair, I will bring to mind the results of my university experience. While some students booed, others were so appalled by this behavior that, for the first time, they began to examine the issues that create the pillars which hold up the stained-glass ceiling. Ironically, the rude response by some students served as a lesson which raised awareness among others—ultimately contributing to further cracks in the ceiling.

—◆—

Water Rights

by Ellen Roberts Young

Daughters of Sarah, March/April 1985. Ellen Roberts Young was then and still is a poet from Ardmore, Pennsylvania.

"and Isaac dug again the wells of water which had
been dug in the days of Abraham his father." —Genesis 26:18

Sister, I've found
one of our mother's wells.
Come quick before our brothers
claim it for their own.
They see it their duty
to guard our sources,
decide which to open,
pour out water for us
fitting their own thirsts.
We have a sorry choice:
to show our mother's gift
and see it closed, labelled
with our father's name
or keep it to ourselves,
unwalled, a little while.
I choose the latter. To this day
our willingness to share has met
misunderstanding and contempt
from those who think the patriarchal
waters should suffice.

— ◆ —

Chapter 4

Women, Theology, & Religion

Theology asks questions which reside at the very core of our being. It seeks to understand who we are and how we relate to the world. It seeks to make meaningful sense of the world and of the sacred. It also informs the way in which religious communities are organized—the structures, leaders, and precepts that guide them.

Men have defined the landscape of Christian theology for centuries. In 1974, when *Daughters of Sarah* began, very few Christian feminist writings were available and "clergywoman" was a misnomer. Feminists were just beginning to redefine the theological landscape and expose the blatant inequities of theological gerrymandering.

And yet is not theology rooted in experience? But whose experience? "What would happen," wrote the poet Muriel Rukeyser in 1973, "if one woman told the truth about her life? The world would split open." So it was when women began noticing the discrepancies between what our churches told us about God, humanity, and ourselves and what we began to realize deep down within our souls. This is the foundational inquiry that feminism brings to theology. Christian feminism examines the questions of theology through the lens of women's experiences—both individually and socially—and tests them against the ethics of feminism.

Christian feminist theology recognizes the experiences of women as a valid source of divine revelation. It challenges social structures as it recognizes Jesus' disregard for the inferior status of women pervasive in his society—how he broke with social custom and welcomed women amongst his followers. It revises the masculine definitions of sin as pride, self-assertion, and rebellion against God, and of grace as self-sacrificial love. It questions the structures of power, authority, and leadership in our churches, and recognizes the legitimacy of the call to ministry experienced by women. It advances interreligious dialogue and ecumenism. It imagines new forms of worship, celebration, and prayer. As feminist theologian Elizabeth Moltmann-Wendel states, "There is a reawakening of sensitivity to the forgotten dimensions, to the spheres of the senses, the psyche, the body, the imagination, which hardly had any status in an abstract intellectual theology. Feminism continues the humanizing of theology in an unprecedented way."

The focus of this chapter is on issues of theology and religion. These few short pages in no way encompass the range of topics which *Daughters of Sarah* published over the years. But they do reflect how Christian feminism provides a crossroads where two seemingly contradictory and incongruent traditions intersect—a place to disentangle threads of hope from thorns of oppression. Certainly social and political change cannot occur without an alternative vision towards which to move. Christian feminism offered such an alternative for theology and churches: theology in tension, but alive with possibilities.

— ♦ —

Feminist Theology in Global Context

by Rosemary Radford Reuther

Daughters of Sarah, March/April 1991 issue on global Christian feminism. Rosemary Radford Reuther holds the Georgia Harkness Chair of Applied Theology at Garrett-Evangelical Theological Seminary. This article is an excerpt from a paper she delivered at the Ninth Biennial Conference of the Evangelical Women's Caucus, July 1990.

Feminist theology has often been seen as a white Western women's movement, while liberation theology is seen as springing from the anti-colonial movements of Latin America, Asia, and Africa. However, women from these regions are increasingly discussing what Ghanaian feminist theologian Mercy Amba Oduyoye called "the irruption within the irruption." By this she means the irruption of third world feminist theologies within liberation theologies.

What Is Third World Feminist Theology?

What are the distinctive issues of third world feminist theology? How do feminist religious leaders from such diverse regions as Brazil and Mexico; India; Korea and the Philippines; and Ghana, Nigeria, Cameroun, and South Africa contextualize feminist reflection in their ecclesial, social, and cultural situations?  Despite this enormous diversity, there are many similarities between feminist writings on Christology, God-language, or church and ministry coming from these regions.

This similarity reflects the fact that these women are Christians who have received their Christianity from Western European and North American missionaries. These women have also been educated in a Western European or North American Catholic or Protestant culture. Their languages of communication came to them from the missionaries and colonialists, Spanish or Portuguese, French or English. In order to become Christians, they or their ancestors were uprooted from their indigenous cultures and religions. They all share some similar problems that come from this history of cultural and socio-economic colonialism and its contemporary realities of neo-colonial dependency and exploitation.

One can analyze several aspects of third world women's development of feminist theology. One aspect is the appropriation of feminist theology and social analysis that has appeared in North America or Western Europe. English speaking women in Africa and Asia might read materials from North America, while Latin Americans often also draw on French feminism. But third world women are often multi-lingual. Korean feminists, for example, are also well aware of German, as well as American, feminism.

Much of the critique of patriarchalism in the church and in society that has been done in the West is quite relevant to these third world women. This same patriarchalism has been exported by the West to Latin America, Asia, and Africa. Women in Mexico or India or Korea or Nigeria or South Africa find themselves confronted with colonialist and missionary versions of patriarchal economic and political patterns and male clericalism. They hear versions of the same biblical and theological arguments declaring that God has created male headship and forbidden women to be ordained. Thus, for example, when a Korean woman does feminist New Testament exegesis, she can draw on the work of Elizabeth Schüssler Fiorenza. The patriarchal biblical interpretation which Fiorenza confronts in the West is the same one such a Korean woman has to confront in her own church and theological school.

A second aspect of third world feminist reflection relates to social analysis. Third world women begin to tell their own stories and reclaim their own histories as Korean women, as Mexican women, as Khosa women in South Africa, or as Filipinas. Here the stories become more diverse and distinctive, although the patterns are similar. For most of these third world women there is a keen interest in the status of women in their native culture before colonialization.

Solidarity with the Poor

The storytelling of third world women also includes their contemporary stories, how their socialization by Christian and Western cultures have made them feel about themselves as Asians or Africans and as women. Middle class women reach out to poor women and create gatherings where these women can tell their stories of poverty and sexual exploitation. Out of these stories third world women develop a social analysis of the issues of women in their context. They move beyond a middle class feminism of "equality" to a liberation feminism, locating gender oppression in relation to the structures of class and racial oppression. Solidarity with the oppression and preferential option for the poor takes on an additional and more specific focus. It comes to mean solidarity with these oppressed and exploited poor women of their own countries. These are the poorest of the poor, the *minjung of the minjung*, to use the terminology of Korean feminist liberation.

Sexual exploitation of women cuts across class lines. For middle class, as well as poor women, there is rape or incest of the female child in the home, wife battering, rape in the streets, and denial of reproductive decision-making. All women bear the burden of sexual stereotyping and domestic labor.

But these burdens are aggravated for poor women by poverty. The wealthy woman can employ the poor woman to alleviate her work in housecleaning and childcare, while the poor woman has to neglect her own children to labor for poor wages and in exploitative conditions in the houses of the rich. The poor woman also faces the dangers of the streets where she may be robbed and raped, or the oppression and health hazards of the factory, as she tries to make some money to support the children she may have had to leave unattended at home.

In their gatherings, third world women share the historically specific aspects of social, economic, and political oppression in their countries and how this affects the oppression of women. Discussion of women's oppression also brings out specific cultural problems. For example, in India, a major focus of feminist organizing has been on behalf of the tens of thousands of Indian women who have died or been severely injured in dowry murders or attempted murders. The dowry has become a way of exploiting the economic relation of the bride's to the groom's family. The low view of the woman as an expendable commodity, to be valued only for the goods she brings with her, is greatly exaggerated under the influence of Western consumerism. The groom's family demands a large sum of money and expensive consumer goods as the price for taking the bride into their family. Once these goods are delivered, together with the hapless bride, kitchen accidents are contrived to burn her to death. The groom and his family then go looking for another bride.

For Korean feminists, the forcible division of their country into two parts after World War II has become a focus for feminist theological reflection. The two parts—North and South, capitalist and communist—are each repressively bad examples of the two antagonist world systems on which they depend. Korean feminists have widened the scope of this analysis to include other antagonistic dualisms within Korean society— urban and rural, rich and poor, and especially male-female hierarchy, with its rigid construction by Confucian social ideology.

Korean feminists have suggested that all these various expressions of dualism are rooted in the foundational model of patriarchy. The liberation of the Korean people must encompass an overcoming of all these antagonistic dualisms, not by setting one side against the other, but by transcending such dualisms in a new harmonious synthesis.

The Problem of Cultural Pluralism

Another difficult issue for third world feminists is cultural pluralism, particularly in relation to indigenous religions and cultures which persist underneath Western Christian colonialism. Indigenous or culturally contextual theologies, such as African theology, have sought to appropriate for Christianity positive traits of traditional religions (see Kofi Appiah-Kubi and Sergio Torres, *African Theology en Route*, Orbis, 1979). The dialogue and even the synthesis of Buddhism and Christianity have become the center of some Asian theologies (see Aloysius Pieris, *An Asian Theology of Liberation*, Orbis, 1988).

But sometimes Christians appropriate indigenous religions and cultures in romantic and unhistorical ways. They treat such cultures as static and unchanging, and ignore negative aspects. For feminists in Asia and Africa, such indigenous theologies are problematic in their failure to recognize the elements in the traditional culture that are oppressive to women.

Many feminists in countries where the indigenous religion and culture is still strong have concluded that they suffer from doubled layers of patriarchal domination. Thus Christianity, instead of liberating women, has become a tool to reinforce the patriarchalism of the traditional culture. For example, in India, Christianity is used to reinforce traditional Hindu restrictions on women. In Korea, a Christian emphasis on the family is used to reinforce a Confucian view of the patriarchal family.

Third world women also find positive resources for feminism in some aspects of indigenous religion and culture. Some Korean women have found helpful resources in Shamanism, where women predominate (see Chung Hyun Kyung, "Han pu-ri: Doing Theology from Korean Women's Perspective," in *We Dare to Dream*, Orbis, 135-146). They also claim the liberating traditions of Christianity as a basis for Christian feminism, even as they protest the failure of the Christian churches to recognize this message.

The relation of third world women to the plurality of their cultural heritages must be complex and dialectical, rather than one of simplistic dualism. Instead of repudiating either culture in the name of an idealized view of the other, they wish to excise the patriarchal elements from both cultures and bring the liberating elements of Christianity together with the wholistic elements of indigenous culture. Third world feminists face staggering difficulties of cultural and social oppression, but the promise of their creative vision is very great.

—◆—

The Prophetic Tasks of Feminism

by Kari Sandhaas

Daughters of Sarah, Summer 1992 issue on prophecy. At that time, Kari Sandhaas was completing her master's degree in feminist theology and ethics at Garrett-Evangelical Theological Seminary in Evanston, Illinois.

The tradition of prophecy is, to me, the place in which Christianity and feminism intersect most directly and harmoniously. In fact, I believe feminism to be the most prophetic voice in Christianity today.

In ancient Israel there were three kinds of religious leaders: priest, sage, and prophet. Jeremiah 18:18 states that "the Torah shall not perish from the priest, nor the counsel from the wise, nor the word from the prophet."

Priests, usually aligned with the monarchy, had the role of preserving tradition and teaching the law, thus maintaining the status quo. Sages gave counsel based on a keen observation of life, the practical experience of the individual, the "order" of the world, and the reservoir of ancient wisdom. Prophets were concerned with the collective behavior of a people, interpreting the signs of the times and calling the people to reform, to remember their roots. Disrupting the status quo, prophets stood in tension with the priestly institution as they called for change and incited rage, mourning, and hope amongst the people.

The priestly office in Israel was composed entirely of elite males. As a woman of Catholic heritage, I often find myself at odds with today's "priests" who place preservation of the church-as-institution over feminist efforts to stretch it towards greater inclusivity and more equitable distribution of power. I honestly wonder if the role of priest is one which can be re-envisioned from a truly feminist perspective.

Though ancient sages teach about Sophia, the fact is that most of the Judeo-Christian wisdom literature has been based on male experience and the order of hierarchy—princes over slaves, rich over poor, husbands over wives, and so on. I feel we are starved for the counsel of wise women, and I search for renewed voices of Sophia.

The male Hebrew prophets raged with concern for the powerless and called down the mighty from their thrones of power. Yet they did not understand women's oppression as women. This is the prophetic task of feminists today—to re-envision the prophetic message inclusive of women's oppression and dignity. Amongst all of the traditions and leadership roles we've inherited, we must assess their accountability to the context and fragility of today's world and to a vision of mutual integrity. The very act of re-envisioning is itself a prophetic one.

In his book *The Prophetic Imagination* (Fortress, 1978), Walter Brueggemann says that the twin tasks of the prophets of ancient Israel were (1) denouncing and grieving, and (2) announcing and energizing. Latin American theologian Tereza Cavalcanti notes a difference in emphasis between male and female biblical prophets—the men tending to denunciation and the women to exhortation, encouraging the people not to give up.

The Christian feminist task today involves all of these emphases, including truth-telling denunciation which removes the gags of silence and the garb of misogynist conformity. One of my seminary professors often described the Hebrew prophets as those "who hear screams in the night and divine thundering." Literally, feminist prophets must bring to hearing the nightly screams which echo forth from the bedrooms and the streets. This is prophetic anger, and we all know anger worn by women has never been considered fashionable. But Christian feminism demands a just rage at injustices left unheard, unchanged.

But, we must also dare to envision another way, a different possibility. Imagination is an essential tool of liberation. "Unless we can imagine something different we remain stuck, says theologian Rosemary Haughton. "[This] is why revolutions are the result not simply of intolerable conditions, but of intolerable conditions plus a voice that cries out that something else is imaginable and possible" (*Song in a Strange Land*, Templegate, 1990). Feminist prophecy requires imagination to a profound degree.

Feminist prophecy is a prophecy of agency. It calls us to behave as if there is something about ourselves and each other worth honoring, worth risking for, and nothing less. Prophetic sisterhood is when one woman's truthtelling provides another with the words to name her own oppression.

I invite you to enter and continue the dialogue and prophetic task that is Christian feminism. Sometimes the dialogue is neither easy nor pleasant. Sometimes it is exhilarating and empowering. As is typical of women, our prophetic voice is not one of a singular heroine, but of many voices, multiple and diverse. Feminist prophecy is a communal prophecy, "hearing to speech" the voices of the many. We must bring not only our voices but our capacity to hear one another as well.

Truly we will hear screams in the night and divine thundering.

— ◆ —

How Can Jesus Save Women?
Three Theories on Christ's Atonement
by Reta Halteman Finger

Daughters of Sarah, November/December 1988 issue on christology. At that time Reta Halteman Finger was editor of *Daughters of Sarah* and a student at Garrett-Evangelical Theological Seminary.

> "I don't have any problems with God,
> because God can be either male or female, but I just can't relate to Jesus.
> You can't get around the fact that he was a man."

In systematic theology, Christology is divided into two areas, the *person* of Christ, and the *work* of Christ. Most of the discussions I have had with women on this topic have centered on the person of Christ (as in the above quote) and how his maleness bothers them. Aside from his relationships with women, less interest is expressed as to whether what he *did*——his saving work—was inclusive and antipatriarchal.

This article concerns the *work* of Christ. I will discuss three models[1] of salvation through Jesus and reflect on how compatible each is with a feminist perspective. All of these models are found in the Bible, and all have had great influence on the church at different times in its history. My thesis is that, by fresh interpretations of orthodox views of how Jesus saves humans, Christian feminists can become even more thoroughly and militantly feminist because Jesus is at the center of our faith.

Substitutionary Model

The substitutionary theory emphasizes the holiness of God and the sinfulness of humankind. Each person stands under the penalty of God's wrath and cannot save herself. Unless this wrath is turned aside, each individual deserves to spend an eternity in hell. By dying an agonizing death on the cross, Jesus became the substitute—the sacrificial lamb—for what humans deserved. God the Father poured out his wrath on his Son instead of on humans. Those who accept Jesus' sacrifice will be saved from hell.

Such an interpretation of Christ's work can be found in church history since the early Fathers. However, it was first formulated as a consistent model by Anselm of Canterbury in his work *Cur Deus Homo?* (Why Did God Become Human?) in the early twelfth century. Anselm developed this theory because he wanted to make his faith logical and reasonable. Substitution remained the dominant model into the nineteenth century. Those with backgrounds in fundamentalist or evangelical churches will recognize this view of salvation as the one they have been taught since childhood.

When interpreted with careful exegesis, this model does not have to be anti-feminist. However, when used as the only model for salvation, I see several ways in which it has not seemed very compatible with feminism.

First, it has been misused as a club to inflict further suffering on women abused by husbands or other family members. Many victims have been counseled by their ministers to sacrifice themselves for their families and take up their cross of suffering as Jesus did. (Such counsel, however, is illogical, for if Jesus offered himself up for sin once for all, there is no need for women or anyone else to keep on doing it!)

Second, the model encourages passivity in the believer. If Jesus did all the work of salvation, what is there to do but sit back and accept it? Such a passive attitude can encourage women to avoid leadership and activism in church and society.

Third, it is too exclusively individualistic. Stress is laid on the sinfulness of each person, but the presence of evil in societal structures and attitudes—such as sexism, racism, and classism—seems to be ignored.

Fourth, an underemphasis on Jesus' ministry and resurrection downplays his revolutionary attitude toward and relationship with women, and their critical presence as the first witnesses to the resurrection.

Illustration from the Ade Bethune Collection, reprinted in *Daughters of Sarah*, November/December 1988.

The Moral Influence Model

According to the moral influence theory, humans are not so much in a desperate situation as they are distant from God, lacking in God-consciousness and moral development. Jesus provides us with a perfect example of someone completely tuned in to God and with a pattern for our own spiritual and moral development. Here the major emphasis is on Jesus' life, which was so committed to God that he persevered unto death. In doing so, Jesus becomes our example of how we need to live and love each other. (Jesus' resurrection is less important and tends to be spiritualized.)

Shortly after Anselm, Peter Abelard suggested the first outlines of a moral influence theory. He argued that Christ's cross was less a propitiation of God's wrath than a demonstration of God's love.

However, this model did not become influential until the nineteenth century. At that time the scientific revolution was pushing many theologians to reject supernatural aspects of Christian faith and to deny or reinterpret Jesus' divinity. Emphasizing the ethical and moral dimensions of Jesus' life was far more compatible with the new scientific worldview than the substitutionary view of salvation. It was also a time (before the two world wars) when western culture was optimistic about the moral progress of the human race. Those from more liberal mainline or Unitarian churches may recognize this model in their background.

The moral influence model can certainly be seen as pro-feminist. Women who have developed a fear and hatred of a stern, wrathful God are deeply in need of this message of love and acceptance. The inclusive, grace-filled love of Jesus, with his treatment of women as full human beings, can be Good News indeed.

However, I have two feminist problems if this is seen as the only theory of salvation. First, since the emphasis is on following in Jesus' steps, it could logically be used against women in the same way the first model is used illogically, i.e., women should endlessly love and suffer just as Jesus loved and suffered even unto death.

Second, I do not believe it adequately recognizes the presence of evil in the world, including the entrenched hierarchical system of patriarchy. Will a benign and loving influence help civilization gradually work its way out of a patriarchal worldview and sexist, racist, classist behavior? Or do we need more drastic surgery?

The Christus Victor Model

The model of the victorious Christ was the dominant one in the church for the first thousand years after Christ, until Anselm. In 1930 Gustav Aulen published a book tracing the history of *Christus Victor* theology, and since then biblical scholars have taken a renewed interest in the model.

Like the substitutionary theory, this model envisions humanity in a desperate situation from which Christ alone can rescue it. Yet the force from which we need to be delivered is not God's wrath, but the bondage imposed by evil powers. Such evil is not simply the absence of good, but an active presence working in the world.

How does Christ liberate humans from bondage? This model focuses not only on Jesus' death, but conceives his entire incarnation, life, death, and resurrection as one continuing conflict with the powers of evil. In his incarnation Jesus was fully human, yet he did not sin, and thus was not in bondage to the powers. The episodes of most active conflict were his temptation in the wilderness and his death. But through his healing, teaching, and exorcism ministries, he was continually confronting the pervasive forces of sickness, negative thinking, demon possession, and the religious and political powers of oppression and exclusion.

But the Christus Victor model is not complete without the resurrection. In killing Jesus, the powers exceeded their limits. God vindicated the way Jesus had lived and died by raising him from the dead. Thus, the last enemy, death, was also defeated.

Human salvation is then effected by putting one's trust in and identifying with this victorious Christ. In our world, the powers are still at work, and we do not underestimate their pervasiveness and ability to poison, cripple, and kill—as violently as a nuclear bomb or as insidiously as polluted water and air. But the resurrection of Jesus is our one hope that evil does not have the last word, and that, in the New Creation, we will be raised like Jesus to witness the final defeat of all powers of evil.

How does Christus Victor relate to feminism? It seems to me that, as our feminist consciousness is raised, we see ever more pervasive and subtle ways in which our global society is caught in the grip of patriarchy—from bride burning and aborting female fetuses in India to widespread rape, marital abuse, and incest rampant in our country; to resistance to inclusive language and women's leadership in our churches. Indeed, the entire assumption that some groups of people or individuals should have power over others or more privileges than others because of race, gender, creed, or class is a patriarchal assumption.

Looking at Jesus' life in the Gospels, we see the boldness with which he opposed patriarchy. Power reversals and liberation of the oppressed were the content of his "inauguration speech" (Luke 4). His identification with the victims of patriarchal subjugation got him into enormous trouble with religious and political authorities.

It is entirely appropriate that women today experience salvation and deliverance through Jesus by first coming to him through the women around him. In his revolutionary attitude toward women, in treating them as full human beings, he directly confronted the evil of sexism. The Gospels portray Jesus' women disciples as utterly faithful, indeed as model disciples. Their presence around Jesus, and especially as the first witnesses to his resurrection, stands as a monument to the beginning of the end of patriarchy and is a prototype of what gender equality and renewed relationships will be like in the New Creation.

By now it is evident where my sympathies lie. I do not reject the substitutionary or moral influence theories. Aspects of both are biblical and speak to human need. However, both seem inadequate as a primary model. Christus Victor deals far better with the theme of conflict portrayed in Scripture. It exposes systemic evils of oppression, such as patriarchy, militarism, and materialism, that the other models ignore.

On the other hand, Christus Victor in no way minimizes individual sinfulness. The New Testament abounds with persons who recognized their own complicity in evil and were forgiven by Jesus; with persons who were freed from demon possession and personally followed Jesus afterward; and with persons who found the price too high and went away sorrowful or angry.

Can we as feminists trust in Christ to deliver us from evil? Can we believe that this man Jesus stripped himself of whatever male rights and privileges a sexist society gave him and engaged in mortal combat with the power of patriarchy? Can we trust that his resurrection in the power of God's Spirit is the beginning of the end of patriarchal oppression? These are the questions I believe Christus Victor answers.

[1] A concise, comprehensive sketch of these three theories can be found in Chapter 16 of Thomas N. Finger's *Christian Theology: An Eschatological Approach*, Vol. I (Herald Press, 1985). I am summarizing his discussion, adding my own feminist analysis.

——— ◆ ———

Models of Love and Hate in the Hebrew Bible

by Lillian Sigal

Daughters of Sarah, March/April 1991 issue on Jewish and Christian feminism. At that time Dr. Lillian Sigal taught English at Grand Valley State University in Grand Rapids, Michigan.

There is a long tradition that has characterized the Hebrew Bible as a testament of hatred and vengeance toward one's enemy. Indeed, the charge cannot be completely denied. Many passages can be cited to support it, particularly those dealing with the conquest of Canaan by the Israelites recorded in Deuteronomy, Joshua, Judges, and Kings.

However, this perception ignores other segments of the Jewish Scriptures that reflect empathy for the stranger and one's enemy, and it overlooks rabbinic interpretations of Scriptures, called midrash, that are sensitive to the suffering of one's adversaries.

As a Jewish feminist, I pay special attention to the presentation of women in the Bible with regard to the theme of compassion versus retribution towards one's opponents. In their zeal to identify strong female role models, feminists often cite female characters who exercise power aggressively, proving that they are not wimps.

Thus they tout such figures as Judith, who cuts off the head of the Assyrian general Holofernes; Esther, who allows the Jews of Susa to engage in not one but two days of slaughtering their foes; and Deborah, who bravely marches forth to battle, shoring up her faint-hearted general Barak against the Israelites' enemy Sisera. Among these three macho-matriarchs, Deborah is the only one who does not use her sexual pulchritude to achieve her aims and accorded the status of prophet. Moreover, her victory song reveals admirable poetic power.

However, the tone of vengeance that pervades the poem of Deborah makes me wince. Her hymn to Yahweh gloats over Jael's tricking Sisera, the enemy general, into believing she will help him and then drive a tent peg into his temple while asleep. Deborah then describes Sisera's mother as she awaits her son's return from battle:

> *Through her window she leans and looks, Sisera's mother, through the lattice: "Why is his chariot so long in coming? Why are the harnessed horses slow?"* (Judg. 5:28 *JB*).

Finally, in verse 31 Deborah concludes her song with the following words:

> *So perish all your enemies, Yahweh! (JB)*

Deborah has just sung of herself as "a mother in Israel" (Judg. 5:7 *JB*). Yet here she expresses almost sadistic glee, rather than pathos for a bereaved mother.

The Song of Deborah parallels Moses' hymn of triumph after the crossing of the Sea of Reeds, which also exults over the defeat of Israel's enemies. However, the spirit of vengeance in the Song of Moses is mitigated at the Passover seder. We recite the ten plagues at our annual ceremonial recounting of the Exodus. But then we recall the midrash in which God admonishes the ministering angels for singing God's praises as the Egyptians are drowning. "The work of my hands is drowning in the sea, and ye wish to chant songs!" (Megillah 10b). Furthermore, as we pronounce each plague, we tip a drop of wine out of our cups to symbolically prevent our cup of joy from running over when our enemies—creatures created in God's image—are suffering.

Peaceable Alternatives

A biblical tale that contrasts sharply with the bellicosity of Deborah is the book of Ruth. This story, like that of Deborah, is set in the period of the Judges, an era of bloody battles for Israelite sovereignty over the land of Canaan. Yet Ruth hints of no conflicting claims of land ownership among the various people who inhabit it. On the contrary, the narrator portrays ancient Israelites living peacefully with their neighbors the Moabites, who elsewhere in the Bible are portrayed as their mortal enemies.

The narrative shows the Israelite family of Naomi and Elimelek leaving Bethlehem to find sustenance in Moab during a famine. They live unmolested among its people, and their sons intermarry with Moabite women. After all the men in the family have died, Ruth accompanies Naomi to Bethlehem. She risks being regarded as a stranger from a despised people. Nevertheless, the book reflects no xenophobia among the people of Bethlehem toward "Ruth the Moabitess." Boaz immediately befriends her and eventually marries her. Moreover, their union produces Obed, the grandfather of David, from whom, according to tradition, the Messiah would one day spring.

In the post-biblical literature of the Talmud, we find a morally mature and sensitive woman by the name of Beruriah. Like the author of Ruth, she also teaches an ethos of magnanimity rather then enmity. Beruriah was regarded as a brilliant scholar by the rabbis and was often approached for advice on matters of religious practice.

One day, upon hearing her husband, Rabbi Meir, pray for the death of robbers in their neighborhood, she admonished him for his harshness. "It is permissible to pray for their deaths," argued Meir, "because it is written, 'Let sins end' (Ps. 104:35). Beruriah pointed out to him, however, that the text reads "sins," not "sinners," and therefore he should not pray for the death of the wicked but for their repentance.

I am one of the many Jews today who deplore the iron-fist policy of the Likud government towards Palestinians in the occupied territories, a policy that follows the model of Deborah rather than that of Ruth. But I am heartened by the numerous organizations in Israel that foster peaceful co-existence between Arabs and Jews. One such group, called Partnership, takes as its motto the rabbinic maxim that asks, "Who is a hero?" and replies, "The person who converts an enemy into a friend."

The story of Ruth prefigures the bonding of women that I saw in Israel in June 1988 when I joined a group called Women in Black who protest weekly in Jerusalem, Haifa, and Tel Aviv against the Israeli occupation of the West Bank and Gaza. Dressed in black, Jewish and Arabic women, from ages seven to seventy, stand stoically silent in solidarity with one another, holding their placards in the face of male harassment. Parallel groups of Jewish women have since sprung up in Philadelphia, New York, and Ann Arbor to express their support of their Israeli and Palestinian sisters.

Both Jews and Arabs have deep historic roots in the land and both cherish it. The book of Ruth, which images ancient Israel living peacefully side by side with the Moabites, points the way towards the possibility of friendship and peaceful cohabitation between modern Israelis and Palestinians.

In addition to the need for reconciliation between Arabs and Jews, I believe in the need for rapprochement between Christians and Jews. One way to further ties between our two faiths is to eschew the triumphalist teaching that dichotomizes the Hebrew Bible as a doctrine of hate and the Christian Bible as a testament of love. Instead, Jews and Christians should emphasize their common tradition of love. Jesus was asked what one must do to inherit eternal life. He quotes the love commands of Deuteronomy 6:5 and Leviticus 19:18 about loving God with all one's heart, soul, and might, and loving one's neighbor as oneself. And when asked to interpret "Who is my neighbor?" Jesus illustrates the concept of love through the famous parable of the Good Samaritan. In this story Jesus teaches that Samaritans, a hated and reviled group in the first century, should not be stereotyped as evil. In essence, Jesus implies that we must treat our "enemy" not as an "it" but as a "thou" (to borrow Martin Buber's terminology), namely, as a human being capable of humane behavior, as someone with whom we can be reconciled, and as our "neighbor" whom we are commanded to love.

As we probe our holy texts for women to admire or emulate, we must be careful not to exalt the behavior of personalities who exemplify the values of patriarchy that treat the enemy as an "it" rather than a "thou." The Hebrew word Deborah means "wasp," whereas the Hebrew name Ruth signifies "friendship." In a world that is imperiled by the threat of nuclear annihilation and environmental destruction, we must ferret out of our sacred literature models of human interaction that teach us not to sting our adversaries. We need rather to explore ways to build trust and mutually search for common ground and peaceful means of resolving our differences.

———◆———

Illustration by Emile Ferris, published in *Daughters of Sarah*, Spring 1994.

Interreligious Dialogue: A Pilgrimage

by *Virginia Ramey Mollenkott*

Daughters of Sarah, Spring 1994. At that time Virginia Ramey Mollenkott had edited *Women of Faith in Dialogue* (Crossroad, 1987). Her most recent books were *Godding: Human Responsibility and the Bible* and *Sensuous Spirituality: Out from Fundamentalism.*

It was the first meeting of a group called Women of Faith, located at the headquarters of the American Jewish Committee in New York City. Inge Lederer Gibel led a group of Jewish, Muslim, Catholic, and Protestant women in an exercise designed to break the ice.

"Suppose," she said, "someone woke you up in the middle of the night, snapping their fingers in your face and insisting that you tell them the first three identifying factors that pop into your mind concerning who you are. Please tell us what those factors would be—factors so deeply ingrained in your concept of yourself that you could respond even while just awakening from sleep."

Gibel's own answer went this way: First, second, and third, I am a Jew. Then, in no particular order, I am a refugee from the Holocaust, a feminist, and a child of God."

I tell that story because it illustrates one of the cardinal principles of good interreligious dialogue: people deal in their own first-hand experience, not in theory or doctrines or attempts to convert one another. Even so, interreligious dialogue would be very difficult for people who hold the conviction that those who do not believe in Jesus Christ in exactly the same way they do will be condemned to eternal flames. Such a conviction puts almost unbearable pressure on the one who holds it, so that it seems cruel and uncaring to enter into friendship with someone from another tradition without issuing periodic warnings and invitations to become a convert. I know the feeling, having believed that way for the first thirtysome years of my life.

But if that conviction were true, wouldn't Jesus have preached such an urgent message all the while he was here on this planet? Instead he urged people simply to fling themselves upon the compassion of God (Luke 18:9-14), encouraged us to love one another (John 13:34), and even implied that love brings about the forgiveness of sins (Luke 7:47). He preached that people of faith would become one in the way that he and the Father/Mother are one (John 17:11), and urged us to be all-inclusive as our Mother/Father in heaven is all-inclusive (Matt. 5:48).

Jesus moved among Jews and Samaritans and Romans and Greeks, including some of the "dregs" of humanity, without ever thundering that they must assent to certain doctrines in order to be saved. They had only to "believe on him"—to relate to Jesus' Source in the same way that Jesus related to that Source. Perhaps, then, some of us, in our doctrinal anxieties, have been trying to outdo Jesus. Our attempts are not only futile; they are divisive and oppressive.

At another of the early Women of Faith meetings, Inge commented that she did not like the term interfaith because there is only one profound experience called faith, even though it is shared by people from all sorts of cultural and religious backgrounds. And indeed, as I was moved by faith-filled stories of my sisters from other traditions, I discovered that Inge was correct.

I saw the fire of faithful justice and compassion burning in the eyes of Dr. Riffat Hassan, a Muslim feminist engaged in the task of proving that the Koran has been misinterpreted in the same ways the Bible has been misinterpreted, and for the same reasons—to protect male supremacy.

I saw the gentle, tender faith of Blu Greenberg, devoted to Orthodox Jewish practice and simultaneously imbued with the feminist awareness that causes many Orthodox to reject her as a flaming radical. (My favorite among Greenberg's books is *On Women and Judaism: A View from Tradition*, Jewish Publishing Society of America, 1981.) Having heard the experiences of women like these, and having lit the menorah with Blu, Norma Levitt, Inge, and others, including Riffat, I could never doubt the reality of God's interrelationship with these, my sisters.

It is because each person shares her own first-hand experience that interreligious dialogue poses no threat to maintaining one's personal religious and theological position. In fact, it was by trying to explain to my sisters in what sense I am evangelical, despite seeming so different to them from evangelicals they had read about or seen on TV, that I came to appreciate the depth of my own evangelical commitment. Otherwise I might long ago have abandoned that good news to the Religious Right.

I explained that I am an evangelical liberationist for at least two reasons. First, because I do not think the gospel should be reduced exclusively to a political theology, since it refers also to a personal faith-experience. And second, because I hold a strong view of biblical authority and have in fact been radicalized by the Bible.

Until I got involved in interreligious dialogue, I had not given much thought to exactly where I belonged on the Christian spectrum. But I was keenly interested in knowing how life looked different for my Jewish sisters if they were Orthodox, Conservative, Reform, or Reconstructionist. So I had to satisfy their corresponding curiosity about where I belonged in American Protestantism and hence how life looked to me. As a result, I came to know my own beliefs more clearly than ever before.

I also came to understand the superficiality of beliefs and customary comfortable rituals as opposed to the depths of the experience we call faith in the One God of all the Universe. Much of that faith-experience takes place on a level which no words can capture. And learning the difference between faith and mere belief-systems is perhaps the most profound lesson that interreligious dialogue can teach.

As I write these words, I have just returned from Minneapolis, where I participated in Re-imagining, a conference of women theologians from all over the world. The conference was wonderful in many ways—a healing, inspiring, and challenging experience. But I was jolted to hear one of the plenary speakers make reference to the "jealous Jewish God," repeating the mistaken liberal perception that the God of the Hebrew scriptures is judgmental as opposed to the loving God of the Christian scriptures. This error was not at all typical of the conference speakers, I am thankful to report, but it was terribly unfortunate nonetheless.

Far more typical was the wonderful urging of Lois Wilson, a past president of the World Council of Churches, that we ask ourselves the question: How can I tell my faith story without telling dirty stories about the others? This is the question that interreligious dialogue forces every participant to answer.

Wilson also stressed that it is better to know a Hindu person than simply to know about Hinduism, better to know a Buddhist than simply to know about Buddhism. Wilson urged that we seek nothing less than a planet-wide community, defining true humanity not in terms of any one religion, but simply in terms of being "one who cares." This is the context in which interreligious pilgrimage would occur, going beyond dialogue to walking together in a faith-filled human journey.

In this regard, my own emphasis at the conference was that, in the worship community, as I re-imagine it, there would be no more attempts to colonize people of other religions by trying to make them believe as we believe. Instead, we would trust the Spirit's work within diverse religious traditions. Therefore, any missionary activities would target only those people who seem to have no sense of the holiness of all creatures, including themselves, and no experience of incandescent wonder.

My ongoing experience in the contemporary college classroom assures me that there is a mission field ripe for harvest. But it is not among those who by their religious or spiritual practice are inspired and empowered to do justice, love mercy, and walk humbly with their God. It is among those who are so stunned by religious hypocrisy and cruelty, or so deadened by scientistic apathy, that they are not able to appreciate the joyous miracle that is the life of the Spirit.

History is replete with evidence that human egos love to latch on to whatever aggrandizement they can grasp: the belief that one's own nation is objectively the best, or even the belief that one's favorite sports team is the only one worthy of support. What does the conviction that one's religion is the only true religion have to recommend it above mere nationalism, or cultural imperialism, or sports-mania, or any other form of ego-enhancement?

I love liberationist Christianity because it is the avenue through which God's Spirit has worked with me, not because it is the only way God's Spirit may ever work with anybody else! Through interreligious dialogue, I have the joy of hearing about the many other ways the Holy Spirit has in fact transformed people's lives with the warm light of faith—and I bear my own witness. Through interreligious pilgrimage, I have the privilege of walking with people of faith from other traditions, all of us working together to bring about a more just society.

——— ◆ ———

Chapter 5

"Our Bodies, Ourselves"

Making the journey to the place where we each see our complete selves as miraculous, holy beings—flesh as well as spirit; matter as well as mind—requires great courage and stamina. We've heard so many ugly rumors about the dark treacheries that might attack us on our way to loving and cherishing our bodies. Our religions have declared our bodies evil; our cultures have treated our bodies as commodities; and our governments have historically viewed our bodies as property, transferrable by contract.

Understanding the reality of the indivisible, vital connection of our body-mind-soul-spirit has always been a crucial component of feminism. The visible, feeling, bleeding body can only be ignored, discounted, or mocked at great peril to us all.

Our God-given lives are beautiful. These lives are encompassed by two very messy physical experiences when the body is definitely at the center of everyone's attention: our birth and our death. We are drawn to focus on the body at those crucial moments without loss of our deep awareness of the presence of spirit in the midst of all the messiness. The question is: Why can't we do that all the time?

The writers for *Daughters of Sarah* articulated their very personal adventures on this hard journey to loving all aspects of themselves with courage, tears, humor, and grace. They walk in beauty, and so can we.

— Introduction by Juanita Wright Potter. Juanita was a member of *Daughters of Sarah's* editorial board from 1984 to 1992 and also served on the executive board.

— ◆ —

Resectioning

by Alice Strain

Daughters of Sarah, January/February 1990. Alice Strain wrote this poem "during the earlier time of separation in my marriage when I was also dealing with cancer surgery, radiation, and chemotherapy." She is now an ordained minister with the Presbyterian Church (U.S.A.).

If they can
Resection a breast
Quadrectomy, lumpectomy,
Mastectomy (partial)
Cut out the rotten part
Malevolent malignancy
Cursed cancer
Pull the cover back over it
Stapled, healing, growing,
renewed
Only a lessening, slender scar
left
Radiate the remainder
Warm it, make it glow
Cast out any lethal lymphocyte

Then couldn't I
Resection my heart
Cast out the broken part
Battered and hurting
Bleeding and wounded
Pull my life back together
Strengthened and restored
Only scar tissue of memories
left
Radiate the rest
Open it to love
The beams of Your searching,
Penetrating presence
Cast out remaining rancor
Cancerous fear.

———◆———

Transition in Childbirth:
Claiming Our Death and Resurrection

by Beth C. Junker

Daughters of Sarah, Winter 1992 issue on birth and abortion. At that time Beth C. Junker owned and operated Expressive Ink, a free-lance writing service in Chicago specializing in works on law, ethics, and society. She was expecting her second child. She now teaches Spiritual Journaling and Stories of God to church groups through Oxenfree Writers' Workshop (oxenfree@mindspring.com).

I will tell you something that has been secret:
that we are not all going to die, but we shall all be changed.
—I Corinthians 15:51

One winter night as the wind suggested the coming of a storm, I wandered through the halls of a Catholic college, searching for the advertised reading of creative writing by women. I was curious about what women from my conservative, bluecollar area of Chicago would write and what they would share publicly. Opening the door to a large conference room, I saw a U-shaped table peopled with writers of all ages, shapes, and colors.

These women—mostly mothers and homemakers—released themselves through their writing and demanded their freedom from the rigid social expectations to which others had bound them. There was something subversive about these everyday artists sharing their selves-in-progress with an audience of family, friends, and strangers.

Amid brave accounts of domestic violence and declarations of lesbianism, an elderly woman named Martha read a short poem describing the birth of her son: the beauty of creation, pain felt with joy, the magic moment of first holding the child, and the subsequent feeling of total completion as a woman-turned-mother. It bore the familiar ring of so many other descriptions of birthing written by women and men over the years that had influenced my expectations of pregnancy and childbirth.

My experience of childbirth, however, contrasted dramatically with this poem. I was puzzled over the apparent disparity in our perceptions, the absence of ambivalent feelings in the poet's memoir, and her innocent correlation between the divine and an event that is purely joyful.

As the applause rose enthusiastically around me, I made a long mental list of women friends whose childbirth experiences differed from that in the poem. It is true that most of their accounts had consisted of superficial details. No one confessed fear, no one described the pain, no one mentioned transition. But pain, frustration, and distress were the underlying thrust of these accounts. We had conspired to continue the silence surrounding the trauma of childbirth, the silence that allows the myth of total joy and easy acceptance to define the meaning of the experience for us.

* * * * * *

In Martha's time, mothers were treated as incidental to the delivery, leaving the miracle to be performed by the closest agent of God, the doctor. "Joyful pain" and the pleasure of waking to see her new baby may have been all the poet remembered of the birth. By contrast, I birthed with very little medical intervention. The pain was far less joyful, and when I saw my boy, my euphoria was quickly overcome by fatigue. Despite the physical difficulties arising from this birthing method, I view it as positive because it returns the entire childbirth experience to the woman, including probably the most difficult part of all, the transition phase.

I learned about transition in a prenatal class on the Bradley method (an alternative to the Lamaze method). Transition is a thirty-minute period at the end of first stage labor when the cervix opens the last of the necessary ten centimeters. Transition turns abruptly into second stage labor during which the baby is pushed out of the womb.

I was instructed that during this stage the physical changes necessary for childbirth would create in my mind a powerful illusion that I am about to die. This illusion cannot be prevented either medically or through forewarning. The feeling that death is imminent, according to the instructor, will have no connection with reality. Coaches were told to remind the woman during this stage that this feeling is a sign that labor is progressing normally and will be over soon. In spite of this warning, I was convinced that, when the moment came, foreknowledge would be stronger than mere illusion, and that my powers of reason would prevail even under the stress of birthing.

Two months later, however, I was clutching my husband's arm during transition, begging him to make the labor stop so I would not die. I had lost control of my body, and the pain seemed to grow beyond all means of toleration. I quickly forgot the child I'd carried most of a year, who now required releasing. Facing into my own ending, I looked for the exit to my survival. When I silently conceded that I did not want to die, even to give my own child life, the physical reality broke in. My body began pushing, with a power I did not understand and could not control, to finish the birth for both myself and the baby.

In the months that followed, I remembered that feeling of imminent death. As I nurtured my perfect son and taught him to smile, I recalled how I forgot him at that sacrificial moment. I could not accept that the sensation of death lingering so close was merely illusion. Every woman with a child must come to a new understanding of herself as mother. But because I could not forget the experience of transition, I had to ask more existential questions. How could I make sense of that death experience so I could rise to a new understanding of myself?

A biologist will tell you that life comes from death in the great ecological cycle. I suspect traditional theologians know this, though they have relocated death to the end, so that resurrection becomes a cure for mortality, and an antidote even for life. Accepting the ecological fact and a broader understanding of the death and resurrection experience helped me to focus on the spiritual reality of birthing.

The Bradley instruction had been accurate: the feeling of imminent physical death during transition was an illusion. I did not die, nor was I likely to die. But I did experience a real and frightening death that was spiritual. In transition, I lost the pre-maternal self: the self that did not yet have a mother's unique responsibilities, the safe self who had loved only adults who could survive my periodic emotional unavailability. In the immediate aftermath of the birth I mourned this loss. And in the wake of night-time feedings and the strangeness of motherhood, I could not see beyond this death.

Yet from the moment I met my child, I was destined to be different from my pre-maternal self. The love I had focused on adults would suddenly shift to one who was entirely dependent for physical care, and trusted completely that I would provide it. My love had to be given absolutely unconditionally.

Unconditional love and responding effectively in trust, of course, are lifetime initiatives. However, I believe I was turned in this direction against my will during transition. Birthing was more than the physical exertion of giving a child life; it was the creation of a self willing to give to this child for a lifetime. Without this change and the corresponding trauma, I could hardly hope to discover the boundless joy that motherhood has indeed brought me.

This spiritual interpretation of transition shifts Christian women away from the tendency toward self-sacrifice. While it was necessary to relinquish part of my self to motherhood, it was not necessary for me to give up my self altogether for my child. Such a sacrifice would hamper the separate personal growth of the child and create a mother who is essentially depleted. Instead, the self is capable of surviving transition and emerging as one unafraid of exploring love in a new relationship.

Scripture is replete with stories and images portraying the death and resurrection of the human soul on its earthly sojourn. We read accounts of acceptance of God's will, confessions of fallenness, and of Christ's ultimate sacrifice on the cross and his resurrection. Yet women are infrequently the subject of these stories.

Surely many stories about women have been ignored or repressed throughout history. However, through voluntary silence, women play into the expectation that our stories are less important than stories of men, that our emotions are less viable than physical realities, and that our own interpretation of experience lacks credibility.

The childbirth experience is both common among women and highly individualistic. Women sometimes share with each other the chronological facts of their birthing, comparing labor times, and birth weights. But we still don't talk to each other about what childbirth does to us, how it changes us. We talk about pain-killers, but never the pain. We remain silent on our feelings of vulnerability, exposure, and the pressure to "do it right." We don't describe our transition, and how it recreates us.

Martha's poem about the birth of her son was disturbing in that it affirmed the long-standing myth that birthing involves no emotional pain, that the physical pain is joyfully felt by women, and that motherhood can be accepted without ambivalence. More disturbing was the enthusiastic response of the audience, with greater applause than ever, blissfully smiling and nostalgically sighing. Clearly, the myth of childbirth would not be challenged by these women. The secret of that pain and death would be allowed to live on a little longer. And the audience approved, perhaps retreating from the challenges of the evening to their emotional womb, hoping to emerge painlessly on Monday morning.

Yet if transition were acknowledged as a deep, spiritual experience in the lives of women, such a reading would mark a most liberating moment. First, the emotional character of childbirth and its physical nature would be reunited. Second, the silence among women about childbirth would be ended, and with it the myths that rob women of the meaning of the experience.

Finally and dramatically, the experience of birth that is uniquely women's could then provide insight into the essential Christian understanding of human struggle as death and resurrection. Through transition we learn that death turns us toward life's lesson of unconditional love.

———— ◆ ————

Sex, Babies, and Other Good Stuff

by Karen Osman

Daughters of Sarah, September/October 1985 issue on abortion. At that time Karen Osman was a free-lance writer from Pontiac, Illinois. Her published work includes humor features, magazine articles, and children's plays and stories.

When I was five years old, a mere child myself, I asked my mother where babies came from. In my little heart of hearts, I was certain the rumors I had heard could not possibly be true. They were ridiculous. No one, I told my young self, would do such a ludicrous and acrobatic thing.

My mother, who has always been good about answering my questions, told me the truth—as she saw it. "You go to church, pray to God, and he plants a seed in your stomach," she said.

Quite frankly, I was confused. I was also very nervous about attending church after that. Every time I sat down to pray, even in the protection of my own room, I made darned sure the subject of babies never came up. I was afraid that if I mentioned them, God would become confused and start a seedling in my stomach. Looking back on it, I guess that was my first attempt to practice birth control.

As I grew older (and wiser), I discovered that the rumors were true and that men did, indeed, play a major role in the making of babies. Oddly enough, though, I no longer found the concept of conception repugnant. I was curious.

I remember when one of my friends in high school finally put the theory we had all been discussing into practice. I hid my virginal shock behind a facade of calm acceptance. "At least you're taking birth control," I said in what I hoped was a very matter-of-fact voice.

I can still see the look on her face. "Birth control!" she cried in righteous horror. "But that's against the teachings of the church!"

Once again, God, sex, and birth control jumbled in my mind like so many building blocks heaped together in a cryptic message.

I took my friend roses when she had her abortion.

Abortion. Now, there's another concept to add to the list of confusions. I envy women who know exactly where they stand on the issue.

If I went to an abortion rally today, I would carry a big sign reading: "Anti-abortion/Prochoice." Everyone would heap insults on my confused head, and I would be lucky to get home with my sign still intact. I can't help it. I am adamantly antiabortion and radically prochoice—I have no friends.

I debate with myself constantly and, consequently, call myself all manner of vile names ranging from murderer to butcher. One part of me screams that life is sacred and should be protected at all costs, and I sit on my well-padded, perfect-for-child-bearing, middle-class tush and make judgments. Abortion is murder, I say, and every fetus is a small miracle waiting to work itself on a lonely world. I hurt when I think of life frozen in the womb, and I feel it is my duty to melt hard hearts.

Then, just when I am ready to take up the prolife banner and march on the nearest abortion clinic, my little angel flies down from her cloud and perches on my shoulder. Her opening line is always, "Seeing only one side of an issue is like not seeing the issue at all." My angel is a pain. She also talks a good game.

"What would you do," asks this tiny bleeding heart liberal, "if you were on welfare, had three children already, and no husband."

"I sure wouldn't work without a net." I counter crudely.

"Not everyone has access to birth control," says the pest.

"Well, I wouldn't sleep around, either," I say.

"Are you sure?" She cocks her angel eyebrow, and continues. "What if you were a young opera singer with a scholarship to college?"

That's closer to home, so I cringe. "I don't know."

"A ballet dancer?" "I don't know. Leave me alone!"

"Would you have an abortion?" she demands like a district attorney at a murder trial.

Then I have to dig down deep. It's hard, this soul searching. I'm not a welfare mother, I'm not an opera singer, and I don't dance anymore. I am me and I don't believe in abortion—I have the luxury of being able to stick to my conviction with ease. My angel doesn't fight fair and I want to trade her off, have an angel transplant.

"I don't know," I say at last. "I can't answer for anyone else. What do I know about opera singers?"

"What do you know about yourself?"

I bite my lip and hang my head. "I know that I am very lucky, and that I should thank God I never had to make that decision."

She smiles. "You may turn out all right," she says grudgingly, "that is, if you stay away from anti-abortion marches. Those women will kill you."

I wonder what the punishment is for choking an angel.

The Elder Sister:
The Struggle for a Personal History of Redemption
by Virginia Wiles

Daughters of Sarah, March/April 1986. At that time, Virginia Wiles (then Nancy Wiles Holsey) was an adjunct instructor in Greek and preaching at Bethany Theological Seminary, Oak Brook, Illinois. She now teaches New Testament at New Brunswick Theological Seminary in New Brunswick, New Jersey.

Martha sat in my office. The perfect seminary student: bright and responsible, sensitive and caring, not the "angry woman" that has so often stormed through seminary. Perhaps a new generation is born, I muse. Maybe this young woman will have a fresh, new story to tell—a story without anger and bitterness, a grace-filled story of her becoming.

And so I listen with hope to Martha's story. What I hear in the hours and weeks to come, however, is not a story that brings hope. It is a story of confusion, a story of nonexistence and of death. My initial perception of her is accurate. It is everyone's perception of Martha. She is bright and responsible, sensitive and caring. She is not angry—but neither is she fully alive.

It is, of course, not a new story. Here is a woman who is everything the church has trained her to be. She is a competent young woman who has thoroughly internalized the church's values. Having read contemporary feminism, she gladly affirms herself as nurturing and relational. But in the process, she has assigned such ultimacy to her relationships that her identity—her beliefs, her emotions, her actions—has been utterly determined by her family, her friends, and her faith-community. She is what they ask her to be. She has no sense of self, except for who she is for others. Martha does not exist except in their relationships to her.

Here she is trapped. The readily available answer does not provide Martha with any real escape from her trap. Psychologists and wise seminary counselors say, "Grow up. Establish yourself as an individual. Leave home."

But this well-trained seminary student knows that to leave home is to commit the sin of the Prodigal Son. To "grow up" means to choose self over others. Those relationships which promise life are suffocating her. But to leave them is to leave her only hope of life. It is an apparently inescapable trap—to stay is a living death; to leave, a form of suicide.

Though this is not an entirely new story, it is nevertheless a death that the church has not often recognized. For the most part, the church has said that sin is pride, and death is the resulting alienation. For such death, the church offers resurrection. The good news is that the waiting father accepts the Prodigal Son.

But Martha's place is perhaps that of the elder brother in that story. And, alas, he is a negative figure, a mere footnote of warning: "Don't be like this." Like Martha, his identity is only in relationship to the *real* protagonist of the story. He is brother, not son. She is sister, not daughter. Martha has no story of her own.

* * * * * *

Perhaps by exploring the power of this story for her brother, Martha can hope to learn how to find power in her own as yet untold story. The parable of the Prodigal Son has been so powerful for this woman's brother because it is true. Psychologists and sociologists recognize its truth. The spiritual dimension of the story expresses the ultimacy of this story about a young man "growing up."

Psychologists trace "normal" (i.e., male) development as moving from an undifferentiated relationship between child and parents, through a process of separation or individuation. Initial separation begins to take place early in an infant's life. This process of individuation expands during the next two or so decades, until the person (the man) comes to that maturity of "knowing who he is." The maturation, however, is costly, for in the process of individuating, one not only distinguishes himself from others, but he cuts himself off from others. He becomes not just *separate from* mother and father, but he identifies himself *over against* mother and father and their values. It's a "healthy" stage we "all" go through. Eventually, the process of individuation comes full circle and the man can reclaim his roots, come to terms with his formation, and reconcile with his parents. He has come home, a stronger individual for having left, but no longer alienated from others, from parents.

The story of the Prodigal Son dramatizes theologically what we "all" recognize to be true about life at its best. In Romans, Paul gives a theological reworking of this developmental scheme. We rebel against Law. It is as normal to rebel against Law as it is for a toddler to test the parent's "No!" Sin is the curse of growing up. Attempting to establish one's own identity (i.e., sin) results in alienation from others and from God (i.e., death). Contrary to modern psychologists, for Paul the problem of "youthful rebellion," of individuating, is not just a "healthy" stage. It is a trap so deep that Paul calls it death. It becomes a trap from which there is no escape. The maturity of "coming home," in fact, does not happen of its own accord. It is graced to the sinner in Christ Jesus. But for the grace of God in Jesus Christ who comes to join him in his death, the sinner would be lost forever in his alienation. He would be hopelessly isolated from the maturity of love and left clinging to a false identity.

And so the Prodigal Son and Paul help our brothers tell their own stories. They can name their sin and their death (pride, rebellion, and alienation), and they can point out grace and redemption (acceptance, love, friendship, community) when it occurs.

But for one who has never left home, who has always said "Yes!" to the Law, there is no such story to be told. And so these "elder brothers and sisters" are left with no stories of their own. Unable to name their participation in humanity's fall (in Adam's and Eve's sin), there is no redemption for them in Christ. They are left to stand and applaud the prodigal's redemption. But for their own experience of growth, their own maturation, their own personal history, they can claim no more than this "secondary redemption."

* * * * * *

Women like Carol Gilligan and Jean Baker Miller are struggling now to tell another story of maturation. Women are beginning to insist that other normal patterns of human choices do exist. The failure of the psychologists to name these patterns has led them to label most women (and some men) abnormal. The failure of theologians to recognize these patterns has silently reduced most women (and some men) to the negative status of "elder sister."

The woman seminary student in my office needs a way to tell her story. She needs to hear her own story. Together, we begin to uncover another "normal" pattern of maturation. We begin to name Martha's (our!) sin and death, and greedily to search for signs of our salvation.

Given the undifferentiated relationship into which we are all born, we are told that one "normally" chooses to limit the relationship in order to establish one's self-identity. This choice appears as rebellion, but it is considered a healthy step in one's growth. Another response, however, is equally possible. One may choose to nurture the relationship rather than choosing to nurture self. Stereotypically,[1] the "boy" is encouraged to choose self, even at the cost of the destruction of the relationship; the "girl" is encouraged to choose the relationship, even at the cost of the destruction of self. In actuality, her choice does eventually lead to loss of self. She becomes enmeshed—a virtual cipher trapped in her highly valued relationships. So, while the "boy's" sin of pride leads to the "young man's" alienation, the "girl's" sin of self-sacrifice (sacrifice of self) leads the "young woman" to enmeshment.

Placed in the context of the Christian tradition, the "boy's" pride is recognized as sin. But the "girl" and her church think her sacrifice of self is virtue. No one noticed her *fall*. And yet her choice, no less than her brother's, leads to a trap that can be described as a death.

Death is an appropriate word for this trap, for it is inescapable. It is experienced as hopelessness and lostness. Theologically, any attempt at extricating oneself from the trap is recognized as works. Paul and consequent Christian tradition makes it clear that works are utterly incapable of bringing salvation. (It is precisely at this point that Christian theology offers a critique to psychological and sociological method.)

* * * * * *

The "young man's" sin of pride led him into alienation. If he now strives for a relationship, he finds that he must sacrifice the self which he has labored so hard to establish. Such an act appears to be psychological suicide. But even if he could do so, would he not find himself enmeshed like his sister?

What the alienated "young man" needs is not a relationship that will swallow him up and eat away his individual identity. He needs loving relationships that nurture and challenge both his identity and those of his covenant-partners.

The "young woman" sinned when she sacrificed her self and she began (with others' help) to weave the web of her own enmeshment. To establish her own independent identity, it appears that she must now deny her relationships. In fact, this is no doubt what her well-trained therapist will eventually tell her. "Enmeshed in a relationship? Leave it. Find yourself. It's your turn to be a person!" But even if she did have enough of a self left to commit this act of apparent homicide, would she not find herself hopelessly trapped in the same kind of alienation which is killing her brother?[22]

What the enmeshed "young woman" needs is not the discovery of self apart from her relationships. She needs the confidence of knowing her own individual identity, of knowing herself as a mutual partner in the relationship. She needs the freedom of seeing that her individual identity both challenges and nurtures those relationships that are so important to her.

But the trap of enmeshment is as thorough as the trap of alienation. No personal maneuvering by either the brother or the sister can defeat their deaths. Salvation is by grace, not by works. A redeemer is needed. "While we were yet sinners," Paul writes, "Christ died for us."

For one who is alienated (from others, from God), Christ comes to join him in his alienation and thereby restores relationship—without destroying his identity (Rom. 5:6–11). Redemption for the "man" is reconciliation that refashions and strengthens a healthy individual identity in the context of relationships.

For one who is enmeshed (with others, with God), Christ suspends the ultimacy of her relationships, without destroying those relationships (I Cor. 7:29–31). Redemption does not lead to the establishment of the "woman's" identity through her alienation. The "woman's" redemption occurs as Christ calls forth her identity in such a way that she can participate in the mutuality of healthy relationships.

Martha does have a story of sin and death. Her story of self-sacrifice and enmeshment and personal identity is as true as is her "brother's" story of pride and alienation and reconciliation. But where he has the parable of the Prodigal Son and Paul's theology in Romans to help him tell his personal history, Martha has neither.

So new thinking must be done about sin and salvation. It is a matter of growing up. Knowing that the story of the Prodigal Son is not our story, women have searched for other scriptural paradigms of salvation. Our search has led us to the Exodus story. Women have been oppressed for too many generations. The Exodus tradition— renewed in Jesus—proclaims that women (and men) can be liberated from the "male" sin of patriarchy (i.e., of corporate pride). Death in the land of Egypt is the result of the oppressor's sin. Women have begun to hear the good news that God liberates the innocents from the oppressive Pharoah. And we have begun to sing Miriam's song of salvation. But even the Exodus has as its sequel the wilderness wanderings. Even the innocents who are liberated eventually come face to face with their own sin and death. Once free of the oppressor's sin, the wilderness compels women to name our own participation in humanity's sin. We are finally free to grow up.

* * * * * *

The sin and death discovered in our wilderness are not foreign to scripture. We catch glimpses of it in the Mary and Martha story (Luke 10:38-42). Martha, enmeshed in her servant role, cannot choose the "better portion." Would-be disciples of Jesus are not free to follow Jesus because they are too tied to such familial duties as burying the dead (Luke 9:57-62). In Galatians 3 Paul warns against the trap of assigning ultimacy to Law. This enmeshment is as deadly as alienation from God. In I Corinthians 7 Paul hints at the sin and death of enmeshment when he fears marriage for the "young woman" because it enmeshes her with worldly affairs.

As we name our sin of self-sacrifice and our death of enmeshment, our eyes become trained to see the light of salvation in scripture. We see a ray in I Corinthians 7:29-31 where Paul encourages a life lived in relationships "as if not." That is, the ultimacy of one's relationships can be suspended—without the destruction of those relationships. In the gospel of John, Jesus is a walking picture of salvation. He is in perfect relationship with God, yet his identity is solidly his own. He builds strong friendships, yet when a friend is sick he is not "trapped into" rushing to heal him. He is separate from his friends while loving them to the point of tears.

We must struggle to name salvation for Martha, for the elder brothers and sisters among us. Such naming will be a critique of the salvation which the church has often offered. If salvation is covenant, we must insist that it is a relationship which grants strong personal identity—that it is not a relationship which enmeshes. If salvation is acceptance and reconciliation, then we must add that it is also the freedom to be in healthy conflict. If salvation is unity, we must also say that salvation is separateness.

Martha can have a personal history of redemption. Christ died for the sins of all. For the one who is alienated, the cross means that Christ shares in the death of alienation in order to bring him (or her) into a loving relationship (Rom. 6:6-11). And for the one who is enmeshed, the cross demonstrates that Christ participated in the values and structures of this world which form her (or his) enmeshment (I Cor. 1:18-2:10). Christ's death defeats the ultimacy of everything and everyone that threaten to enmesh us, and thereby delivers us into Life.

Martha is not an "elder sister." She is a daughter of God.

---

[1] In western culture, the dominant pattern is the pattern of rebellion and alienation. The male is encouraged to protect self; the female, to protect relationship. In actual experience there are males who fit the so-called female pattern of enmeshment and females who fit the so-called male pattern of alienation. In nonwestern cultures, it is not unusual for the dominant pattern to be enmeshment. The patterns are culturally determined; neither pattern is inherently "male" or "female."

[2] Though one must admit that at least the death of alienation is one the Christian community can recognize as death. Enmeshment is usually labeled as a lack of maturity, not accorded the status of death. At least in her alienation she can hear and hopefully receive the story of the Prodigal Son. But with no story for her own death, she is forced to go through this double death before hearing good news.

Building an Altar

by Carol Tyx

Daughters of Sarah, May/June 1991. At that time Carol Tyx, of Greenville, Ohio, was teaching herself and college freshmen how to write while working on a master's degree in English and women's studies.

I have not listened
to my Inner voices,

I have trampled
on sacred ground.

I have chosen to tie up
the strong woman

and allowed my house
to be robbed.

Let this place be marked

I will gather stones,
heavy and rough-edged,

and build an altar, here,
at this place in my life,

to honor the Spirit
who has led me

to this sacred ground where
the strong woman listens

to her Inner voices.

Or again,
how can anyone
enter a strong man's house
and carry off his possessions
without first
tying up the strong man?
—Matthew 12:29

Illustration by Kari Sandhaas, published in *Daughters of Sarah*, May/June 1988.

Will Size 22 Fit
Through the Pearly Gates?

by Janet Tanaka

Daughters of Sarah September/October 1989. At that time Janet Tanaka was a free lance writer, civic activist, and volcanic hazard management consultant who freely admitted her age (fifty-three) and dress size (22-24W). A similar article by the author, with the same title, appeared in the October, 1988 issue of *BBW* (Big Beautiful Women) magazine.

And it came to pass that Richard Simmons was electrocuted by a faulty switch on his treadmill. After several moments of clinical death he was revived.

"Food! Food!" he shouted, sitting up. "Raspberry tart, chocolate truffle!"

The startled paramedics listened in amazement to the tale of his traumatic, near-death conversion experience.

"I saw God," Simmons cried. "I saw GOD, and SHE'S FAT!"

Lord, let it be…

Once it was preached that dark skins were a divine punishment, and that women had no souls. Respectable church-going society has now found a new "nigger"—fat people. Listen to C. S. Lovett in her diet book *Help, Lord, The Devil Wants Me Fat* (1980), "Whenever you see a fat Christian, you're looking at (one) who is not walking with the Lord.… Most subtle is the way the devil gets us to defile our bodies with food."

As if there weren't enough eager entrepreneurs getting rich by damaging the bodies, minds, and emotions of large people, now there are holy hucksters peddling diet books preaching that thinness is next to godliness and faith can remove mountains of you-know-what. The message, whether blatant or subtle, is that fat-is-sin-and-the-righteous-are-thin-amen.

Well, sisters, it's a lie. It's the weight-fanatics who are committing sins: sexism, prejudice, idolatry, selfishness.

Much of the weight loss business is a sexist put-down. Without denying that fat men are also pressured, it is an inescapable fact that the pressure to be thin lies heaviest on women. At the root of society's weight obsession we find male doctors, male exercise gurus, male fashion designers, and males running companies that profit from diet foods and fads. Yes, groups such as Weight Watchers were started by women. But why?

Illustration by Kari Sandhaas, published in *Daughters of Sarah*, September/October 1989.

In response to a male-dominated culture that has for centuries lived in awe and fear of the big, powerful, mysterious Earth Mother.

Breasts and behinds are the stuff of pornography because there they can be admired without being respected. Bellies, however, will never be "in" because they are the undeniable proof of woman's supreme power-giving life itself through pregnancy and childbirth. Childbirth, of course, represents sex with responsibility—from which those males who are emotionally immature and spiritually stunted have always fled.

Kim Chernin, in her book *The Obsession: Reflections on the Tyranny of Slenderness* (Harperperennial Library reprint, 1994), draws an enlightening comparison between terms used by feminists and by weight-watching groups.

Feminists	Weight Watchers
acquire weight	become lightweight
abundant	small
widen	narrow
be expansive	shrink
grow	diminish

"These metaphoric consistencies," says Chernin, "reveal a struggle that goes beyond concern for the body." While the essence of feminism is woman's freedom to be herself, the weightists want to conform our outward and inward selves to someone else's concept of who and how we should be. Societal pressure to reduce women's bodies is the modern version of ancient Chinese foot-binding.

"Equal rights" has become a way of turning women against ourselves. The dominant culture proclaims that it is all right for women to "get ahead" in the business or professional world as long as we become clones of men. Looking like men means flat chests, flat bellies, and small rears. Acting like men means suppression of those qualities identified with women: compassion, tenderness, patience, modesty, etc.

As long as our inherent power and gifts are tied up in ourselves, we present no threat of change. The sexist/weightist wants us to concentrate our energy on losing pounds instead of winning elections. Keep us counting calories, jumping around in front of exercise videos, agonizing over the scale, and we won't be campaigning to clean up toxic waste. They must divide us against our large-bodied sisters, because united, women will change the world!

Some of the authors of Christian weight-loss books seem to have been true compulsive overeaters. Perhaps their approach has helped them live happier, healthier lives. They may not regain their lost weight, but ninety-eight percent of dieters do. If they do, they will heap new loads of guilt upon themselves for something that is virtually beyond their control.

These books falsely generalize that all fat people are compulsive overeaters, and they proceed to do what Christians have been explicitly told not to do: judge the state of other people's souls. May some angel appear to them in a dream and command them to write Matthew 7:1 ("Do not judge, so that you may not be judged") a thousand times on the back of their calorie charts!

Weight fanatics violate the First Commandment by making an idol of appearance. They bow down and worship diet and exercise gurus, the tenets of their weight-watching clubs, and their doctors. All have become infallible.

When the scale, the tape measure, the calorie chart, and the other sacramentals of dieting become the standards by which we measure not just our bodies but our souls, we are worshipping at the wrong altar. We have become so obsessed with perfecting our finite bodies that we have ignored the perfecting of our immortal souls. We have become the priest and Levite who pass by the victim in the gutter because we are afraid to break our jogging stride.

It's my body that must get smaller. It's my mind and my emotions that control my destiny and worth. From the first peek at the scale in the morning till the last grapefruit at night, we are consumed with me, me, me!

What a strange focus for the woman who claims to follow the One who said not to be anxious about what we should eat, drink, or wear. How can the woman whose daily moods are controlled by the figures on the bathroom scale, whose days are filled with denial and resentment, whose sole motivating purpose in life is to wear a smaller dress size, justify her lifestyle to her Lord who asked in Matthew 6:25-27, "Is not life more than food and the body more than clothing? Which of you, by being anxious can add one cubit to [her] span of life?" Jesus might add today, "and why are you worried over subtracting one inch from your waistline?"

But what about health? Isn't obesity a disease? Abundant medical research shows that God did not intend one size to fit all. Body size, shape, and chemistry are largely genetically determined. Permanent weight loss is virtually impossible for anyone except those who were true compulsive overeaters and those willing to live in a state of semi-starvation. Dieting does little but mess up the metabolism and cause stress—which in turn causes most of the illnesses usually blamed on fatness.

The weight-obsessed woman suffers from a false conception of herself. Healing begins with a resolve to discover the true self. God's creation is good, in all sizes, shapes, and colors. The beauty of a garden comes from diversity, not sameness. Some of us are slender daffodils, and some are big fluffy chrysanthemums, but we are all cared for by the same Gardener. (Unfortunately, we are all also hip-deep in the same male-bovine-excrement. Does that mean a little manure is good for growth?)

Did Jesus care what size clothing Mary and Martha wore? Did Paul, in all his discussion about women, mention body size? Ridding ourselves of prejudices is not easy, especially when the KKK (Kalorie Kutting Klan) keeps tempting us with designer sheets, and diet evangelists preach that fat is the root of all evil.

Whether we are persecutors or persecutees, we need to be healed. Concentrate on being physically healthy. Eat the right foods in moderation and limit fats, sugars, sodium, and other foods harmful in excess. Stop smoking. Drink alcohol sparingly or not at all. Enjoy regular exercise. Get enough sleep. Our bodies are temples, and we must care for them lovingly whether they resemble roadside chapels or Gothic cathedrals.

Concentrate on being intellectually and emotionally healthy. Read solid medical research and good books for and about large people. When a thought of body hatred comes, replace it instantly with thoughts of love and acceptance. When we realize how wonderful we are, our goodness will expand and crowd out the faults. Seek out God's abundance in nature: big snow-capped mountains, glorious oceans, giant Sequoias, and round, sweet apples.

We become spiritually healthy by forgetting what the scale says and living by what God says. Remember that genetically ordained biochemistry has nothing to do with the sin of gluttony. Read Scripture showing God's love for us and how we should love each other. When we concentrate on expanding love and service, we worry less about reducing our thighs. Exchange the diet club for a peace group, give the gym fees to charity, and get exercise chasing toddlers in a day care center for low-income mothers. If we fast, let it be because we gave to the neighborhood food bank!

Then if we still believe that being thin is the ultimate goal of existence, we can volunteer in a hospice for terminal cancer or AIDS patients. We'll meet lots of very thin people who'd gladly swap for a large, healthy body.

Save real guilt for real sin; wearing size 3XL is not a matter for confession. Jesus' response to those "Christian" diet books can be found in Matthew 15:11: "It is not what goes into the mouth that defiles a person, but what comes out of the mouth, this defiles..." When we are called to our final accounting, it will be for the shape of our souls, not our bodies.

— ♦ —

"Sin & Grace," Illustration by Kari Sandhaas, published in *Daughters of Sarah*, January/February 1990.

Chapter 6

Women and Abuse

When *Daughters of Sarah* first called for articles about women and domestic violence in 1987, we received more material than we had ever received for any other topic. Many manuscripts were personal stories from those who had been battered wives, women sexually abused as children, or therapists working with women who had suffered violence at the hands of husbands or fathers or ministers. The two issues of the magazine that we eventually published with these tragic stories and soul-searching discussions were also the most frequently requested issues.

Confronting the reality of such close-to-home abuse is not easy. It thrives on silence, fear, denial, shame. In many cases, the abuser is a respected church member, a pillar of the community. Only at home is the inner rage allowed to explode.

Where does the rage come from? Why has there been so little public discussion about what seems to be a very common occurrence in so many of "good Christian homes"? Our discussions over these troubling manuscripts led us into territory that left us with more questions than answers. Does the traditional teaching of male leadership in church, society, and home lead some men to think they have the right to hurt their wives and children? Does a main theological tenet of the Christian faith—God the Father asking Jesus the Son die for everyone else's sins—somehow, unconsciously, justify violence among some of the faithful?

Why do some people feel they have the right to wound most deeply those who love them the most?

The authors of the articles that follow gave voice not only to the truth of their own experiences but the experiences of many who still suffer in silence.

— ◆ —

The Lost Coin

by Lonni Collins Pratt

Daughters of Sarah, Winter 1992. At that time Lonni Collins Pratt was an often-published freelance writer and print media specialist living in Lapeer, Michigan.

My ex-husband, an evangelist and pastor, beat me regularly for fourteen years. Slowly I sank into a state of feeling lost, isolated, and completely separated from any sort of loving presence—especially the male god who seemed to silently condone my bruises, bloody face, and scalded body.

Since escaping that nightmare marriage, I have frequently counseled other battered women. Often, after a session with such a woman, I must remind myself that this woman feels totally lost. When I become frustrated with her for not doing something about her situation, it is her lostness that I should remember.

She is not lost in the sense that a sinner is separated from God without Jesus. She is lost, as I was, like the coin in the parable. "Suppose," said Jesus, "a woman has ten silver coins and loses one. Does she not light a lamp, sweep the house and search carefully until she finds it? And when she finds it, she calls her friends and neighbors together and says, 'Rejoice with me; I have found my lost coin....'" (Luke 15:8-10 *NIV*).

In this parable, God is the Woman who values something that has been lost in the debris and darkness of a home. The lostness described here is a different kind from the lost son or the lost sheep. The coin didn't wander off; there is nothing willful about its separation from the Housewife. Through no fault of its own, it is isolated in a dark corner.

Illustration by Kari Sandhaas, published in *Daughters of Sarah*, Winter 1992.

Why would Jesus include such a picture of lostness? If we have lived long enough in the ranks of humankind, we know that most of us create our own problems and are completely responsible for being "lost." But there are extreme cases when this isn't true, and extreme cases are not uncommon.

Domestic abuse is a good example of this, as is sexual abuse. I'll only address domestic abuse, yet most of what I say applies to sexual abuse as well. The lostness that results from wife battering is a helpless sort of separation from others and God. The woman can do nothing about it. Yet there is hope because God is scouring the house to find and rescue the coin.

Church, society, even her own sisters have tied her hands. Male pastors say, "Go home and be good, don't upset him and he'll stop. You know what sets him off, just don't do it." Recently a battered wife recounted to me that she had asked a mature Christian woman, "Isn't it sin for him to hurt me?" Her advisor replied, "You're not being submissive, I can tell by your attitude. You wouldn't be asking these questions if you were submissive." Every time the coin wants to become unlost, more debris is piled on, until it finally rolls into a corner and silently bears the debris, buried in oblivion.

In the middle of the many pictures of lostness, we find this message about God as a determined Homemaker who will not rest until She finds the coin. It is her coin and it matters. Jesus includes this parable while teaching about the general lostness of all humans. It shines as a message of hope to those who feel trapped in a hopeless situation not of their own making. God will find them in their oblivion.

Too often the church has chosen to ignore the lost coin and God's search of it. I have my own memories about the way many religious people twist scripture to encourage battered women to remain in their situation. I was hospitalized after a severe beating. I couldn't sit up or turn my head because of several well-aimed kicks to my neck, so the minister had to lean over my bed when he said softly, "All things work together for your good. This is the cross God has called you to bear. Think of how glorious it will be when you see your husband conforming to what God wants for him. It will happen if you just continue to love him. He's God's man and the devil is after him, but we aren't going to let old slew-foot have him, are we?"

Before his arrival, I had determined to end the marriage and abuse. But influenced by pastoral advice, I returned to the home, certain that it was God's will. Six months later I miscarried in my third month of pregnancy after a severe beating.

This time the pastor was enraged when he learned I had been pregnant. He said I did not have to stay with a man who killed his own child. But his counsel was confusing and didn't ring of truth. After all, my husband had been killing *me* for years.

So murder isn't grounds for divorce, I thought. I was too dead to move, too dead to protect myself, too dead to believe that I mattered to God. I felt like a stick person without insides.

Years passed. Years of hot coffee in my face, bruises, bloody noses and lips, twisted arms and legs, blows and kicks, one after another, year after year. I rolled into a corner to be buried beneath the debris of my marriage—lost.

Then something else was wrong in my body, beyond the battering. The diagnosis was cancer. My husband said I could not undergo chemotherapy. He was a pastor by then and pastors' wives "...don't go to man for healing, they go to God. If it's God's will, you'll live. If not, well, you'll just have to accept His will."

Wait a minute, whispered an internal voice that I thought had been silenced long ago. He wants you to die! He's supposed to love you like Christ loves the church and he is actually going to keep you from getting the treatment that could save your life. He wants you dead. You've survived all these years and now he thinks God will do the job for him. He thinks God is his hit man.

If I obeyed my husband, it would mean my death. It would mean he had his way at last. When I looked into his eyes, I knew I was finished. If it meant the church deserted me, if it meant God hated me, if it meant losing everything, I would do what was best for me. I would fight for my life. Life was suddenly worth fighting for.

I didn't see into the spiritual world where God had used my illness to move aside the dust balls and shove away the furniture. God shone a light on the lost coin and the light seemed to come to life inside me. As this man I had lived with for fourteen years demanded my life on the altar of his religious ego, the will to live was birthed inside me. God had found me. The divine Housewife stooped over and clutched me in Her fingers, pressing Her fingerprints into the silver of my life and declaring, "Mine!"

It is up to God the Housewife to find the lost coin, the precious, valuable one who waits to be found. Sons can decide to go home, sheep can bleat loudly. But the cries for help from a battered woman are frequently silenced.

It is time for the church to become part of the finding of the coin, to move the furniture with God and to search with lamp and broom as God's partner for those too dead to cry anymore.

——◆——

Liturgy for a Lost Childhood

by Marty Green

Daughters of Sarah, September/October 1987 issue on incest. At that time Marty Green was the pen name of an Iowan who had written on spiritual and mental wellness, including three books for young people. She works with families and the elderly at a social service agency.

When, after more than thirty years of amnesia and three years of therapy, I finally was able to remember the abuse of my childhood, part of me longed for some ritual to bring closure to this part of my life, to celebrate the present, and to prepare the way to get on with the future.

I discovered a longing for those social customs someone receives who has had a child die, because a part of me, my child, was killed. In our area, it is the custom to have announcements printed up on little cards telling of a person's death and funeral services. These cards are placed in local stores and mark the public acknowledgment that a loss has occurred. I wanted that public acknowledgment. I wanted the neighbors to bring home-baked goods to the house, to have a wake and funeral. I wanted my family to grieve with me. That wasn't going to happen.

Instead, a prayer emerged from inside of me. It is for incest survivors, not incest victims. We *were* victimized. But now we *have* survived and can begin to heal. This prayer has helped my healing process. I offer it here, for any others who need a ritual of closure to a similar past.

The Memory

he is here. he is with me. i lie on his arm. i like that, then he lies on my arm.
i don't like that so much. it hurts. it is too heavy. but he is with me.
he pays attention.
now we play that game again. he is here. there. close. closer. it feels good.
now it doesn't feel good.
now I don't feel at all.
then he goes away. i don't know what i did. mama is mad and daddy is gone.
i must have been so bad he left. i just can't remember what i did.
and mama hates me for being with daddy.
i don't know the words for this.
but inside, my body remembers, down there, where memories still hurt.

The Prayer

God, all of these years I have felt evil, only I never quite knew why. I've tried to convince myself and others of how bad I am. I always thought it was confession I needed, but it never took away the guilt. Now that I've remembered the incest, I know it is healing I need from you, not forgiveness from others. I thought I needed to say, "Bless me, Father, for I have sinned." Now I know I need to say, "Bless me, for my father sinned."

Marty, you are not alone. Turn to me within yourself, search for me in community. Healing is possible. Keep trying, Marty, I am near to broken hearts and I am close to you.

God, my heart is surely broken. It is so hard to trust others, even you. Help me be open. Help me understand about anger. I'm so angry at *him* for what he did to me. I'm so angry at *them*, that I never even knew I deserved their love.

I was taught that anger is a sin. Admitting this rage makes me feel evil all over again. I need to learn it is part of being human, not a sign of my wickedness.

Marty, listen to me. You have a right to your anger. Your loss is tremendous, but I do understand. I will help you heal.

But God! I missed out on so much, I want to have had a happy childhood. I want a mother and father who love me. Oh God, I want what I can never have.

What they did to you is wrong. But now you are making your own choices for the future. You are building a new life in the light of my love. I am very proud of you. Do not despair I have been with you and I promise to remain with you.

I want to believe. Each day I choose for the future, but it was so hard to remember the pain and anger that sometimes I can't let it go for fear of forgetting again. How do I live without pain, without anger, without a family? I just can't do it by myself.

I promise you this: I am your light and your salvation. You need not fear. I will never leave you. I will never desert you. Even though your father and mother deserted you, I will always care for you. You can believe me; you will see goodness in life. Put your hope in me. Be strong.

I do try, God, but I feel such overwhelming failure. Again and again, I slip back and no longer want to live. Please, God, are you sure it's worth the struggle? Do you even remember that I'm here?

Hush, Marty. Does a woman forget her baby, or fail to cherish the daughter of her womb? Yet even if these forget, I will never forget you. It will be all right. I'm here.

Okay, I will begin again. While the incest was forgotten, I could not heal. Now I know. Thank you, God, that now I know. Thanks for the memories. You always did know and you never left me. I don't understand that very well, but thank you. I will try to believe in you and—so much harder—believe in myself. Together we will heal, one day at a time. Thanks, God, for sticking around.

Epilogue

I still hurt
sometimes, God.
I know, Marty.
I cannot, in
this scheme of things,
stop the hurting.
But, my child,
I can
I will
I do
hold you
close
to me
and
My Touch
you can trust
for ever
and ever.
Amen.

———◆———

Illustration by Kari Sandhaas, published in
Daughters of Sarah, September/October 1987

Karissa (four poems)

by Kaiona Anthony Koeninger

Daughters of Sarah, Summer 1993 issue on racism and womanist concerns. At that time Kaiona Anthony Koeninger taught history and poetry at Marymount College in Rancho Palos Verdes, California. He has published five books of poetry, the most recent being *Poems for Billie Holiday* (1993). Kaiona now teaches Mexican-American history at Cuesta College in San Lui Obispu, California.

Karissa Don't Taste Honey

Karissa heard no jazz
There was no reggae or funk
leapin
down C Street
as he pressed
up against her

Karissa did not taste honey as he
forced his mouth
on her mouth

There wasn't any taste
of sweet lemon drops

No violets
or forsythia
      blossomed
from her tears

Karissa Take Care

Karissa just come back from clinic,
next to the high school,
over on 30th Street

She thank Jesus she ain't pregnant

She got bruises on her arms, on
her breasts
*And she got bruises she just don't
talk about*

Karissa cries

but she thank the Lord she ain't
pregnant

Karissa Takes Line 42 Downtown

She got 8 dollars & 93 cents
to buy something for her children

Karissa not gone buy taffy,
not chocolates
naw, she gone pick out
    something special
at Tiny's Thrift Store
for her children to keep & say
mama gave us this

maybe she buy woolen blanket,
or beads,
or Kwanza cards

she wraps gifts awful pretty

Karissa Got Some Gumption!

*Start with what you know
and build on what you have*
—Kwame Nkrumah

Karissa, raised in Babylon,
estranged from peace,
she always near flame,
got some idea, new, keen,
about how she gonna innovate,
improvise

mmm, how she gonna pull
something real pretty
outta the ashes.

———◆———

Illustration by Kari Sandhaas, published in *Daughters of Sarah*, July/August 1987.

"As For Me"
Making Choices When Threatened with Acquaintance Rape
by Dorothy Samuel

Daughters of Sarah, July/August 1987 issue on domestic violence. At that time, Dorothy T. Samuel, a writer and teacher on issues of women and religion in the Minnesota area, was giving programs on women in the life and teachings of Jesus and the early church.

The fastest growing violence against women today is acquaintance rape. It fits none of the usual stereotypes associated with criminals and criminal behavior because the rapist is, quite literally, the boy-next-door—or in the next chair at school, or waiting for the next dance at a private party.

Some women have recognized that the abyss between an unknown attacker and a surprised victim can sometimes be bridged by a human response that is neither threatening nor terrified.* They are stymied in situations of date rape, however, for they are already relating to their attacker on a warm, human basis of trust and respect. It is because of that open relationship that they are in a position to be threatened.

Susan is an example combining the elements of many true stories. She came to a large university from a midwestern town of ten thousand. She felt a little lost, but she liked the other students and her professors. After the first math quiz, she showed her D paper to Tom in the next seat. He had an A. And when he suggested cokes in the Student Union to talk about the math problems, she was grateful.

After an hour of math, they reached for their coats. "Look," Tom suggested, "I have a manual in my apartment that just steps through the process without all the excess words in the textbook. Want to stop by and borrow it?"

Susan thought that was a really generous gesture, and she eagerly agreed. They laughed and chatted as they walked the few blocks under the darkening autumn sky.

His room was on the top floor of an old mansion-like house, rundown now and carved into student rooms. He unlocked his room door and carefully closed and relocked it behind him. After switching on the record player, he came up behind her to take her coat.

"Oh, I can't stay," she objected, keeping her arms around her books. "I'm due at the cafeteria. Just let me take the manual, and maybe I can ask you some questions tomorrow after I've tried working with it."

Tom laughed. "We've already had homework time," he said. "Just have a drink before you leave."

"I don't really drink," she murmured.

"Well, hell, you're not going to just pick my brain, take my book, and run, are you?"

He was smiling broadly, a nice wide smile on a nice tanned face. And it did seem a bit ungracious after all the tutoring he'd given her.

"Well—maybe—do you have any Pepsi?"

"Coming right up. Just let me take your coat or you'll freeze when you leave."

So he took her coat and somehow wedged it into his closet, insisting she sit down. The chairs were piled with clothing and books, but there was an open corner on the couch. He opened the refrigerator and took out a can of Pepsi and a liquor bottle. After pouring the Pepsi, he held out her glass and kept a smaller one for himself. He clicked glasses jovially with a toast to "many more times together."

Susan laughed and took a swallow. "Tom, you put something in this…," she began.

"Oh, drink up. It's just a drop, and it'll make everything better."

His free arm was suddenly around her shoulders, and she had to struggle to keep her glass from spilling. "Careful!" she burst out.

"Well, drink up then!" He gulped his own drink, set down the glass, and brought his hand across to clasp her waist.

Small town girl, unfamiliar social situation, isolation, mores under attack—it's a common situation on campuses across the United States where date rape is the greatest fear. And many of the college men don't even see it as a crime. Their earnest rejoinders ring with sincerity.

"They know what they're doing when they come to a guy's room…."

"All girls do it….."

"Girls really want it but they want to be coaxed…."

There are two kinds of Susans, and neither of them is guaranteed safety. But the Susans who are trapped in social politeness and the desire to be approved by their peers seldom walk away untouched. Their ineffectual, uncertain arguments and their hysterical pleadings titillate and then challenge the increasing expectancy of the male.

Some Susans do walk away. This Susan set her glass down quickly and paid no attention to the spilled liquid. And she rose, so quickly and firmly that she was on her feet before a surprised Tom could regroup his arms.

And that might have ended this scenario had it not been for the locked door.

"Wait—your coat," he said, and marched to the closet.

As she fumbled with the key, he came to her holding out the coat. It seemed he was now ready to forget it, forget her, too, of course. So she stretched out her arm for the coat, and suddenly he was holding her in football hardened hands.

"You didn't really think you were going to play games with me, did you?"

"I'm not playing games."

She stood quietly erect, neither softening nor fighting under his grip.

"Oh, yes, you are, you little tease. And you're not going to get away with it!"

He shook her slightly, but she didn't respond.

"You know I can make this pleasant for you or damned unpleasant."

And she knew he could make things extremely unpleasant. But she knew, too, that she wasn't going to help him do it.

"You will just have to do what you think is right for a man like you," she said quietly. I can't make *you* do anything."

"You're damned right...." he began.

"But I'm going to do what I think is right for me, too, and that is to leave."

He opened his mouth for the familiar lines of his well-learned script, and the lines didn't come. She stood apart, even though his hands were holding her tight. She looked unblinkingly up into his eyes, and she might have been some strange woman looking at him from across a room.

Angrily, he shoved her coat at her, wrenched open the door, and pushed her into the hall. The door slammed as she caught her balance, and she heard the lock turn sharply behind her.

There is, of course, no set of words or actions that can be guaranteed to produce this result. But those who walk away seem to demonstrate a kind of centering familiar to religious experience. Perhaps they are not overwhelmed with terror in crisis because their inner self has not already been eaten away by fears about being accepted, approved, fitting in—or being polite.

A detailed study of attitudes toward sex at the University of Connecticut in 1983 revealed very different presuppositions in male and female students. But one college male unconsciously described the typical mindset of the easily victimized female.

He told of being repeatedly called upon by a young woman across the hall in their coed dorm to play the heavy boyfriend when her dates got out of control. Apparently he responded to the signal for awhile, frightening the date-rapers off. And then he got fed up. "Here I am putting on this furious jealousy bit, and she smiles at the guy and apologizes sweetly instead of just telling him to get lost!"

Women who want to walk away with their reputation for charm and pleasantness as intact as their bodies seldom maintain either. The confused male is left feeling he'll score the next time. The Susans who walk away know their own values and limits. They assume a value system in the man—even while knowing it may be different from theirs. Susan asked nothing of Tom, nor did she threaten him with screaming or blows. She recognized his physical ability to control her body, but made it quite clear he had no control over her inner self. He could not reduce her to terror or compliance or hysteria. Tom was faced with a situation for which he had no script.

But these date rapers are boy-next-door types, who in other circumstances are generous, kind, decent, and polite. It was this other set of response patterns that was activated by Susan's suddenly appearing to him as a person rather than "fluff." Tom did not go around beating up on persons, and in the confusion between his roles, he was glad to be rid of her. Only her nonthreatening stance, however, gave him that option.

Susan's response rings out like Joshua's of the Old Testament: "Choose you this day...but as for me...." (Joshua 24:15 *RSV*). There is something Jesus-like about this centeredness under attack. Jesus, too, did not become a different person under attack or abuse. Many times the opposition melted away before his calm centeredness. When it did not, even death did not change his center.

I believe we are called to two challenges in situations of danger. The first is for ourselves—to know who we are and what values we hold, and to center even more strongly when threatened. The second is for the other—to recognize what we Quakers term "that of God in every person," and to call upon it by our very recognition.

Psychologically, it is this grounding in one's own self, one's own values, one's own faith that dismays the attacker. The scenario is disrupted, expectations are shattered. The abuser is confronted with a human being, not an objectified victim. He must then respond as a human being—whatever kind of human being he really is underneath the posturing and role playing. In many cases, he will be pushed back to a fundamental decency and humanity.

---

* Dorothy Samuel's book, *Safe Passage on City Streets*, Word Books, 1975, illustrates this bridging as achieved by a variety of centered people who encountered criminals on the streets and walked away unharmed. Though out of print, it can still be ordered directly from her for $3.95 plus $1 postage: 1207 14th Ave. S.E., St. Cloud, MN 56301.

—— ◆ ——

Daughters of Sarah's Summer 1992 issue included a symposium which stemmed from a concern about the religious roots of child abuse and whether images of the cross and human sacrifice feed into a patriarchal cycle of violence. The leading essay by Joanne Carlson Brown, asserted that glorification of Jesus' suffering led to the abuse of women and children, both in the church and in the home. Response essays from varying perspectives followed Brown's article. Perhaps more than any other topic printed by Daughters of Sarah*, this one prompted numerous strongly opinioned letters to the editor, ranging from an enthusiastic, yet pained, "Yes! Yes!" to an equally passionate, but fierce "No! This goes too far." Following Brown's essay below are a sampling of the forum's responses. —Editors*

Divine Child Abuse?

by Joanne Carlson Brown

Daughters of Sarah, Summer 1992. At that time Joanne Carlson Brown was an ordained United Methodist minister and Professor of Church History and Ecumenics at St. Andrew's Theological College and United Church of Canada Seminary in Saskatoon, Saskatchewan. She is now minister of United Church in University Place, Washington, and adjunct professor at The School of Theology and Ministry, Seattle University.

In our society, women have been acculturated to accept abuse, believing it is our place to suffer. We only come to realize this as the silence about the victimization of women is broken through women's literature, theology, art, social action, and politics. I believe that Christianity has been a—sometimes *the*—primary force shaping our acceptance of abuse. The image of Christ on the cross as savior of the world communicates the message that suffering is redemptive. If the best person who ever lived gave his life for others, then we should likewise sacrifice ourselves. The right to care for our own needs conflicts with following Jesus.

Further, our theology says that Christ suffered in obedience to his Father's will. This "divine child abuse" is paraded as salvific. The child who suffers "without raising his voice" is lauded as the hope of the world. Thus many in the Christian tradition feel that sacrifice and obedience are an integral part of what it means to be Christian.

In both church and society, women have been assigned such a suffering servant role, denied of our personhood and our rights. We have been labeled sinful, the Other, and reminded of our inferior status through theological concepts of original sin. In order for us to become whole, we must reject the culture that shapes our abuse and disassociate ourselves from the institutions that glorify our suffering. This can lead to the conclusion that we must leave the church.

Yet many women do not leave. We stay, trying to rework the tradition by finding feminine undercurrents and countercultures, doing new quests for the historical feminist Jesus, writing women back into the Bible and the tradition. Some enter the ordained ministry, but they pay so high a price that they begin to resemble the very people they want to redeem. All the while, they call to their crucified lord to understand their suffering and support them in their times of trial and martyrdom.

Women who stay in the church are as victimized and abused as any battered woman. Their reasons for staying are the same as those of women who stay in battering situations: they don't mean it; they said they were sorry and would be better; they need me; we can fix it if we try harder; we have nowhere else to go. A Christian theology with atonement at the center still encourages victimization. Internalizing this theology, we are trapped in an unbreakable cycle of abuse.

The only legitimate reason for women to stay in the church will be if the church condemns the glorification of suffering. Only if it is a place where cycles of abuse are named, condemned, and broken can it be a haven of blessing for women.

Atonement Means Suffering

To understand how Christianity is abusive, we must examine its central metaphor: the idea of atonement. Classical views of the atonement have asserted that Jesus' suffering and death is fundamental to our salvation. Critical views have formulated the issue of salvation in different terms, but have not challenged the central problem of the atonement—Jesus' suffering and death, and God's responsibility for it. Perhaps this basic tenet of Christianity upholds actions and attitudes that glorify and even encourage suffering and abuse. Perhaps the glorification of suffering is so central to Christianity that we will never be redeemed and liberated until we leave it.

In classical orthodox theology, the death of Jesus is required by God to make God's plan of salvation effective. Though there are many interpretations of how we are saved by Jesus' death, no classical theory of the atonement questions the necessity of Jesus' suffering. And every theory of the atonement commends suffering to the disciple.

There are three classical views of the atonement. Though I cannot discuss them thoroughly here, I want to make a few observations about each one.

The *Christus Victor* tradition sees the death of Jesus as a mortal confrontation with the powers of evil that oppress human life. Jesus' death represents the apparent triumph of evil, but his resurrection from the dead reveals that God is the greater power whose purpose will finally prevail. Redemption is liberation from evil forces and is brought about by the power of God. The *Christus Victor* theory encourages people to endure suffering as a prelude to new life. God works through suffering, pain, and even death to fulfill God's divine purpose. Suffering is to be looked on as a gift.

Such a theology has devastating effects on human life. In reality, victimization never leads to triumph. It can lead to destruction of the human spirit through the death of a person's sense of power, worth, dignity, or creativity. It can lead to actual death. By denying the reality of suffering and death, the *Christus Victor* theory of atonement trivializes tragedy and defames all those who suffer.

The "satisfaction" (or substitutionary) theory of the atonement, exemplified by Anselm in the eleventh century, says that Jesus died to "pay the price" or "bear the punishment" for human sin. He sacrifices himself in our place to satisfy God's sense of justice. Thus God's wrath is turned away, and the requirements of his honor are met. Then God can relate to human beings without compromising God's principles that sinners should suffer for their sins.

Within this theory, suffering is sanctioned as an experience that frees others. The imitator of Christ may choose to endure suffering because she has become convinced that through her pain another whom she loves will escape pain. Such logic may encourage woman who are being abused to be more concerned about their victimizer than about themselves. It may confuse children who are being abused by a parent, when love and violation seem to go together. And when parents portray God as demanding the total obedience of his son, even to death, what will prevent the parent from engaging in divinely sanctioned child abuse?

As long as our culture images God as a father demanding the suffering and death of his own son, it is sanctioning abuse and it is abandoning the victims of abuse and oppression. Not until this image is shattered will it be possible to create a just society.

The "moral influence" theory, put forth by Abelard, emphasizes God's love and mercy. Jesus' death on the cross is a divine demonstration of that love. God loves us so much he is even willing to die for us. The barrier to our redemption, then, is not in God's nature (as in the satisfaction theory) but in human nature. People's hearts are hardened. Looking at the cross can move us to accept God's mercy and dedicate ourselves to obedience to God's will. The moral influence theory is founded on the belief that only an innocent, suffering victim—for whose suffering we are somehow responsible—has the power to confront us with our guilt and move us to new choices.

Theoretically, the victimization of Jesus should suffice. But women are often viewed as Christ figures, and the actual deaths or violations of women are as necessary to the system as was the death of Jesus. Holding over people's heads the threat that, if they do not behave someone will die, requires occasional fulfillment of the threat. Thus women and others who end up as chosen victims of society live in fear of rape, murder, attack, verbal assault, and denial of their rights and opportunities.

God Suffers with Us

Contemporary critical theologians have directed severe criticism at the traditional atonement concepts, seeing them as contributing to oppression. They have seen their task as one of freeing God from the charge of Divine Oppressor and then to join with this liberated God in laying the axe to the root of oppression. Suffering, they say, must be regarded as negative and not ordained by God. All, that is, except Jesus' suffering! Here the critical traditions fall short of pushing their challenge to its logical conclusion. There is not space here to fully examine these critical views, but I will mention three major trends.

God suffers with us. Edgar Sheffield Brightman and Jürgen Moltmann, among others, have put forth this view. This is progress. It changes the face of theology, but it doesn't necessarily offer liberation for those who suffer. To the question of "how shall I interpret and respond to suffering in my life?" the answer is the same: patiently endure, and suffering will lead to greater life.

The suffering God theologies continue a new form of traditional piety. Because God suffers and God is good, we are good if we suffer. If we don't suffer, we're not good. This theology is offensive because it suggests that acceptance of pain is tantamount to love and is the foundation of social action.

Suffering is inevitable in the struggle for liberation. The concept can be seen in Martin Luther King, Jr., and many Latin American liberation theologians. Instead of making the straightforward observation that those in power resist change by using violence and terror to intimidate those who question injustice, these theologians say that suffering is a positive and necessary part of social transformation.

The cross is still an image of liberation. The third trend critiques the notion of redemptive suffering but insists on retaining the cross as an image of liberation. This view is represented by such theologians as Jon Sobrino, William R. Jones, and Carter

Heyward. There is a tendency to focus on the cross as an example of commitment to justice and liberation. Death on the cross is the result of working for justice. Jesus' example enables us to endure.

In times of severe persecution, such as presently exists among Christians in Latin America, this idea is understandable. One needs to remain courageously committed to the struggle in the face of the despair and grief such suffering brings. But to sanction the suffering and death of Jesus, even while calling it unjust, so that God can be active in the world, only serves to perpetuate the acceptance of the very suffering against which one is struggling.

Liberated from Patriarchy

I still maintain that Christianity is an abusive theology that glorifies suffering. If it is to be liberating for the oppressed, it must itself be liberated from this theology. We must do away with the atonement, this idea of a blood sin upon the whole human race which can be washed away by the blood of the lamb. This blood-thirsty God is the God of patriarchy who at the moment controls the whole Christian tradition. We do not need to be saved by Jesus' death from some original sin. We need to be liberated from this abusive patriarchy. If in our struggle there is suffering, it will be because people with power choose to use their power to resist and oppose the human claim to freedom.

So the key question remains: if we throw out the atonement, do we still have Christianity? I believe we do, if it can be affirmed that:
- Christianity's heart and essence is justice, radical love, and liberation.
- Jesus is one manifestation of Immanuel but not uniquely so, whose life exemplified justice, radical love, and liberation.
- Jesus did not choose the cross but chose integrity and opposition to injustice, refusing to change course because of threat to his life.
- Jesus' death was an unjust act. Its travesty is not redeemed by the resurrection.
- Jesus was not an acceptable sacrifice for the sins of the whole world, because God demands not sacrifice but justice. No one was saved by the death of Jesus.
- Suffering is never redemptive, and suffering cannot be redeemed.
- To be a Christian means keeping faith with those who live God's call for justice, radical love, and liberation.
- Resurrection means that death is overcome in those precise instances when human beings choose life, refusing the threat of death. Jesus climbed out of the grave when

he refused to abandon his commitment to the truth, even though his enemies threatened him with death. On Good Friday, the Resurrected One was crucified.

— ♦ —

SAMPLE RESPONSES to "Divine Child Abuse?"

Jesus *Did* Suffer

by Weaver Santaniello

Daughters of Sarah, Summer 1992. At that time Weaver Santaniello was a Ph.D. Candidate in the Northwestern University/Garrett-Evangelical Theological Seminary Joint Program, Evanston, Illinois.

Joanne Brown states that Christianity has been a primary force in shaping women's acceptance of abuse, for the central metaphor of Christ on the cross as the Savior of the world communicates the message that suffering is redemptive. Her underlying conviction is that Jesus' death is *not* necessary for revealing the theological truth that God suffers with us. She regards Jesus' death as an unjust, unnecessary, violent death, which was final. I agree, as do many contemporary theologians that she criticizes. The problem with Brown's critique of the atonement is that she fails to realize that Jesus' death can be seen as redemptive and revelational without being considered a necessity or as a model that we should necessarily suffer with others. In her criticism that the cross sanctifies social suffering, she misses the heart of the matter which is that Jesus *did* suffer with others and that this suffering is *descriptive*, not necessarily *prescriptive*.

The cross is central to Christianity inasmuch as it is a historical fact which is an essential part of the Christian religion. It is a fact in the sense that it requires theological reflection by the community to go beyond the fact of death in an attempt to create new life. Although, as Brown shows, many classical atonement theories *have* glorified suffering, to say, for instance, that viewing the cross as an example of justice and commitment constitutes the "glorification of suffering" is an overstatement. It seems accurate to assume that as human beings, we suffer and are going to suffer. One of the eternal problems is how we will respond to this condition. Suffering can create us, destroy us and others around us. It seems, therefore, that the metaphor of the cross *should* say something positive about suffering and how it can relate to what is truly divine. To view all types of suffering as "negative" is to deny the human condition—in which pain, loss, and death are inevitable. To say, for example, that one can acquire spiritual strength through suffering is not to glorify suffering; it is only to say that suffering *can* be transformed into positive qualities.

The crucifixion illustrates the tension between self-sacrificial suffering and violent opposition to it, neither of which are desirable nor resolve the paradox of aggression and abuse. More than anything, the cross illustrates that life *is* suffering, and that despite it, we still have the power to become caring persons and/or hostile creatures.

Although Brown's essay is commendable in exposing how the cross has contributed to the victimization and subjugation of women, abolishing the metaphor of the cross is not the answer to the problem of suffering. Rather, the cross should be maintained as a vital Christian symbol and interpreted in ways that illustrate, promote, and perpetuate life, not death.

Both the suffering we endure and the suffering we inflict will not disappear by burying the cross, but by reflecting upon ourselves (and others) in relation *to* it, for it serves to convey what it means to be all-too-human.

Diving Down Many Layers

by Shelley Wiley

Daughters of Sarah, Summer 1992. At that time Shelley Wiley was a Ph.D. Candidate in the Northwestern University/Garrett-Evangelical Theological Seminary Joint Program, Evanston, Illinois. She is currently a pastor in Durham, North Carolina.

"Divine child abuse." Those three words have struck chords. I have seen anger on the face of a seminary professor: "Just what is this divine child abuse? It is a gross misrepresentation of the tradition."

I have seen humor on the face of one who has shunned Christianity: "That's great! It's about time someone said it!"

I have seen concern struggling with recognition on the face of the clergywoman familiar with the realities of spouse abuse in her congregation: "I am beginning to see why this issue is important."

It is this last comment that is most intriguing to me. The first one refuses to honor the real experience of so many abused women and children in our churches. The second voice doesn't know the complicated history that leads to the phrase. But the third, the one filled with real pain—that is the voice to which I must respond.

I, too, am a clergywoman. Now, however, I am finishing my dissertation on atonement. Mostly I spend a large portion of my time talking with friends who pastor churches, especially women friends. I listen to their attempts to be responsible to the traditions they have embraced while at the same time communicating wholeness and holiness in their work. Many of them have reacted strongly to "divine child abuse."

When those of us so deeply aligned with the church read an article like Joanne Carlson Brown's, we are struck by several things. First, we agree with the criticisms of the traditional atonement theories. We can see how the divine work interpreted this way is child abuse. If we are honest, some of us can see the parallels between being an abused partner and being a woman in the church. But uneasiness comes when we consider our own pain and the pain others have gone through and survived.

My clergywoman friend told me, "Knowing that God goes with me into my times of pain and suffering is one of the most powerful elements of my theology, and nothing expresses that like the cross." She argues that the words "divine child abuse" are woefully inadequate to her experience.

And yet later she calls me with the story of a woman who, even today in 1992, is being told by her pastor to endure physical abuse by her husband as Christ bore his abuse. And she says, "I am beginning to understand why this article is important."

What is going on? I think what Joanne Carlson Brown has done is to name something we aren't ready to hear. She has reached down through unexplored layers and wrenched out a truth that isn't yet true for us. And we don't know how to respond.

On one hand, Brown says that our various atonement theories really amount to divine child abuse. The standard response is, "But that's not what the theories were meant to say; they're being misused." But theological reflection has only recently begun to say that perhaps the lived-out consequences of a particular theory are, in fact, part of that theory. We aren't used to thinking of resulting actions as part of a theory.

On the other hand, Brown insists that atonement theories themselves are the problems, and that they need to be thoroughly rooted out of Christianity. But we take a look around our world, seeing the pain and brokenness, and we say, "We are not at one." We do need a concept of atonement—just not one based on Jesus dying for us.

Throughout church history, the symbol for becoming whole has been almost solely the crucified one. But if we acknowledge that the cross alone is not enough, we need another symbol, one that empowers us to live out of Divine wholeness. And we don't have such a symbol.

Further, what are we to say about sin? After all, atonement theories offer an explanation of how we cross that sin caused chasm between God and humanity and between one another. Does part of Brown's solution rest on the denial of original sin? If so, how do we explain our own, at times, less-than-adequate behavior?

Digging deeper, if sin is part of the systemic evil that works to enslave and degrade some at the expense of others, how do we continue our critique of these systems? The entire subject of human sin, of what it is, of how it works with divine graciousness, of our role in it and its role upon us, is a layer not yet explored.

Personally, I don't so much disagree with Brown's article as I think we don't have adequate foundations in place to receive such statements. I think the insight that makes the connection between glorification of suffering through the cross and abuses in our society is absolutely crucial. I am thankful it has been named. My quibble with "Divine Child Abuse?" is in where we go from here.

We are not 'at one.' And I don't believe we'll get there on our own. We need our communities, our friends, our lovers, our actions as well as our theories, and perhaps even our interaction with the divine, to find that place of reconciliation. And as much as I'd like to see it happen overnight, it won't. We'll have to work very hard to get there. Joanne Carlson Brown dove down through many layers, and provides us with one guiding vision of where it is we might end up.

Readers' Responses — *Daughters of Sarah*, Fall 1992 and Winter 1993 letters from readers

I am grateful that *Daughters of Sarah* is a forum in which Christian feminists can disagree with one another, as seen in your recent series of articles on "Divine Child Abuse." One of my continuing frustrations is the assumption that all Christian feminists...think alike. Thank you for giving us a forum in which to learn from one another. —*Peggy A. Haymes, Greensboro, North Carolina*

This was the first time I had encountered the idea of "divine child abuse".... My initial response is that perhaps Christ's atonement has been misinterpreted just as other biblical material has. As a former student of Phyllis Trible, I can remember how freeing it was to hear her reinterpret the story of David's daughter Tamar, among others. Her thesis was that the biblical story had been the victim of misogyny for centuries and that it was up to us to continue the Judeo-Christian tradition of rediscovering God through scripture.

In that case, then, what if Jesus' suffering was not as a helpless victim? What if he made a choice to enter human life to demonstrate that the power that produces victims can be overcome? Think about his confrontations with religious authority..., or the ways he taught about the misuse of earthly power and wealth.... If we take Jesus' resurrection as part of a full process,... then we can see God entering into oneness with those who suffer in order to show God's answer to the kind of power that makes victims and produces abuse. *—Marcia Dorey, Maryville, Missouri*

As a Roman Catholic woman, I was interested in and troubled by Brown's essay. I know first-hand about institutional abuse. I can barely attend my church because of its attitude toward women and the sexist language in its liturgy....

Among the responses, I most identified with Weaver Santaniello's "Jesus *Did* Suffer." While I agree with Brown that most suffering isn't redemptive and that the Church has glorified suffering, particularly among women and the poor, I *don't* agree that acceptance of all suffering is masochistic. After all, Jesus did suffer, and so do we.

As an adult woman, I have a responsibility to grow beyond the sinful attitudes of my church, just as I can see my parents as imperfect and not try to repeat their mistakes. But life involves suffering. It is a necessary component of learning to live with each other's differences, to see ourselves not as the center of the universe but as a part of a larger whole. That isn't masochistic. That is redemptive.

Jesus' actual death *was* unnecessary. Yet avoiding his death because he could see it coming would have been to avoid his moral responsibility to follow truth as he understood it. He might have saved his physical life, but he would have given up his freedom to live a valid life. Jesus' acceptance of the consequences of his actions makes redemptive sense, just as those who protest nuclear arms buildups accept arrest and jail, however unjust those consequences are.

When we can alleviate our sufferings, of course we should. But when they can't be changed unless we are unfaithful to ourselves, then we must accept them. That is redemptive suffering. *—Mary F. Hazlett, Akron, Ohio*

— ◆ —

Chapter 7

Women, Love, & Family

What is a family? What are women's and men's roles within the family? Are we willing to support democracy in the family as we do in our public institutions? How do women, who biologically birth and breastfeed babies, find a balance between mothering and vocation? How seriously should men take their fathering roles?

Family configurations have also drastically changed since the first half of the last century. Single-parent families, blended families, childless families, foster parenting, lesbian and gay families (with and without children), and numerous other combinations raise new issues and questions within the church at large. The current rate of divorce in America traumatizes many children, women, and men, and challenges biblical attitudes toward divorce and remarriage.

Some articles in this section recognize such tensions without coming to dogmatic conclusions. Several biblical articles make clear egalitarian assertions.

— ◆ —

Illustration by Kari Sandhaas, published in *Daughters of Sarah*, Winter 1994.

A Tall Tale of a Working Wife and Mother

by Charlotte Jones

Daughters of Sarah, March/April 1988 issue on work and family. At that time Charlotte Jones was a free-lance writer living with her husband and son in Boulder, Colorado. She is the author of seven award-winning nonfiction books for children and over 125 adult and children's articles.

Once upon a time there was a very poor, very unappreciated, and very rut-bound woman. No one said thank you to her. No one said, "You look very pretty today." She earned no gold dust as a cabinwife.

One day the poor, unappreciated, rut-bound woman went to the marketplace. She and two other women were the only ones buying goods. "Where is everyone?" our heroine asked. "Employed," another woman responded. "They've all taken jobs. I'm interviewing for one this afternoon."

Our peasant woman went to the church for the Lady's Club meeting. But she and the treasurer were the only ones there. "Where is everyone?" she asked.

"Employed," the treasurer responded. "They've all taken jobs, I'm interviewing for one tomorrow."

The poor, unappreciated, rut-bound woman started toward home. On the way, it was time for the changing of the guard at the king's castle. The woman halted to watch. She noticed that not only was the guard changing, but other people were also getting off work. Here came the women she usually saw at the marketplace and at Lady's Club meetings.

But none of the women were dressed in dayclothes, as she was. They were wearing lovely gowns and beautiful hats. One even carried a pouch of papers. They were busy talking about their work and didn't have time for our lady. No one cared about the babes or the new porridges or the bargain on mutton at the corner vendor.

The poor, unappreciated, rut-bound woman listened as the employed women

Illustration by Kari Sandhaas, published in *Daughters of Sarah*, March/April 1988.

passed. Some were catering dinners for the king. Others were designing fine garments for the queen and princess. Some were tutoring the royal children. Still others were writing messages for the king to send abroad.

More employed women passed. They were speaking of their riches—discussing vacations to foreign kingdoms, investments in the king's C.D.s (cattle deals), and of all they would purchase with the gold dust they earned.

The poor, unappreciated, rut-bound woman rearranged her shawl to hide the patches in her day clothes. Then she clumped toward home. As she trudged along, she thought about her family. Her husband worked hard, yet his income allowed the family to just barely survive.

There was more that concerned our heroine. Majesty, the family horse, was aging. He had been part of her wedding dowry, but soon Majesty would be sent to the glue factory and a younger model purchased. That would be a great expense.

Their middle daughter was exceptionally talented, but she would soon need expensive, advanced lyre lessons. Their second son had a bad foot, and our countrywoman shuddered at the cost of future medical treatments. Their income was quite limited.

And then there were Frizzy and Lizzy, her husband's two best goats. The lady's eyes clouded over, recalling that terrible storm when they were both killed by a bolt of lightning. And the miller just raised his prices for milling wheat. Where would it all end?

In bed that night, our lady made a decision. The next morning she walked to the town square and read the notices posted on the public board. There was a job opening at the castle. She hurried home and attired herself in her only fine dress. Then she rushed to the castle. The Personnel Director interviewed and tested her. They needed an accurate counter—to count the king's wealth. Our heroine counted very well. She was hired!

The next morning she began her new job. Every day she counted. She counted gold coins, rubies, and emeralds. She counted both of the king's diamonds. She counted cattle and sheep, cats and children. She counted slippers, fireplaces, and subjects. She counted everything the king owned.

Soon she had lovely gowns, just as the other employed women wore. She had beautiful hats. But our heroine didn't spend all her earnings. She opened a savings account at the Royal Credit Union.

Meanwhile, the lady's husband came home many nights to discover his dinner was not ready. He had worked hard and was hungry. He was also displeased with his wife's strange talk. Why was she more interested in the king's holdings than in drying catgut for the violins he made? And why did she insist on counting when she could make cheese from his goats' milk?

The oldest son soon discovered no one had washed his tournament socks, so he had to wash them himself at the river. The second daughter found no one had packed bear grease into the wheel of the family cart, so she had to pack the wheel herself. The second son had to soak and wrap his bad foot without any help. The youngest daughter soon realized there was no food in the house. She went to the marketplace and learned to barter with the vendors.

Our careerwoman (for that was what she had become) was very proud of her family. Her husband's cheese was twice as good as hers. The children were taking responsibility. And she was proud that she could earn so much gold dust and look so nice. Even the king once said how pretty she looked and how well she counted.

But life was not perfect for our heroine. She often worked overtime, and her family was already asleep when she got home. Other nights she was so tired she collapsed in bed right after work. The king had much to count, so she could never get time off. She missed her youngest son's first sword duel and her middle daughter's lyre recital.

"I'm sorry I missed your activities," she apologized, "but I have good news! I am earning much gold dust. With it we can take a trip this June. How would everyone like to go to Dizzyland?" She was very excited and proud of the opportunity she offered. But if she expected accolades, she was soon disappointed.

"I can't go to Dizzyland," her husband objected. "Who would feed and milk the goats and make the cheese? Who would stretch the catgut?"

"I can't go to Dizzyland," her oldest son howled. "We have Kingdom tournament playoffs the whole month of June. I can't miss."

"I could never walk around Dizzyland with my bad foot," the second son moaned.

"I can't go to Dizzyland either," the middle daughter said. "I start advanced lyre lessons in June. If I'm not there, the master will take another student."

The next morning the youngest daughter was ill. "I can't go to lessons today," she complained. "I'm scared to stay home alone. What if a bear comes in the house?"

Our heroine felt her daughter's forehead. "I'll get Widow Brown to stay with you," she said. She hurried to her house, but a neighbor said Widow Brown had taken a job at the docks, cleaning fish. She hurried down another lane to ask Widow Larson to sit with her ill daughter. But Widow Larson said, "I'm sorry, but I'm selling cosmetics and I have to make deliveries today."

Our good woman finally found Crazy Mary, the village eccentric. Crazy Mary said,

"Sure, I'll take care of the little girl. I have a new brew I'll try on her." Our career woman arrived at work late and worried all day about her daughter and Crazy Mary's brew.

That evening when she returned home, the ailing daughter said, "I wish you didn't have to work." The rest of the family was eating leftovers and each agreed.

Her husband said, "Life was less hectic and easier when you stayed home."

"I liked it better when we were poor," said the middle daughter.

"Everyone's always in a hurry," the youngest son said.

"We never have time to talk," the second son said.

"We haven't had clean clothes in a month," the youngest daughter complained.

"Besides, Mom," said the oldest son, "you're cross-eyed from all that counting."

Our friend faced a decision. Should she give up her job and return to the role of cabinwife? Should she resume being very poor, very unappreciated, and very rut-bound? There would be no more new gowns and nowhere to wear the ones she had. There would be no professional conversations, few compliments, less gold dust.

On the other hand, by returning to her role as cabinwife, she would be free to be more creative. Her schedule would be flexible and she could give more time and love to her family. And her husband would be a happier man if she were home every day managing his meager existence.

But, she reminded herself, the family was more secure with the gold dust she earned. She had purchased a horse. She had paid for advanced lyre lessons for the middle girl. And she almost had enough saved for the second son's medical treatments. The children were becoming more self-sufficient and responsible.

Should she risk sticking with her decision? Should she sacrifice her family's happiness for her own feelings of satisfaction and self-worth?

Our good woman turned to the Bible. She turned the pages and found the story of Lydia in the book of Acts. Lydia, the businesswoman, wasn't home scrubbing floors and ironing all day. She read of Priscilla, a tent maker. She read of other working women. Then she turned to Proverbs 31 and read the attributes of a virtuous woman.

Our heroine thought and contemplated. She weighed the advantages against the disadvantages. She considered her options. Finally she made a decision based on her own values and circumstances. She made it wisely, guided by the words, "Know thyself."

Moral: *There are no easy answers. Life isn't perfect. Everyone must decide what is best for herself.*

———◆———

Making Family

by Allison Stokes

Daughters of Sarah, Winter 1994 issue on women and family. Allison Stokes is founding director of the Women's Interfaith Institute in the Berkshires and co-author of *Defecting in Place: Women Claiming Responsibility for Their Own Spiritual Lives.*

Clergy in the United Church of Christ gathered from all over New England and New York to discuss "Family Life in the Nineties" at the 1991 Annual Pastor's Study Conference. Some ministers expressed disappointment in the topic. The previous year's focus, "Sexuality in the Faith Community," had drawn large numbers and was perceived to be cutting-edge material. "Family Life" was not.

As the invited "conference preacher," I gave much thought to the problem. I eventually decided that reasons for the topic response were twofold. On the one hand, we in the Protestant mainline—or "old line"—make the mistake of letting the religious right claim and define "family." On the other hand, we make the mistake of thinking we know about families because we belong to families. We do not feel a need to inform ourselves, to study family issues in the way we might study other issues. The key question for all of us, it seems to me, is: will we overcome old stereotypes, rethink our concept of "family" in the light of demographics in our country today, and tackle the challenges head on? Or will we allow nostalgia for family life of the 1950s (father-mother-kids-dog-cat) rule?

Jesus himself re-defined family when from the cross he said to Mary, "Woman, behold your son," and to John, "Behold, your mother." John writes, "And from that hour the disciple took her to his own home" (19:27). No blood ties would bind the two together in that home, but rather, ties of love and service.

And when Jesus asked, "Who are my mother and brothers?" he taught us that what is ultimately important is not kinship ties, but ties of love and service to God. Jesus redefines family for us just as he redefines "neighbor." "Who is my neighbor?" A neighbor is not the one who lives in proximity. Rather a neighbor is one who extends love and caring, however distant in place or culture. Following Jesus, we might take a broad and inclusive view and say, "A family is a circle of people who love you." (I recommend to you a little picture book by this title, written by Doris Jasinek and Pamela Bell Ryan and illustrated by Caroline Price, CompCare, 1988).

Given the newly configured family life in the nineties, what might be our response as women in ministry? I am convinced that if we are to deal with family issues effectively, we must first commit ourselves to ongoing study, reading, and learning. From historians we learn about the very different models of family life over time. (The "traditional" family is really the Victorian family.) From sociologists we learn about the social construction of family life. From psychologists we learn about the dynamics of family life and about family systems theory. A remarkable book that pulls together historical, sociological, and depth psychological learning in a readable way, and does it from a feminist perspective, is Deborah Anna Luepnitz's *The Family Interpreted*. (Basic Books, 1988)

Second, I suggest that in the face of rapid social change we as clergy need to maintain "a non-anxious presence," a concept I borrow from Rabbi Friedman, author of *Generation to Generation, Family Life in Church and Synagogue* (Guilford Press, 1985). Let us entertain the notion that God may be doing "a new thing" with families, and that the social order, despite its apparent disarray, may not be collapsing into chaos. What if we were to minister in the present and look to the future not with anxiety, but with confidence?

Unrelated people living in committed relationships of love and service—in families—may not be a bad thing. As the concept of family is freed up, we are beginning to understand that the so-called "traditional" family life of the fifties was often detrimental to the health and well-being of mother. The fact is, the women's movement came out of the 1950s. Feminists are showing how new roles for women and subsequent shifts in family life can benefit not only women, but men and children as well.

Third, women in ministry can respond to the new configuration of family life by speaking out with courage. We can be open, affirming and supportive of people who choose to live in loving, committed partnerships that are not the norm. I am thinking particularly here, though not exclusively, of same sex partnerships, of gay and lesbian family households. As a United Church of Christ pastor I am proud of the progressive stand our denomination has taken on issues of human sexuality. And I agree with William Sloane Coffin, Jr. when he says that the church's treatment of gay and lesbian persons is the litmus test of justice in our time.

Fourth, we women pastors can respond to the newly configured family life in the 1990s by "making family" in our congregations. I credit Penny Long Marler, sociologist at Samford University in Birmingham, Alabama, with the term "making family," an alternative to "building family." I know that there are pastors who resist putting together the words "church" and "family." They would rather speak of "church fellowship" or "church community." But Rabbi Friedman speaks of the congregational family system and with very good reason. In the 1990s countless people look to church not to serve the family, as in the 1950s, but to *be* family.

Recently at a luncheon at my church a single mother asked the man seated across from her, "Would you be a big brother to my son?" She is forty-four. Her son is three. She has no family at all. She came to our church seeking a network of caring for herself and her son. The man with whom she spoke and his wife are middle-aged. They are childless and will remain so. He wants nothing more than a connection with children. Later when this single mother watched the man stroll off down the street with her son perched high on his broad shoulders, she realized that the boy had never before been carried by a man. "Think of it!" she wept.

Today's world of single parents, childless couples, and people living alone calls us to "make family" in our congregations. We need to rethink our churches' ministries and programming now that the traditional family is not the sociological norm.

Finally, as women in ministry we can be there to empower and equip others to do the work of ministry in our newly configured world of families. It is the whole people of God who will make the world a more just, fair, loving, nurturing place. I can touch a person's life and make a difference, even when I have not met that person. This happens when I am a source of support, inspiration and insight for a member of my congregation who is out in the community working in one way or another with children, parents, or families under stress. Sally, the school bus driver; Mary, the food bank volunteer; Audrey, the community health nurse; Jean, the kindergarten teacher— all have been empowered in their ministries by my preaching of God's Word.

Today we clergy women are addressing from the pulpit controversial social issues like the changing family. And we are interpreting scripture out of our lived experience. So doing, we preach "Sermons Seldom Heard." (See Annie Lally Millhaven's edited collection by this title, Crossroad, 1991.) At the same time we clergywomen are addressing women's pastoral care needs in a new way as we counsel "Women in Travail and Transition." (See also Maxine Glaz and Jeanne Stevenson Moessner's edited collection by this title, Fortress, 1991.) As increasing numbers of women become ordained religious leaders and as their voices are heard and their influence felt, we can count on women's experience of family life shaping culture. God is doing a new thing.

—— ◆ ——

Head: What Does It Mean?

by Nancy Hardesty

Daughters of Sarah, July/August 1976. Nancy Hardesty, of Greenville, South Carolina, is Professor of Religion at Clemson University. Her books include *Inclusive Language in the Church* and *Women Called to Witness: Evangelical Feminism in the 19th Century*. All biblical quotations are from the *Revised Standard Version*.

"But what about headship?" Invariably the question arises in any discussion of biblical feminism. Behind the query usually lies the assumption that the Bible teaches that "the husband is the head of the home" or "the husband has unilateral authority over the wife" or "the husband makes the final decisions." The Bible actually teaches none of these things. Nor does it teach, as some extremists say today, that all unmarried Christian women must be under the "headship," i.e., authority, of a male elder or pastor.

The Bible says nothing at all about some abstract concept of "headship"; it simply says, "the husband is the head of the wife as Christ is the head of the Church, his body." This verse is found in the midst of Ephesians 5:21-33, the only real discussion of the head/body image in relationship to marriage. (The only other mention is in I Corinthians 11:3, which says simply, without explanation, that the head of the woman or wife is the man or husband—the words are interchangeable.)

To understand what Paul is trying to say in Ephesians 5, one must read carefully through both Ephesians and Colossians (the books are very similar in thought patterns), paying close attention to the use of such words as "head," "body," "one," holy," "grow," "knit," "fit together," "built," "fullness," "baptism." These words form an image-cluster which can also be glimpsed in Romans 12, 1 Corinthians 7, 11, 12, and 15 as well. One cannot begin to understand Paul's use of "head" apart from an understanding of this image pattern as a whole.

A writer uses an image to evoke the mental representation of a sensory experience which illustrates the point he or she is making. Images may be "free" or "tied," "figurative" or "literal." A "tied" image is one whose meaning and associational values are nearly the same for all readers, while the meaning of a "free" one is not so fixed by its context so that various people may give it various interpretations. A figurative image is one which involves some "turn" on the literal meaning, while a literal one involves no necessary change or extension of the obvious meaning of the words.

For example, in Exodus 19:4, God says, "I bore you on eagles' wings and brought you to myself." This is not a literal image; God does not have feathery wings. It is figurative, suggesting that God enabled Israel to flee Egypt with the swiftness and freedom of an eagle's flight. The image is, however, "tied" to the association with a literal eagle; the reader is not "free" to conclude that, as all Americans know, the eagle is a symbol of the United States and thus this is really a statement that those who reside under the spread-eagle of U.S. sovereignty are closer to God!

Likewise, Paul uses the word "head" as part of a "tied" and a "literal" image, referring simply to the unity of head and body in a living human being. The context makes it clear that he does not intend to suggest some figurative interpretation; Ephesians 5 in particular spells the meaning out so clearly that readers should not have felt "free" to add other associations. Paul is clearly using the references to head/body as an "image" to refer to the physical objects and not as a "symbol" to connote some abstraction such as "authority" or "Order of Creation "or "Chain of Command."

One reason readers have misread authority into the head/body image regarding men and women is that they have misunderstood the image as Paul applies it to Christ and the church. Certainly "Jesus Christ is Lord" over all earthly powers (Eph. 1: 21; Col. 1:16). And his lordship over the world may be included in the associations which the word "head" is intended to have in such verses as Ephesians 1:22. But throughout these letters Paul stresses not Christ's authority over the church but his *union* with it, not Jesus as Lord but Christ as *savior*, not the church's submission but its *exaltation*. As Paul says in Ephesians 2:4-6, God has "raised us up with him, and made us sit with him in heavenly places," which puts us "far above all rule and authority and power and dominion" (1:21) which are "under his feet" (1:22). Similarly, Paul speaks of individual believers as "chosen before the foundation of the world" to be "holy and blameless," (1:4) "filled with all the fullness of God" (3:19); able to attain mature personhood "to the measure of the stature of the fullness of Christ" (4:13).

A second reason some readers have argued that "head" means "authority" is because they read I Corinthians 11: 3 as a hierarchy ranging from God down through Christ to males (husbands) to females (wives). This is an extremely opaque passage and scholars disagree even on its basic thrust, but it seems to have something to do with the appearance of women when they take part in public ministries. It is not a discussion of marriage. Even a cursory reading of verse 3 shows no "chain of command." It begins with what would be the middle terms (Christ and males) and ends with the first term, God, working more in a circular than a linear fashion. In fact, verses 10-12 make the case against a hierarchical understanding even more clear. The most grammatically plausible reading of verse 10 says that "a woman ought to have authority over her own head." Verses 11-12 argue that Christian men and women are to be mutually interdependent with each other and equally dependent on God.

This same thrust appears in other New Testament references to male-female relationships. "Authority" is used regarding the marital relationship only in I Corinthians 7:3-4 where Paul states unequivocally that each spouse has authority over the body of the other. He goes on to say that even if one spouse is unbelieving, the other (whether husband or wife) should defer to them and continue to live in peace with them, because the Christian spouse can make the non-Christian "one with the saints," and can make their children holy (presumably through the one-flesh relationship). In Ephesians 5:21 spouses are told to submit themselves one to the other. This is a constant theme for all Christians throughout Paul's writings: "forbear one another in love," "be friends with one another, and kind, forgiving each other as readily as God forgave you," "teach and admonish one another in all wisdom," "have a profound respect for each other," "in all humility count others better than yourselves, " "seek to do good to one another" (Eph. 4:2, 32; Col. 3:13, 16; Rom. 12:10; Phil. 2:3; 1 Thess. 5:15). Mutual submission is clearly the teaching of the New Testament for all Christians, including married ones.

Even if Paul is not using the head/body image in a figurative way, could not it literally refer to the brain's direction of body functions, implying that the husband is to make decisions for the wife? No. If Paul were trying to say that, he would have depicted the husband as the heart because that is the organ with which first-century people associated such functions (Eph. 1:18; Matt. 12:34). To read our knowledge of the central nervous system back into the head/body image of Scripture is anachronistic. Nor is the concept theologically accurate when it is inferred from Christ's relationship to us as members of his body the church. Christ makes no decisions for us. We are each responsible to God for ourselves, and response-able to make our own individual decisions to accept and use or to reject God's gifts.

What then does "head" mean? Actually, by itself it means nothing. The whole point of Paul's use of the head/body image is in its organic unity, its oneness. Apart from our acceptance of Christ's death for us, we are estranged from God, dead in trespasses and sin. But through baptism (Eph. 4:5, 5:26; Col. 2:12; 1 Cor. 12:13; Gal. 3:28) we are made one body with Christ and we "come to fullness of life in him" (Col. 2:10). Our union with Christ is the source of our life. Jesus himself used another image to convey the same idea: "I am the vine, you are the branches" (John 15:5).

Time and time again the Apostle stresses oneness (Eph. 2:14-18; 4:3-6, 25; 5:31; Col. 1:17; 3:15; 1 Cor. 12:12ff.). He speaks of the church as one body, one building "fitted together" (Eph. 4:15-16; 2:20-22), "knit together" (Eph. 4: 16; Col. 2:2, 19), "built together" (Eph. 2: 20; 4:12, 16; Col. 2:7), above all "growing" (Eph. 2:21, 4:15; Col. 1:10; 2:19), growing into "fullness" (Eph. 1:23; 3:19; 4:13; Col. 1:9; 2:10), maturity (Eph. 4:13; Col. 1:28), becoming "holy and spotless" (Eph. 1:4), "holy, pure and blameless" (Col. 1:23), "with no speck or wrinkle or anything like that, but holy and faultless" (Eph. 5:27).

What then is Paul trying to say in using the head/body image to illustrate the relationships between Christ and the church, between husband and wife?

First of all, the relationships come into being because of voluntary self-giving on the part of each of the parties. Christ freely gave himself for our salvation (Phil. 2:1-11), and we freely choose to give ourselves back to him. "He is our peace, who has made us both one"—Jew and Gentile, slave and free, male and female (Eph. 2:14; Col. 3:10-11; 1 Cor. 12:13; Gal. 3:28; Acts 2:17-18). Husband and wife submit themselves freely and voluntarily to each other, and "the two become one flesh."

Second, Paul's focus is not on any abstract concept of "headship" or even on heads and bodies per se, but on the living organism formed by a united head and body. To concentrate on husbands as "heads" is to miss the point; to identify husbands with Christ in his role as Lord and God is idolatrous.

Third, the purpose of the relationship is to build up, foster growth in, and achieve fulfillment for the individual believer, the church, the wife. Undoubtedly, wives have responsibility to nourish, support, and build up their husbands on the basis of general Christian principles. But the weight of Ephesians 5:21-33 is certainly on the husband's responsibility to the wife who has voluntarily become one with him (three verses are addressed to wives; nine to husbands). Husbands are to nourish, cherish, look after and foster the mature growth of their wives as they would their own bodies. As "head" they are to be a source of life, emulating Christ the Savior who "loved the Church and give himself up for her, that he might sanctify her...."

Obviously this message was revolutionary in its day and unfortunately it still is in ours. In a patriarchal society only men are to achieve fulfillment; women are to pour all their energies into "helping their man succeed." Jesus, however, taught another way: "those who lose their lives for my sake will find it" (Matt. 10:39). It is as we each give our lives in service to others that we find abundance of life ourselves.

—— ◆ ——

One Role Model for All
The Biblical Meaning of Submission

by Phillip Cary

Daughters of Sarah, September/October 1986 issue on men and mutuality. At that time Phillip Cary lived in New Haven, Connecticut, and was a student in philosophy at Yale University. He is now Associate Professor of Philosophy at Eastern College, St. Davids, Pennsylvania.

It has traditionally been assumed that the Bible promotes a special feminine role for women. Yet we are immediately faced with the problem: what model shall women emulate? Eve? Mary? Sarah? Mary Magdalene?

In the New Testament, Jesus is held up as the one model for both men and women. This central biblical teaching can in one stroke expose as a purely human invention the idea of special "feminine" roles for women. To take Eve as a model of "true feminism," for example, would be like taking Adam as the example of "a real man." Both of these represent the old humanity, which must be mortified so that we can put on the new self which we have in Christ Jesus.

To my mind the lack of special feminine roles is nowhere more striking than in those New Testament texts which have traditionally been used to bludgeon women into submission. But to see this we need to reject both liberal and fundamentalist hermeneutics. That is to say, we must understand these texts as culturally relative, but not dismiss them as merely "cultural" and therefore irrelevant.

The greatest help I have found in this hermeneutical ground-clearing operation is John Howard Yoder's book, *The Politics of Jesus* (Eerdmans, 1972). A work of solid but accessible scholarship, it shows, among other things, how understanding the relationship of the early church's teaching to its culture makes its relevance to us more, not less, apparent. I would recommend this book to Christians fighting any kind of oppression, with the proviso that they be willing to subject their own ideological commitments to the scandal of the Cross, which Yoder carefully preserves. I can convey only a few of Yoder's lessons in this article, but everything I'm about to say is shaped by years of reading the New Testament with his comments in mind.

Traditionalism Old and New

The scholars call the texts we are concerned with *haustafeln*, or "household tables," They consist of a series of admonitions addressed to people in roles of socially defined superiority/inferiority, such as parent/child, husband/wife, and master/slave. They were traditionally interpreted as if the New Testament authors were instituting God-given roles. More recently, social conservatives have gone so far as to justify wifely submission as God's plan for feminine fulfillment.

Now as far as I am aware, this notion that women are supposed to enjoy submission is of relatively modern vintage; I can't think of any examples before the Victorian period. Nevertheless, it is a central claim of the New Right's campaign for supposedly "traditional values." I'd rather call it "submission for the Me Generation." (It's almost as preposterous as the Army advertising itself with the jingle, "Be all that you can be.")

In an earlier and soberer age, of course, theologians did not try to fit the household tables into the mold of pop psychology. Among authentic traditionalists, there could be no point in pretending that submission was fun. Like it or not, slaves, women, and children were property of their social superiors. No one in the society of New Testament times would have pretended differently, and wisdom lay in submitting to this divinely instituted order of things. At least so runs the traditional interpretation. And you have to admit, this was at least more honest than the New Right's assertions.

How Wives Were Like Slaves

The first thing for Christian feminists to notice in these texts, therefore, is the parallel between the admonition to wives and the admonition to slaves. It is a parallel which modern fundamentalists must try hard to ignore, for it makes clear that wives, like slaves, were not expected to find "fulfillment" in their inferior status. Even children were not expected to find fulfillment until they reached the age to be free from the authority of others (cf. Gal. 4:1ff).

On the other hand, we can also notice something that traditionalists of previous centuries often tried to ignore—that slavery was no part of Creation, but a product of human social history. Likewise, we can note that male domination of women derived not from Creation, but from the Curse (Gen. 3:16): it is of the same order as death, toil, and labor.

Submission to the established order of things, then, is not wise or virtuous, for this is not what God meant it to be. What then is the purpose of the household tables? Are they enjoining a hopeless resignation to the incorrigible status quo?

Again, traditional interpretations (not modern day Me Generation conservatism) can give us a clue to the real meaning of these texts. A century and a half ago, whether you believed in slavery or not, it was obvious that Africans did not find "fulfillment" on Southern plantations. Thus pro-slavery theologians argued that slaves had their reward in heaven.

Now as soon as we stop thinking of the kingdom of heaven in a pie-in-the-sky fashion and start understanding it in the eschatological context of the New Testament—a context which scholars like Yoder have been working to uncover for most of this century—then a radical shift emerges in our interpretation of the meaning of this reward, and with it the meaning of the household tables.

The Eschatological Context

The New Testament epistle-writers called the established order of things "this present evil age" (Gal. 1:4, cf. 2 Pet. 1:4), and believed that it was already passing away (I Cor. 2:6), because in the Cross of Christ its powers and principalities had already suffered a decisive defeat (Col. 2:15). However, since they are not yet completely in subjection to the new reign of God (I Cor. 15:24-26), the church is still engaged in warfare against them (Eph. 6:12). This tension of the victory which is already won but not yet consummated is the fundamental condition of the world as the apostles understood it. This is often obscured in English versions of the Bible, which translate "the age to come" as if it meant "the other world," the traditional but unbiblical place of reward up in the sky.

In the eschatological view of the New Testament, then, we are not supposed to be resigning ourselves to the present form of the world, which is passing away (cf. Rom. 12:2). On the contrary, we who participate in Christ's victory have already been freed from the basic principles of this world or age and should no longer allow ourselves to be dominated and defined by them (Gal. 4:3ff, Col. 2:20). Instead, we await the day when our freedom shall be revealed in glory (Rom. 8:19-21), like children waiting to come into their inheritance.

This age does not understand who we are in Christ, and so it defines us as master or slave, husband or wife—but this is like thinking the underage heir is really only a slave (Gal. 3:26-4:7). These social realities are already done away with in Christ and shall melt away entirely when he reigns supreme and we reign with him in life.

In this eschatological context, the ethical admonitions of the epistles focus on how we can make use of our time of waiting to be witnesses of the coming realm and its righteousness. The problem addressed by the household tables is that of oppressive social structures. How does someone freed in Christ deal with the social reality that she is the property of her husband or master? The central principle here is the central principle of all Christian ethics: we bear witness by following and imitating Christ.

There is no special slaves' ethics or feminine ideal, but one ethic for all Christians, which takes different forms depending on the individuals' social position. A slave imitating Christ has a different concrete task than a master, precisely because they have both received the same command, which is to imitate Christ in his obedience, servanthood, and suffering. Hearing this one command, a master may have the task of freeing his slaves (cf. Philemon 15ff), and a slave may have the very different task of submitting to a harsh master (I Pet. 2:18).

Peter's Household Tables

Consider, for example, the household tables which take up I Peter 2:13-3:22. This particular text is especially revealing, because it is quite frank about the oppressive nature of these social relationships. It does not include admonitions to parents and children like the household tables in the Pauline letters, but instead deals at length with the relationship between a persecuted church and the political authorities. Peter tells the whole church the same thing he tells slaves oppressed by harsh masters and wives belonging to unbelieving husbands: don't rebel, submit.

Now obviously Peter is not telling people to submit because that's how God meant things to be. Rather, he is formulating a tactic in our spiritual warfare against this present evil age. Significantly, the tactic is chosen, not for its effectiveness, but for its meaning. In submitting to suffering, we point to Christ's victory by imitating the way he won it: "To this you were called, because Christ suffered for you, leaving you an example" (I Pet. 2:21).

When Christian slaves submit to their masters, then, they are not resigning themselves to their inferiority in God's scheme of things. They are enacting their freedom in the same way Christ did when he freely emptied himself to take on the form of a servant (Phil. 2:6ff). Like all Christians, their freedom takes on concrete form in servanthood. "Live as free people...live as servants of God" (1 Pet. 2:16) is the rule for all Christians.

This becomes clear in the admonition to women as well, if we take note of a fact which many translations of the Bible serve to obscure. In I Pet. 3:4, a "gentle and quiet spirit" is commended to women. Sounds like the feminine ideal, doesn't it? But in fact it's the ideal for all Christians. The Greek word translated "gentle" is the same as the one translated "meek" in the beatitudes: "Blessed are the meek, for they shall inherit the earth" (Matt. 5:5). (For quietness as a characteristic of all believers, see Ps. 131). A "gentle and quiet spirit" is thus not a mark of femininity, but the sign of all heirs of the kingdom.

Now this was unheard of in that society, which as a rule allowed only free men to be heirs (especially heirs to a kingdom!). Yet Jesus and Peter, urging meekness upon women and slaves, were reminding them that they too are heirs of the realm of God.

Enough then with the lie that women are to find fulfillment in "femininity." It serves the same purpose as the old lie that some people were born to be slaves: it justifies the powers with which we are at war.

The Enduring Scandal

The household tables do not propose a special ethic for women and slaves, nor do they constitute an "adjustment" of the Gospel to social realities; they show how Christians in difficult situations can partake in Christ's victory. This is the biblical meaning of submission, in contrast to liberal or traditional glosses: it is a tactic in our spiritual warfare.

Of course, in the two millennia since Peter's time, the shape of the battle has undergone some changes. Men no longer own their wives, at least not in the West, and economic exploitation takes different forms than slavery. Hence we may have reason to adopt new tactics, or rather, reemphasize old ones—tactics such as nonviolent resistance, or crying out for justice, or exposing the lies which prop up the power structures of our age.

Yet, though tactics change, the war remains; whatever tactics we find necessary, they are still to be chosen not for their effectiveness, but for their meaning. We are not commanded to accomplish something, but to follow Christ. Hence the biblical meaning of submission remains of urgent relevance to us, even as our tactics change.

Peter's command did not outline a method of "feminine fulfillment," but it did not set forth a program of social change either. It enjoined an altogether strange set of tactics, designed not to win the war but to point to the one who had already won it. And the only way to point to him is to follow him—even to the taking up of a cross.

This nearness to the cross is the enduring scandal of the household tables and of every other part of Christian ethics. We are not called to build a better world or grow as persons, but to follow Christ, no matter what the cost. And let us make no mistake: the cost for a first-century wife or slave could include all sorts of abuse and brutalization. The cost for a first-century master or husband to free his slaves or treat his wife as his own body meant giving up tremendous personal and political power and ego enhancement.

To take up our cross and follow can be unhealthy, is often bad for the development of our inner potential, and is not necessarily calculated to produce constructive social change. It makes no sense in any terms other than our belief that Christ won his own victory this way.

It is scandalous when the Gospel tells us that through our suffering Christ is made manifest. But it is also the source of our hope: we cannot tell what earthly good our tactics will do, but we know that all the suffering and servitude they impose upon us brings us closer to Christ and his victory. As Yoder says, "The relationship between the obedience of God's people and the triumph of God's cause is not one of cause and effect but one of cross and resurrection."

For us Christians, cross and resurrection, scandal and hope, lie very near one another. But we must not confuse them. The cross is at the heart of the Christian life, and it is not a means to social change or personal growth, but a way to die. We will find the strength to follow Christ even to a cross, only if we remember the resurrection and new life to which we are heirs. For an heir may look to all the world like anything but an heir—a mere child, an overworked slave, a non-macho man, a battered wife, or some other sort of stifled, undeveloped personality. But they know they are heirs and all their slaving and suffering and submitting are their active ways of waiting for the day when their true identity, now hidden in Christ, is revealed in all its glory.

—◆—

A Long Time Grieving:
Recovery from Unwelcome Midlife Divorce

by Letha Dawson Scanzoni

Daughters of Sarah, January/February 1989 issue on divorce. Letha Dawson Scanzoni is a professional writer specializing in religion and social issues. She is the author of *Sexuality* and coauthor of *All We're Meant to Be; Is the Homosexual My Neighbor?*; and *Men, Women and Change: A Sociology of Marriage and Family.*

The car was packed so full I could barely slip in the fly swatter I found at the last minute. I took one final look at the house I had just put up for sale after calling it home for ten years. I started the engine and backed out of the driveway. My neighbor, who had come outside to pick up her Sunday newspaper, stood in her bare feet and bathrobe waving goodbye one more time. I knew I'd miss her and her family and all the other good friends who had made the neighborhood such a pleasant place to live. But now I was on my way to a new home—a new life.

The date was October 2, 1988, exactly one week before my fifty-third birthday and only one day short of five years from the date of the divorce that had left me so devastated. Now I was taking advantage of an opportunity to purchase a new home with a friend who had accepted a university position in Norfolk, Virginia. I was excited about the prospect of living in a bustling seacoast area where from the front yard I could see the bright blue of one of the rivers that empties into the Chesapeake Bay. And it seemed almost too good to be true to know I'd be only a short walk away from both a well-equipped university library and an excellent public library. I was becoming eager to move on in my writing career once again and was thrilled to know I'd have easy access to good research and reference materials.

My sons and a number of friends had been urging me to move from North Carolina for years, but until this year I had felt hesitant and afraid to take risks. I wanted to cling to the security of the familiar—even with all the excruciating memories.

As I drove along, I thought about all the people who had wished me well in this new venture and who applauded my courage in putting the house up for sale and doing something I wanted to do—not something others expected or wanted me to do. I thought of the strangers who cheered me on, telling me they had "been there" too.

There was the woman at the bank who said she was so glad she had made the decision to move to another area after her divorce; the woman who fitted my new eye-glasses and told of seeing her thirty-two year marriage end in divorce ten years ago, but was now delighting in her independence; the grandmother working at the dentist's office who told of trying to start over amidst her anguish and anger over her husband's leaving her for a younger woman. I thought of the woman in her fifties who phoned to say she had pulled out in front of a truck on a crowded expressway. She wondered if the near accident was an unconscious attempt to act out the suicidal feelings she had been having since her husband announced his desire for a divorce.

Like me, these women had seen their dreams shatter, their self-esteem plummet, their feelings of security disappear at a time when they least expected it. I knew I wasn't alone. Although two-thirds of the marriages that end in divorce are dissolved within the first nine years of marriage, a little over eleven percent involve couples married twenty years or longer. Government statistics show that one out of five wives whose marriages end in divorce is forty years old or older.

As the miles rolled by that October day, the gray clouds began to lift and the sun lit up the sky, reminding me of the poem I had memorized in the rural Pennsylvania two-room schoolhouse of childhood days, "October's Bright Blue Weather." An orchestral arrangement of "Safe in the Arms of Jesus" began playing on the car radio, and I found myself humming along with it. I began feeling a lightness, freedom, and confidence I hadn't felt since the wrenching agony of the marital breakup.

I had read somewhere that, when a long-term marriage ends, the spouse who didn't want the divorce will find that the grieving and healing process will also be long-term—that it might take as long as one year for every five years of marriage. When John told me he was no longer in love with me, felt trapped and dying inside, and wanted a life apart from me, we had been married twenty-five years (although the divorce took place two years later).

"Why Don't You Just Get Over It?"

It struck me, as I sensed the degree of healing I was becoming aware of that October Sunday of 1988, that the one-year-of-grief-for-every-five-years-of-marriage formula for "getting over" a breakup was turning out to be true for me. It was a revelation, because there were times I thought I'd never heal from it.

"Divorce, at any age, is a stressful life event. For mid-life and older women, the transition from married life to single life can be particularly difficult," emphasizes a special booklet entitled "Divorce after Fifty," prepared by the American Association of Retired Persons.

This transition is especially hard for mid-life women who neither wanted nor expected to ever be divorced, but who found themselves faced with a husband's choice to leave the marriage—whether to "find his true self," experience the single life, have experiences with other women, or for any other reason. (Women who themselves have initiated a marital separation and who experience relief over ending a bad marriage will, of course, react differently than the women I'm focusing on here.)

The reason divorce recovery can't be hastened after a long-term marriage ends is that the uncoupling process is so complex. The couple has a long shared history. "In order to uncouple, two people must disentangle not only their belongings but their identities," writes sociologist Diane Vaughan. "In a reversal of coupling, the partners redefine themselves, both in their own eyes and in the eyes of others, as separate entities once again" (*Uncoupling*, Oxford Univ. Press, 1986, Vintage Books ed., p. xvii).

But the woman left by her spouse of many years may not want to redefine herself as single. To give up her socially esteemed title and role as wife may be perceived as a great loss. (I wore my engagement and wedding rings for over a year after my husband moved out.) Women experiencing divorce in mid-life entered marriage in an era when being a good wife was heralded as the loftiest aspiration a woman could have. All other interests were to be secondary. Such a wife devoted her energies and best years to being a loyal, loving helpmate, trying to anticipate and meet her husband's every need, putting his career concerns above hers, being willing to move wherever his job dictated, and so on.

A wife who is left at mid-life has formed an image of herself that doesn't fit with "Marital Status: Divorced." She is likely to feel terribly betrayed—not only by her husband but by the church and society whose rules she followed so carefully and faithfully. Instead of being rewarded, she is deserted, as though all her efforts are worth nothing at all. Still, after so many years of thinking of herself as married, she finds she cannot accept herself as unmarried without great difficulty.

Others in her life may have the same problem. They may feel betrayed because a marriage that they considered ideal has ended. They may have looked upon the couple as a role model for their own marriage and thus feel let down. They may also worry that their own marriage could be in jeopardy. After all, if this couple got divorced after so many years of what appeared to be a good marriage, what might happen to them? The mid-life divorcing woman may find friends avoiding her whether because they don't wish to "take sides," or because they don't know what to say to her, or because they can't bear listening to her grief, pain, and anger.

Not only does the mid-life divorced woman find it necessary to form a new self-image and personal sense of identity, she may also find herself being forced to form a whole new world view. Sociologists Peter Berger and Hansfried Kellner in their oftquoted article, "Marriage and the Construction of Reality" [*Diogenes* 46 (1964):1-25], speak of the ordered way of looking at the world that emerges from the daily interaction of the married couple. A common reality is formed—a sense of "the way we see this," "the way we feel about that," "what we think about them," and so on. "The couple thus constructs not only present reality but reconstructs past reality as well, fabricating a common memory that integrates the recollections of the two individual pasts," write Berger and Kellner.

Questions of Personal Identity

But when the marriage breaks down, all this changes. The mid-life wife who thought she knew so well the man she had lived with all these years may begin feeling he is a total stranger. The beliefs, values, and views she thought they held in common may now be discredited, disowned, and derided by him. The shared reality is no more. She may begin feeling she's going crazy. The sense of order is breaking down, and life may cease to make sense. What the middle-aged woman had thought was settled for life—her feelings about herself, her relationship with her husband, her perception of her world—have become uncertain and chaotic. And it seems so late in life to have to rethink everything.

Dealing with personal identity questions is difficult enough at any time. But for the woman faced with an unwanted divorce at the mid-life stage, such self-examination and rethinking hits her at a time when energies are already drained by innumerable decisions and demands.

There are legal and economic matters to attend to. There are plans that must be changed. Perhaps she had expected to at last have "her turn" at this stage of life after putting off her higher education and career aspirations until the children were grown and her husband was well established in his career. Can she still pursue her goals or are they financially infeasible? Does she have present skills for the job market, or are they rusty and outdated, forcing her into lowpaying jobs with no benefits? What will she do about health insurance when she is no longer on her husband's plan? She may have a history of health problems that make it difficult to find insurance on her own. How many jobs would she have to take to be able to afford to buy out her husband's half of the house and keep up with the mortgage payments?

So many practical matters require attention just when she needs time to think and grieve. She may develop physical problems exacerbated by the stress. Her children may be going through their own problems and yearn for Mom's support just when she needs theirs. At the same time, her aging parents may need her assistance.

During my own marital breakup, I was responsible for my mother's care through an amputation, a cardiac arrest, colon cancer, other hospitalizations, and at the end, a stroke. My own grieving had to be put on hold many times.

But the hardest thing is the feeling of being rejected, cast aside by the person who had been so loved. I remember telling someone that in the past when I felt sad, hurt, or afraid, I had gone to my husband's arms for comfort. It was strange to realize that not only could I no longer go there, but that this person who was once the source of my comfort was now the source of my suffering. I often read Psalm 55:12-23 where the writer laments a companion's violation of a covenant. And I thought about God's own understanding of what rejection feels like and God's promises to heal the brokenhearted and bind up their wounds.

One woman says that her "mirror" is gone—that she had previously formed her view of herself by looking to her husband. Her self-esteem was battered by his rejection of her, and her self-confidence was slashed apart by his cutting, demeaning, humiliating comments. In spite of all this, she finds it difficult not to continue looking into that same "mirror," seeing herself now as all the negatives her ex-husband has said about her, an undesirable person unworthy of his love.

Part of the problem is that Christian wives have been so conditioned to think husbands are right about everything that many wives will accept even insulting, abusive comments as the truth about themselves. But as Howard Halpern emphasizes in his helpful book, *How to Break Your Addiction to a Person* (Bantam paperback, 1983), a real love relationship is mutual, helping each partner to feel better about himself or herself, not worse.

We need to be gentle and patient with the person going through an unwanted midlife divorce. The grieving cannot be rushed. Much time was invested in the marriage; it will take much time to recover. As one woman said after her friends criticized her for grieving so long after the death of her son, "Every grief has a life of its own." What is true of death is also true of divorce.

———◆———

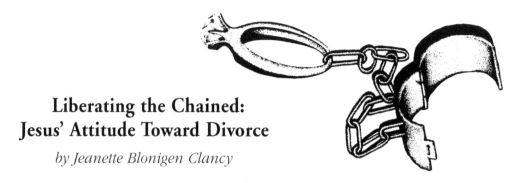

Liberating the Chained:
Jesus' Attitude Toward Divorce

by Jeanette Blonigen Clancy

Daughters of Sarah, January/February 1989 issue on divorce. At that time Jeanette Blonigen Clancy was pursuing a masters degree in systematic theology. Since obtaining the degree she has read widely in theology, spirituality, mythology, and comparative religion, as well as writing and presenting on these subjects.

If as a Christian feminist you think you have problems understanding Jesus' statements on divorce, rest assured that you are not alone. Lately I've been reading the experts—biblical scholars and exegetes—and they sound just as perplexed as the rest of us. They can't reconcile an absolute prohibition of divorce with the facts of our culture any better than we can.

Traditional exegetes have done their best to discover what exactly Jesus said, why he said it, and what he meant by it. But they have been unsuccessful in overturning the interpretation that Jesus meant to say divorce in itself is evil. Such an interpretation is problematic given the necessity and reality of divorce in modern society.

Jesus certainly spoke out against divorce. Unfortunately, the most stringent interpretations of his words have influenced church practices and attitudes, damaging the lives of many. But what exactly was his message?

There are five different New Testament passages which go back to a particular saying of Jesus. They come out of various oral traditions, and so they have various forms. The passages (from the *RSV*) are given below. Boldface print indicates variances.

Matthew 5:32— "Every one who divorces his wife, **except on the ground of unchastity,** makes her an adulteress, and whoever marries a divorced woman commits adultery."

Matthew 19:9— "Whoever divorces his wife, **except for unchastity, and marries another,** commits adultery."

Mark 10:11-12— "Whoever divorces his wife **and marries another** commits adultery **against her**; and if **she** divorces her husband and marries another, she commits adultery."

Illustration by Tom Corlette, published in *Daughters of Sarah*, January/February 1989.

Luke 16:18— "Every one who divorces his wife **and marries another** commits adultery, and he who marries a woman divorced from her husband commits adultery."

I Corinthians 7:10-11— "To the married I give charge, not I but the Lord, that **the wife** should not separate from her husband (but if she does, let her remain single or else be reconciled to her husband) and that the husband should not divorce his wife."

Since Jesus never left any written record, we cannot be sure that any of these sayings are his exact words. Biblical scholars' debate on this issue reveals why Jesus was concerned about divorce.

Adapting Jesus' Words to New Audiences

Of the four New Testament books in which the saying appears, the earliest is First Corinthians, so this passage might be expected to give Jesus' own words. But scholars point out that Paul adapted the saying to his Gentile audience. It is addressed primarily to women, and assumes that a woman would be able to get a divorce. But in the Palestine of Jesus' day, women could not legally divorce.

The second earliest writing is generally assumed to be the Gospel of Mark. But this passage is also ruled out for being the closest thing to Jesus' own words, because it also addresses the prohibition to the woman.

We may understand this Jewish double standard better if we note Deuteronomy 24:1: "When a man takes a wife and marries her, if then she finds no favor in his eyes because he has found some indecency in her, and he writes her a bill of divorce and puts it in her hand and sends her out of his home...." Implicit here are two unquestioned assumptions: divorce was perfectly acceptable, and it was entirely the man's prerogative.

Rabbinical debates over the grounds for divorce operated out of these assumptions. The grounds for divorce were things like childlessness or unattractiveness, or even burnt food. A woman under Jewish law was essentially a nonperson with regard to rights. Nevertheless, she received the blame for adultery, and it rendered her forbidden to her husband.

Another puzzle that inadvertently throws light on the subject is the peculiar phrase in Mark, "against her." This perplexes scholars because it seems to express a sensitivity to women that would be, at the least, extraordinary from the Jewish viewpoint of that day. It introduces the novel possibility of a woman being wronged by adultery. Imagine a piece of property having rights!

A reasonable solution to the puzzle is that this phrase in Mark is an awkward translation from the Aramaic which always follows the verb "to commit adultery" with a preposition. The sentence simply means, "commits adultery with the second woman." The linguistic analysis throws light on the issue of woman's place.

The debate over the saying's most original form yields an interesting argument by Catholic scholar Bruce Vawter. He thinks Matthew 5:32 must be closest to Jesus' original words. There Matthew omits "and marries another," which appears in the other Gospel passages and is paraphrased in Paul. By not mentioning remarriage, Matthew 5:32 links divorce itself with adultery.

Vawter reasons that such linking reflects a tradition thoroughly steeped in the Palestinian context. A man having sexual relations with a woman other than his wife did not commit adultery unless that other woman belonged to another man. He could not be "unfaithful" to his wife because women were chattel. By the same token, divorce even without remarriage constituted adultery for him, because he was giving up his property to be violated by another. Vawter's reasoning illuminates the utter insensitivity to womanhood in the Palestinian milieu.*

Returning to the exegetical debate, we find that another Catholic biblical scholar, J. A. Fitzmyer, disagrees with Vawter about the divorce saying in Matthew 5:32. Fitzmyer uses historical-critical methods of form, source, and textual analysis to present the convincing opinion that Matthew's formulation is not true to Jesus' own words. The significance of that is Matthew's phrase "except for unchastity." That exception, says Fitzmyer, was Matthew's adaptation in response to a troublesome pastoral situation.

Another New Testament writer who made his own exception to Jesus' teaching is Paul. In I Corinthians 7:15, he writes that if "the unbelieving partner desires to separate...the brother or sister is not bound." The Greek vocabulary in this sentence definitely implies divorce and remarriage.

Scholars are not in agreement over the details of Matthew's and Paul's pastoral situations, but they have focused on these exceptions as promising avenues for reconciling the New Testament divorce passages with contemporary life. If the early church considered practical pastoral modifications appropriate, so can we, they declare. The Spirit who moved in their modifications is no less active today.

---

*Abuse of women *was worldwide*. We must not assume that the Jews were exceptional misogynists surrounded by cultures that treated women fairly. Outrageous gender injustice was not only a Middle Eastern phenomenon. The purpose of establishing insensitivity in the Palestinian milieu is to describe Jesus' life setting; to try to see what Jesus saw.

But no amount of exegetical study modifies the sense that, whatever Jesus' own words, he condemned divorce harshly. In fact, more thorough study gives the divorce sayings even more impact.

For instance, the exceptions in Matthew have been popularly interpreted to mean that, in the case of adultery, divorce is all right. However, the scholarly consensus speaks strongly against interpreting *porneia*, the word translated "unchastity" in the *RSV*, to mean "adultery." Matthew uses *moicheia* to mean adultery, and clearly distinguishes between *moicheia* and *porneia* in this passage and others. Therefore Matthew's Jesus, even with the exception, was denouncing divorce in general.

Another divorce saying of Jesus, distinct from the saying which has been the concern of this article, gives us an added look at his attitude toward divorce. In the passages of Matthew 19:3-9 and Mark 10:2-12, Jesus says, "What therefore God has joined together, let no one put asunder" (*KJV*). Together, the two sayings express clear, even vehement, disapproval of divorce. In the passage introducing this saying, Jesus accosts the Pharisees for accepting divorce and upbraids them for hardheartedness.

As uncomfortable as it makes exegetes and the rest of us, there is no reason to doubt that Jesus was emphatic about the wrongfulness of divorce. The multiple appearances of the teaching and the teaching's radical break from Jewish law are indications of its authenticity. Jesus was very forceful when he said it, and he made a great impact. He was obviously overturning a commonly held assumption. In our milieu the teaching defies common sense—unless we rethink the traditional exegetical approach.

Curiously, Fitzmyer and Vawter argue contrary positions for the identical reason: that in Jesus' life setting, women were chattel and Jesus' original saying would reflect that. It is even more interesting that in this case biblical experts base their determination of a saying's authenticity on its *similarity* to Jewish tradition. Usually one criterion for determining the authenticity of a Jesus saying is its *dissimilarity* to his culture.

Divorce Law Oppresses Women

The question is, what was Jesus overturning? Why was he so forceful and insistent in challenging the traditional practice of divorce?

I think that traditional exegesis overlooks the most valuable fruit of its own research. It reckons with a patriarchal milieu that degrades women, and it assumes that Jesus implicitly endorsed that. But the Palestinian divorce system is not just a quaint, outdated curiosity or a cultural peculiarity useful for the work of historical criticism. It was horribly oppressive, and it must have outraged Jesus.

Elizabeth Schüssler Fiorenza and Leonardo Boff draw the only interpretation of the saying which makes sense in light of the human suffering caused by destructive marriages. The urgent message is not the indissolubility of marriage, but the immorality of victimization. This reading is the only one which accounts for the force of the language and what we know of Jesus' attitude toward the abuse of power.

The question of the saying's original form and even the focus on the exceptions are relatively unimportant. What is important is the presupposition in Jesus' culture that a wife was property. A person who broke the taboos of his culture to uplift women as Jesus did could not be expected to acquiesce in the treatment of women as property. If we believe that Jesus was sincerely relating to women as equal persons, we have to conclude that he would object to their abuse by the divorce practice. We do not know what became of divorced women in first century Palestine, but in a culture where women were dependent on men for economic and social survival, their situation must have been grim indeed. We know enough to understand what must have informed Jesus' condemnation of divorce.

Jesus was addressing the practice of owning women and getting rid of them for trivial reasons. He was not laying down the law for future Christians. What we have are his words to oppressors. We do not have his words to the victims of oppressive marriages in today's more equalized climate, where divorce can be a liberator as well as an oppressor. But we can guess what they would be. It is inconceivable that the Word of God would prohibit the most effective means that some victims have of escaping their oppressive situations. Jesus consistently empowered the powerless and liberated the chained. He would not denounce the freedom to divorce and remarry.

Jesus' prohibition of divorce is less important than the reason for it. To deny divorce and remarriage today on the basis of his saying is to violate the spirit of the law for the sake of its letter. If we are to comply with the spirit of his saying, we will allow a repentant transformation of our hardened position on the "evil" of divorce. We will encourage prisoners of destructive relationships to end those relationships and be free to enter life-giving relationships.

A proper reading of Scripture sees Jesus as a radicalizing and revolutionary presence who was not interested in setting down rules that would become encrusted and calcified with age. The challenge of the Reign of God is renewal and growth, not enshrinement of laws. Rules are not everlasting; love is.

— ◆ —

"Two Married Girls": A Lesbian Couple Making Family

by M. J. Rinderer

Daughters of Sarah Winter 1994 issue on women and family. M. J. (Nikki) Rinderer is a writer living in Brookfield with her partner Barb.

Recently Andrew, a four-year-old friend of ours, was on his way to our house with his mother for dinner. On the way, he asked his mother, "Are Nikki and Barb married?"

"Well, sure," his mother replied.

"To who?"

"To each other, of course," she said.

Andrew thought about this for a minute, and then said, "Yes! Two married girls! I've been telling all my friends at school, but no one believes me! "

> *"Gonna build a little home*
> *for two or three or four*
> *or more in Loveland,*
> *for me and my gal."*
>
> —from "The Bells Are Ringing"
> as sung by Holly Near

How gays and lesbians make family, it seems to me, is the same way that anyone else makes family. The process is the same. That is, we live and love and share and care together over time through all the ups and dawns, ins and outs, joys and sorrows of daily life. We face the issues and questions together and are committed to working out the solutions together. We build traditions and rituals; we establish networks of extended family and friends and church and community. This makes us "family." However, even though the form is the same, the substance is different. The way we solve and answer the problems of daily life is necessarily different from the ways in which people in traditional relationships solve them.

Barb and I have been making our family for over ten years. In that time we have had to face and answer for ourselves many of the kinds of questions that have to get answered in the process of making any family.

On Marriage

At some point in most ongoing relationships, two people who love each other begin to think about commitment. Should we get married? If you are a gay/lesbian couple, this question takes on a variety of twists and turns. Church and government generally won't "marry" lesbians/gays. Is marriage even the right word? If we believe in commitment but can't get "married," do we just live together? Families rarely sanction and support these unions. Friends don't think of having a "shower." If we had a ceremony, who would come? What would it look like? What words would we say? What would we wear?

Barb and I decided, after living together for two years, that we wanted to affirm our commitment to one another with a ceremony. We wanted to make a public declaration that we were partners for life. At that time we were out to very few people, so we had a small, private ceremony in our own apartment with two friends, one of whom gave a message, and the other did a reading. We didn't exchange rings but did exchange lockets (easier to keep secret). (By the way, in case you're wondering, I wore a sweatshirt that said "Merry Me" with red suspenders and blue jeans.)

One of the things a guest said at that ceremony stuck with us. She said that marriage is a difficult task even when family and society support it. It would be even harder for us, she said, because if and when we have problems, people will suggest we should not stay together and will do little to try to help. In a heterosexual relationship, when one of the partners gets angry and goes home to mom and dad, the parents will likely send him or her back to work things out. For a gay/lesbian person, that parent will just as likely say, "You stay here. It's for the best. I always knew that kind of relationship couldn't work out." In addition, legal structures don't work to help gay/lesbian couples stay together. We aren't legally married, so we don't have to get legally divorced. We can just get up and walk out. Our friend asked us to make a commitment to come to her if we were in difficulty, before we dissolved our union. Knowing that we have people in our lives (many more now than back then) who will work to help us keep together has been important to us. It's provided a support for us that we're not certain our families of origin can or will.

On Children

Barb and I have elected not to have children, but many gay/lesbian families make a different choice. Some couples choose to adopt children, having to do so as single parents, because adoption agencies don't recognize the legitimacy of gay/lesbian unions. Some lesbian couples opt for artificial insemination, but the courts have been slow in allowing the non-birth partner to adopt the child. Some gay and lesbian couples hook up together and form a two-couple family, with a partner from each couple serving as birth parents. Some couples have children from previous heterosexual relationships that they bring into the new family. And some couples' children are taken away from them by the courts. Do we have children? How do we have them? Are we both trying to be legal parents? What do we tell them and when? How do we present ourselves to their teachers, their friends, their pediatricians? These questions can be very difficult for the gay/lesbian couple to answer.

On Extended Families

And what about our extended families? Do we tell them about our relationship? Are we willing to risk losing our family ties? There are multitudes of horror stories out there about rejection from family members who want nothing to do with gay/lesbian relatives, or who won't let them near their children, etc. That's a big risk to take. And if you draw up wills, and healthcare and property powers of attorney as we have, will your extended family honor your choices, or will they subject your partner to a painful court battle? Sadly, too often a person driven by the need for honesty with the people about whom she/he cares most finds the pearl of honesty trampled underfoot by fearful or moralistic family members who consider it their duty to "set the person straight." (No pun intended.)

And how do we spend our holidays? For many years, Barb and I had told only my mother. None of her family knew, and my father and my siblings didn't know. Each year we would dutifully split up at Thanksgiving and Christmas and go off to our respective "families." And each year we got more and more miserable doing so. We were violating the truth of our love for one another and spending our vacations and holidays apart. So, we started alternating. One year we would both go to her parents for Thanksgiving and then to my parents for Christmas. The next year we would do it the other way around. This has worked somewhat better.

There are still some painful times—unconscious moments such as when someone decides to have a family photo taken and decides that Barb should take it (after all, she isn't "really" part of the family). Or the Christmas letters that go out and mention all the kids and their wives except for Barb. And of course, at Barb's parents' home, I continually feel like everyone is wondering what in the world I am doing there. Nevertheless, the area of extended family has gotten much easier for us and is significantly better than what many of our friends face in their extended families.

On Religion

One final area I want to touch on is religious practice and affiliation. Barb and I have been committed Christians all of our lives. We believe in the saving grace of Jesus

Christ, and we have been active in church for as long as we can remember. We believe that spiritual faith and practice is an important element in the making of a whole and healthy family, and we strive to keep our faith an integral part of our lives. I have to say, though, that some other followers of Christ do not make this easy.

Barb and I struggled a great deal in the church we attended when we met. Both of us had been very active church members for more than ten years, holding significant positions of leadership on the church staff and the church board. When we finally decided to be honest with our so-called church family, the ever-wise elders of that institution decided that because they viewed our relationship as sin, we were welcome to sit in the pew on Sunday morning (pew-potatoes) but not to participate in leadership. Barb and I believe in truth, love, and service, so that church became an intolerable place for us to stay. Luckily, we have found a wonderful church whose philosophy states that their job is to love whomever comes in the door. It is a church which actively works to be sure that it is not guilty of the sin of turning any of God's children away from a house of worship. Many gay/lesbian people are not so fortunate, and countless people who could be wonderful disciples and followers of God have been forced into atheism or agnosticism by the church's self-appointed moral police. Finding your way as a gay/lesbian Christian is not easy. The actions and words of many Christians make it a wonder that any of us even try.

In Conclusion

There are many other issues which could be dealt with in an article like this if space permitted, such as questions of finance, home ownership, insurance, legal protection, pets, vacations, neighbors, or displays of affection. We have only touched on a few that seem central to the concept of "family" from a Christian perspective.

Barb and I are as happy together today as the day we got married. We know there are lots of questions ahead of us, but we look forward to working through them and growing old together, secure in our love. Right now we are planning a ceremony to renew our vows—yes, in our church. We have over one hundred fifty people we want to invite to this ceremony—wonderful friends and family members who love and support and cherish us and our love for each other. We are buying matching rings, and some of our friends have already mentioned giving us a shower. I wonder if I can still fit into my wedding sweatshirt?

— ◆ —

Chapter 8

Women & Human Rights

"There is no longer Jew or Greek, there is no longer slave or free; there is no longer male and female. For you are all one in Christ Jesus" (*NRSV*). This baptismal formula quoted by the Apostle Paul in Galatians 3:28 cuts deeply into our ingrained, worldly assumptions about who is superior and what groups have more power and prestige than others. The abolitionist movement of the nineteenth century and the civil rights movement of the twentieth exposed not only the evils of racism in our church and society, but also the crippling injustices of sexism.

As the feminist movement gathered strength in the 1970s and 80s, and as male privilege was challenged, other forms of discrimination became more obvious. Feminist women of color challenged the racism of their white counterparts and preferred to call themselves womanists or *mujeristas*. Classism, ageism and heterosexism were also identified as endemic in our culture. Women in the two-thirds world challenged the oppressive practices of Western feminists and non-feminists alike.

Most of the articles and poetry in *Daughters of Sarah* challenged these "isms" (or at times unconsciously participated in them). The following representative examples confront international prostitution, racial stereotyping, ageism, and garden-variety Sunday School sexism among children.

— ◆ —

Where to Find Them

by Sandra Lake Lassen

Daughters of Sarah, Fall 1994. At that time Sandra Lake Lassen lived and wrote in Daytona Beach, Florida. She now lives in West Jefferson, North Carolina, where she pursues dual careers as a genealogical researcher and high school teacher.

"Shortage of 60 Million Females Worldwide; Infanticide, Neglect, Fetal Selection Blamed"
—*Boston Globe*

You will find the female children
in the bottom of birthing pails.
A few inches of water will suffice.
In the absence of water,
    in continuing drought,
pinch nose and mouth
    between thumb and finger
until the wriggling stops.

If a mother breeds more than
    two girl babies
burn her like kitchen refuse
and marry the groom again.

Pretty daughters may be sold
    to bamboo brothels
in Bombay,
    where you will find taxi-drivers
eager to show the way.

If selling of females is forbidden
by more progressive laws
neglect will yield a fine result.

Wrest girls early
    from their mothers' breasts,
while older brothers nurse.
You will find them crawling in the dust,
    too weak to stand.

The ones who live are found
tottering on tiny feet in rice fields
    or in cattle pens
where boys steal food
    from their bowls
and mothers look away,
    pretending not to see.

Pretending not to see
also yields a fine result.
In time, you will find them
not at all.

"I know my work is wrong, but…"
Hospitality Women and American Sailors

by Jan Lugibihl

Daughters of Sarah, January/February 1987. Jan Lugibihl was in the Philippines from 1984 to 1987 with Mennonite Central Committee working in Olongapo City with prostitutes and street children. She is currently the Executive Director of Bethany Brethren Community Center in Chicago, which provides before and after school programs, a summer camp, a leadership development program for adolescent girls, and a seniors program.

August 15, 1985. I have lived in Olongapo City, the Philippines, for four months now. This is only the beginning of two-and-a-half years here. So many things have become normal to me. The planes from Subic Bay U.S. Naval Base flying overhead. The bars that line the street leading from the main gate of that base. The dancers, hospitality women, and streetwalkers—about 15,000 Filipinas—who work on that street and the side streets leading from it. The rhythm of their lives here—four to six weeks when only a few of the American sailors stationed at Subic Bay come out to the bars, followed by four to six days when a U.S. aircraft carrier arrives with its support ships. Then 8,000 to 10,000 U.S. sailors on leave flood the streets looking for rest and, mostly, sexual recreation.

This cycle repeats itself year after year. It is during those times of no activity that the women get bored and have time to talk.

Four months. Not a very long time at all, but enough to raise one very troubling question, a question for which I must search for an answer if I am going to continue to live here. It's a question the women themselves bring to me in many different forms. "Am I a sinner?"

Perhaps the easiest way for you to understand why I have no ready answer for that question is for me to tell you one woman's story. The essentials of it differ only in specific detail from those we have heard from many other women here. Multiply it hundreds, thousands of times, and you will begin to experience the Olongapo I am coming to know.

Dee is the first woman we met when we visited almost a year ago. Since then we have sat with her often, laughing and crying with her, learning to know and love her.

Bar sign in Olongapo, Philippines

Photo by Pam Hasegawa, published in *Daughters of Sarah*, Winter 1993.

Dee is thirty-one-years old. She came here from Manila three years ago to work as a maid. Her hope was to make more money here than she had as a city bus conductor in Manila—money she would send to her poor family. Soon, however, the woman she worked for told her she would help her find a better paying job as a waitress in one of the restaurants on the strip, the bar-lined street leading from the naval base. Dee found such a job. Then about a year-and-a-half ago, she moved to her present, even better-paying job as a hospitality woman (i.e., prostitute) in another bar.

During those days when an aircraft carrier is in and she has customers, Dee has food to eat, can pay her rent, and even has money to send to her family. A sailor pays 250 pesos (about $13 U.S.) to her club for her time, she receives 170 pesos of that. When no ships are in, she receives no salary and she is often broke and hungry, along with most of the other women in Olongapo. The women in her bar, however, share what food they have with each other, so no one starves. They are all simply underfed together.

Dee's bar is not fancy, nor is she. She shares the dream of the other 14,999 Filipinas working in Olongapo: to meet a sailor who will love her, marry her, and take her to the States where all will be well and she will be rich, as everyone there is.

Sometimes Dee talks of what she would really like to do—study to be a pre-school teacher. All of her extra money, however, goes to her family, so she cannot save any for the future.

Sometimes, too, she talks of returning to her family. In her more realistic moments she believes that is impossible. Being a prostitute, no matter what the reason, is a cause for shame and embarrassment in the Philippines. Even those families who know the source of the money their daughters send them each month often pretend ignorance. Some families who know where the money comes from accept it, but tell their daughters they never want to see them again. Others, like Dee's, pray for their daughters and try to convince them to leave Olongapo. Dee knows. however, that if she left she would have to lie about her past and that her chances of marrying a Filipino and living a normal life would be slim, since virginity in a woman is highly prized by men looking for a wife here.

Of course, there is much more to Dee than those facts. Dee almost always has a customer when a ship is in, often someone she has known before, a sailor who returns to her each of the two or three times a year his ship is in port. She never forgets any of the men she meets and speaks of them as a sister might talk about a favorite brother. She advises them, washes their clothes, helps them ease their loneliness, and gives them the sex they pay for. Her women friends tell her she is too nice to the men.

Sometimes she wonders about that. "It seems like the women who take advantage of men and steal their money are the ones who get married and go to the States while I stay here. Maybe they're right—I am too nice."

Dee also believes in God. Sometimes when she has no customer she asks us to pray for her to have a man. Other times she says, "I give my hands and heart to God and God uses me. When people say God brings war and suffering, I say, 'No, what God wants for the world is more love.'" Then she says, "I know my work is wrong, but I believe God has never left me."

I bring that statement home with me every night. We hear it, in different forms, from almost every woman we talk with here. I struggle to find a response. Perhaps you can help me.

A part of me, the part I am most comfortable with, wants to affirm what Dee says. I know I could do that with integrity because I came here believing, and still do, that Dee and the others would not be in Olongapo if they were not driven here by poverty. If the United States, my country, removed itself from Filipino affairs and removed our military bases from this country, Olongapo and the lives of the women would be very different.

I am a feminist who believes God wants me to work for liberation for women and other oppressed people, and I know what happens to women here in Olongapo is not liberating. Women are exploited here by the U.S. sailors who pay for their bodies, and by an overwhelming poverty that makes working as prostitutes in Olongapo seem like their last resort for survival. I believe that exploitation is a sin and must be spoken against here and in the United States.

But I also wonder if that response is enough for Dee and the others. Are they also searching for a different kind of response, one that touches them as individuals and affirms them as special, cared for by God?

Certainly they know the evil that lies within the political and economic system better than I do, for they are daily victimized by it. But they also know many Filipinas as poor as they who do not choose to come to Olongapo. They know women who instead choose to sell newspapers and candy at the small stands on every street corner. Women who stay on farms. Women who scavenge in garbage dumps and sell the scraps they find. But Dee and my other friends are here and, once here, leaving seems impossible for them. In light of all that, a response outlining only the structural sins that bring them to Olongapo seems partial, and perhaps even patronizing.

So I find myself struggling with the question of personal sin. I believe sex without commitment is wrong, destructive to those involved. I have little difficulty saying American sailors are sinning here. But what do I say to these women who are becoming my friends?

I find I cannot so easily say to them, "Prostitution is sin. Nice women are not prostitutes." For they are nice women. I feel great caring and love coming from them to me, and I see it at work among them. Often I feel God's presence and grace when I am with them. Not the least, I shrink from telling them I think they are sinning because I know my own relationships are not always healthy.

I wonder, however, if I can say with integrity, "Yes, what you do here is sin, but I believe there is power and healing in naming our sins, repenting for them, and accepting the grace and forgiveness of God?"

Four months in Olongapo of hearing the stories of women, being invited to share their lives, growing to love them. Four months of great joy and confusion. I know now that no matter how the expression of that confusion makes me sound to you who care about justice, it is time to ask for your help. So I share my confusion with you, my sisters and brothers. I wonder if it is possible to search for a response to personal sin in a situation where the structural sins are so obvious and overpowering. How would you respond to Dee's statement: "What I do here is wrong, but I believe God has never left me"?

— ◆ —

Pardon My Fangs

by Karen Osman

Daughters of Sarah, July/August 1987 issue. At that time Karen Osman was a regular contributor of humor to *Daughters of Sarah* and writing her master's thesis on the Buddhist doctrine of non-self.

When I was in kindergarten, Robbie Blakeman pulled a chair out from under me. I apologized.

When I was in grade school, Augie Zinser hit me in the arm because I won the spelling bee. I apologized.

When I was in junior high, Dean Lawler told everyone I was gay because I wouldn't kiss him. I apologized.

When I was in high school, Mrs. Williams got mad at me because Jerry Watkins kissed me on the school bus. I apologized.

When I was in college, I apologized to Bret Johnson because I had breasts. I ran from his car in tears, climbed the four floors to my dorm room and cried some more. Then, as I lifted my tear-stained face to the mirror and surveyed my swollen, blood-shot eyes, something inside me snapped.

"Wait a minute," I said to my trembling reflection. "Let me get this straight. You go out to the movies with this guy, you go for a pizza, come back to the dorm parking lot, reenact the Rape of the Sabine Women in the front seat of his car, fight for your virtue like Pauline in the Perils of, then apologize to the jerk? What in heaven's name is wrong with you?"

That was the wrong question, of course.

The right question would have been. what in heaven's name was wrong with the person who ripped the buttons off my favorite blouse, pinned me under the steering wheel of his car, blamed me for arousing desires in him, demanded satisfaction, then called me a child? That was the real question.

But I was young. There I was, little Miss-Buttons-to-the-Chin-Original-Catholic, about as seductive as your basic ballpoint pen, hating myself because I had breasts.

Breasts, of course, are the root of all evil (i.e. Eve had breasts. Pandora had breasts. Lilith had breasts. I rest my case.)

It was obvious to both Bret and me that men were perfect, and never, under any circumstances, had sexual urges except in the evil presence of seductive female breasts. In other words, we both knew that his actions were my fault.

Well, wipe the blood off my fangs and call me vampire, but at that moment, standing in front of the mirror in my dorm room, I forgot that I was evil incarnate. "Who?" I asked myself. "Who in the history of womankind ever told that man I would stand idly by, take his abuse, and then take the blame for it?"

Then I laughed.

It was me. I was the one who told him that. When I apologized to Robbie, when I apologized to Augie, when apologized to Dean, and when I apologized to Jerry, I had said, "It's all right. Blame me. Make me feel like a worm." I was holding up an age-old tradition. I had taken on the role of the original apple vendor.

As a sex, it seems that we women tend to think it is more demeaning to assign blame than to accept blame for things we never did in the first place. It is, somehow, noble. We say things like, "Gee, Fred, I'm sorry I made you hit me and that I bled all over the new carpet." "Gee, Gary, I'm sorry I'm so ugly and boring that you had to have an affair;" and "Gee, Harold, I'm sorry I'm such a loser that you can't treat me like a human being anymore."

It's as if the female mouth is incapable of forming the word "jerk." We can be Eve, Pandora, Lilith, and Lizzie Borden all rolled into one person, but our men must be made in the image of God. Their blamelessness is our treasure in heaven.

We take blame. Our mothers take blame. Our sisters take blame and we accept it as the status quo. We say: "Why did you let him hit you?" "Why did you let him hurt you?" "Why did you...?"

It's time to stop, to stop blaming ourselves and each other. Before we utter a single word of doubt or recrimination, we need to look down at our own breasts. We need to decide if we see them as beautiful instruments of nurture or a blemish on the image of God.

Illustrations by Kari Sandhaas, published in *Daughters of Sarah*, July/August 1987.

Lessons from Sunday School

by Christine Dubois

Daughters of Sarah, Winter 1992 issue on women and mental health. At that time Christine Dubois was a freelance journalist whose work had appeared in more than forty publications.

Michelle," I said sternly, "if I hear you put yourself down one more time, I'm going to make you stand in the corner."

Her blue eyes widened in surprise. It was obviously not the sort of thing she expected to be punished for in Sunday school. Making students stand in the corner may be an outdated form of discipline, but I was fed up with hearing this bright, talented girl continually degrade herself. Her paintings were "ugly," her achievements were "nothing," her ideas—when she did venture to share them—were "stupid."

I used to think we women were making great strides. That traditional, sexist attitudes were disappearing and a new dawn of equality and justice was just around the corner—if not for us, then certainly for our daughters. But after four months of teaching Sunday school, I'm not so sure.

Last spring my husband Steve and I took the intermediate children (fourth, fifth, and sixth grades) at a local Episcopal church. We had two classes: a boys' class and a girls' class. The differences were revealing.

One day we talked about Jesus' command to love God, our neighbors, and ourselves. The girls had no trouble thinking of ways to show we love God and our neighbors. But when it came to loving themselves, they were stumped.

The boys had no such problems. Their answers were typical for their age—"I'd buy myself a Porsche"—but, unlike the girls, they were comfortable with the idea of doing good things for themselves.

After the oil spill in Valdez, Alaska, we drew masks expressing our feelings about this despoiling of God's creation and discussed what we could do about it. The boys filled the chalkboard with possibilities, everything from "nuke Exxon" to "write to Congress." The girls had a hard time thinking of anything that would help. They felt powerless, immobilized, unable to take action in the face of the enormity of the tragedy.

The classes also differed in the way they responded to our authority. The girls obeyed either of us equally well. The boy would listen to Steve or our male helper, but treated me as if I were invisible. It was a new, uncomfortable feeling. I'm used to being taken seriously, used to being respected. The men I work with may not think that having women in the workforce is a great idea, but they know better than to show it. These boys had learned early that women don't count, but hadn't yet learned the social value of pretending that they do.

The church has changed a lot since I was a child. Today we see girls serving as acolytes and women priests celebrating the Eucharist. Women serve as committee heads and run parish councils. We even have a new nonsexist hymnal where "Rise up, ye men of God" has been replaced by "Rise up, ye saints of God."

How, I asked myself, could these girls still be locked in attitudes of powerlessness and self-hatred? How could the boys have such entrenched sexist attitudes? Hadn't any of them absorbed the gospel message of justice and freedom? Where did they learn to act like this?

The answer, of course, is: they learned it from us. We talk about justice, equal opportunities, the dignity of women, and so forth. Then we go home and do eighty percent of the housework. We're caught in a changing society, and it's no wonder we give our children ambivalent messages.

My mother is mystified when my sister and I talk about our struggle with self-criticism and doubt. "We fought hard so you girls wouldn't have to suffer from those things like we have," she says. "You've had so many opportunities that we didn't."

Girls like Michelle will have even more opportunities than my sister and I did. But they'll struggle with the same demons. We can't assume that our children or their children or even their great-grandchildren will see the society we dream of.

Thousands of years of oppression can't be erased overnight, but we can make progress. Our best hope for change lies not in what we do for our children, but in what we do for ourselves. The way we live will be the loudest message they'll hear.

— ◆ —

Color Me Purple

by Silvia Cancio

Daughters of Sarah, March/April 1989 issue on racism. At that time Silvia Cancio was a doctoral student in sociology at the University of Cincinnati, and a member of the Greater Cincinnati Women-Church.

I am a Cuban-American woman. I am a Christian feminist. This is how I choose to name myself. I have some strong reactions to the term "women of color." I far prefer a longer phrase such as "women of various ethnic, racial, and religious backgrounds." Let me explain.

Over the last few decades, various strands of feminism have wrestled with issues pertaining to the rights of all women in all areas of life. Understanding the experience of minority women is crucial when transforming existing oppressive structures of society.

But feminism was initially born out of a middle-class, educated, mainstream segment of society. Sometimes it was not successful in dealing with issues of race, ethnicity, and class, neither within its own movement nor within society itself. In their efforts to understand the triple oppression of sexism, racism, and classism, feminists have classified a large group of minority women as "women of color." This is meant as a way of expressing solidarity and including them in the feminist movement. I cannot help but wonder, however, if such classification is valid, and if in the long run the consequences will prove negative. Here are some of my objections.

Will the Real Color Please Stand Up?

First, I see confusion about the usage of "women of color." Often it is used to include women of African, Hispanic, Asian, and Native American origins. Other times it refers exclusively to Black women—and is a term with which Black women identify. This is understandable when we look at the civil rights movement, the large number of Black women in higher education, and the vast body of research produced by our Black sisters. Studies of other cultures' minorities are somewhat lagging behind, possibly due to the lesser involvement of other minorities in the women's movement.

If You're Not This, You Gotta Be That

My second and main objection lies in the dualistic nature of this division. By putting women in two categories, we are placing them at ends of a continuum. It is a given in philosophy that classification implies mutual exclusivity. Members of the same group cannot belong in both categories. Simone de Beauvoir in *The Second Sex* makes the point that this classification of "the one" and "the other" is at the core of the division and devaluation of female characteristics.

This is how stratification occurs in society. When we point to differences between categories, we place them in a hierarchical value system, and certain characteristics become more desirable than others. Beauvoir points to the peculiarity of women's situation in that they live in a world where men compel them to assume the status of "other." One can readily see the parallels with our classification of women as "white" and "colored" and the harm this may cause in the women's movement.

Along with the hierarchy of categories comes the problem of language, which reflects the value system of our culture. Our ritual and our terminology tends to develop a life of its own. In our Western culture, white is associated with goodness, purity, and spirituality. The lack of whiteness speaks of evil, ugliness, and the shadowy parts of our beings. Word associations are made unconsciously and lie deep in the transmission of our myths. We may be applying this deeply-rooted symbolism to our categories.

Don't Blur the Richness

Third, it is a given in the social sciences that the broader our categories, the less they explain. We can argue, for example, that "white women" does not say much about the diversity within this category. Their experiences are influenced by class, education, family background, place of birth, sexual orientation, employment, and social networks. And all of these aspects are interconnected.

By the same token, "women of color" does not say much about Japanese or Korean women's experiences. It says little or nothing about what constitutes an Argentinian, a Mexican-American, or a Native American. Both "white women" and "women of color" tend to assume a homogeneity that does not exist. Instead, these terms blur the richness of these women's lives, ignoring their perceptions of themselves and the world.

It is often offensive to be described by others with a term not part of our self-perception. Being raised Catholic, I have often been amused by the division of the world into Catholics and non-Catholics. I have yet to find a Lutheran or Episcopalian who describes herself as non-Catholic. Catholicism is not their point of reference. Similarly, being a "woman of color" is not the point of reference for women of other racial and ethnic groups.

Peach, Olive—or Hispanic?

This concept is further rendered meaningless when we realize we are all women of color, except for albinos. Indeed, where do we draw a line? Where, for instance, do we place southern European women, Jewish or Italian women, who are often quite dark? Or better, how do they perceive themselves? One then begins to wonder if these concepts do not betray hidden and unspoken assumptions.

Using such terminology also introduces an element of confusion between race and ethnicity, as in the case of Hispanics. A couple of decades ago, the U.S. Census Bureau used this term to classify our population into White, Black, and Hispanic. This fostered the notion that "Hispanics" are a race, and that the three classifications are mutually exclusive.

The term "Hispanic" refers to those who speak Spanish or have a Spanish surname, but it poorly describes their incredible heterogeneity. Latin Americans differ from one another as much as the English and the French, the Belgians and the Greeks. A traveler to Latin America would find the continent teeming with ethnically and racially diverse people speaking many different languages.

To Name Is to Have Power Over

In the biblical tradition, naming means to contain and limit, to exercise power over. When we name others, we take away their freedom of self-definition.

Our "either-or" world is a given of our Western mentality. But it does not define the totality of the human experience. The complexity of our lives as women defies simplistic dichotomies.

The women's movement calls us to be truly counter-cultural, to expand our understanding of the world. I believe some ideas, such as the concept "women of color," have outgrown their explanatory usefulness. If our approach is holistic, let us look at what unites us, not at what divides us. Let's look at African-Americans, Mexican-Americans, Japanese-Americans. Let's hear what each has to say, rejoice in our diversity, and drop concepts that may lead to alienation and division. Let's empower women to name their own experiences.

I agree it's a mouthful to say "women of various ethnic, racial, and religious backgrounds." But if it tells us more, why not say it? In the meantime, I intend to color myself purple. It is the color Alice Walker uses to describe the woman experience. It is also the color I turn each time I hear the term "women of color."

What Was That You Called Me?

by Virginia Ramey Mollenkott

Daughters of Sarah, May/June 1988 issue on lesbians. With Letha Dawson Scanzoni, Virginia Ramey Mollenkott wrote *Is the Homosexual My Neighbor? Another Christian View*, updated and expanded in 1994 (Harper San Francisco). Her most recent book, *Omnigender: A Trans-Religious Approach* (The Pilgrim Press, 2001) provides a view of sex/gender orientation that modifies certain statements in this article.

Is it possible to have biblical or ethical reservations about homosexual behavior without being homophobic? As a person who has been engaged in the struggle for gay and lesbian liberation for many years, I think the answer is yes. It is unfortunate that the term homophobia has sometimes been applied to people who are merely heterosexist, or even perhaps accepting, but who fall short of outright approval and affirmation of gay women and men in general. I should like to argue for a more judicious use of terms, a use that would more fairly represent the variety of attitudes gay people may encounter among Christians.

Homophobia

In my opinion, homophobia is a term that should be applied only to those who manifest phobic responses toward homosexuality. A phobia is, of course, an exaggerated and usually inexplicable and illogical fear of a particular object or class of objects. Homophobes are people who suffer from such intense fear of homosexuality that they feel shaken, nauseated, or enraged by the very mention of the topic.

But those of us who have frequently spoken in public concerning homosexuality have discovered that, very often, homophobia is not as inexplicable or illogical as many other phobic reactions seem to be. The causes may be unconscious, but they are not totally illogical. We have found that homophobes are often people who are unsure of their own sexual orientation, desperately trying to deny to themselves the possibility of their own gayness or bisexuality. By attacking, excoriating, or perhaps even killing a person assumed to be gay, homophobes seek to reassure themselves of their own "normalcy."

Heterosexism

By contrast to homophobia, heterosexism is a pervasive social system, a set of attitudes that are so widespread that they seem to be a necessary and universal aspect of reality, and therefore "the will of God." According to the heterosexist thought-system, people must be heterosexual or at least appear to be so in order to deserve first-class citizenship.

A single lifestyle is acceptable as long as due respect is paid to heterosexuality. For instance, if a single woman is asked why she has not married, heterosexist society will tolerate her if she admits ruefully to having a tremendous career drive and expresses sorrow at being forced to forego marriage because of that drive. She will receive full approval if she shrugs and remarks with downcast eyes that, in her case, "Mr. Right" has not yet come along. But she will mar both social and career opportunities if she responds that she is lesbian or that she actually considers herself "married" to a female life-partner.

Heterosexist society denies protection of civil rights to homosexual persons on the assumption that their rights are protected like everyone else's as long as they are "discreet" about their orientation, which is often trivialized by calling it merely a "sexual preference." (A bisexual may prefer to relate to the same sex at one time of life and to the other sex during another period, but a predominantly or exclusively homosexual person is able to relate sexually in an authentic fashion only with the same sex. It is a matter of unchosen orientation, not a matter of whim or preference.)

Getting back to civil rights: the assumption that gay people must be "discreet" is heterosexist because it insists that decent society must appear to be one hundred percent heterosexual. Heterosexual persons unconsciously flaunt their sexuality by public displays of affection, wedding rings, the title Mrs., and constant references to and pictures of boyfriends, girlfriends, or spouses. But gay women and men are expected to keep their orientation and erotic relationships strictly in the shadows.

In fact, if they insist on the integrity of a public recognition of who they are in private, they must forego the protection of their civil and human rights. They become instant outlaws in many states and therefore subject to the whims of law enforcement officers. Except in the few communities that have passed specific gay rights legislation, they can be denied jobs and housing.

On the other hand, if they submit to heterosexism and try to pass as heterosexuals, their personalities and relationships suffer severe strain, and they are vulnerable to accusations of hypocrisy, pretense, and insincerity.

Christian churches play a major role in the heterosexist system. Although many of them support civil rights protection for gay people, most national churches do not practice this basic democratic principle in their own internal policies. Gay people are welcome to become clergy as long as they pretend to be heterosexual, but (ironically) integrity is not tolerated.

Any lesbian woman who publically identifies with her own being and the welfare of gay people (her own people) is promptly evicted from the active ministry or relegated to a special and severely curtailed ministry. A gay man may progress into the highest echelons of his church, but only if he is willing to keep his identity secret. (William Stringfellow told me years ago that he could name forty four gay bishops in the Episcopal Church.)

Another manifestation of "Christian" heterosexism is denial that a person can be both gay and Christian. This is a refusal to believe the gay Christian's first-hand testimony concerning her or his personal experience.

Still another manifestation is the insistence that Christ can and will "cure" the homosexual of his or her orientation. Such "cures," however, occur to people who are bisexual or nearly so, and therefore have an authentic choice of relating to their own or the other sex. There is no evidence that a predominantly or exclusively homosexual person has ever been changed to a heterosexual, and plenty of evidence that certain highly touted "cures" were fraudulent.

Acceptance

Acceptance is the term I would suggest to describe the attitudes of people who are willing to respect the self-definition and integrity of gay Christians, willing to love and befriend them individually, and willing to support their civil and human rights. They feel, however, that they cannot give approval to gay unions because they have biblically based questions about the morality of same-sex erotic relationships.

There are, of course, many resources available to assist people in settling their biblical questions. For Christians, perhaps the most compelling would be Tom Hanks book, *The Subversive Gospel* (The Pilgrim Press, 2000). To the degree that heterosexual Christians really do accept their gay sisters and brothers, they will take seriously the need to achieve clarity about their biblical concerns.

Acceptance is an important term because it is something every parent owes to every child. We cannot know our children's characteristics in advance—not even their sexual orientation. Like Jesus, we must learn to receive the children who come to us. We can try to help them live responsibly and caringly, but we cannot control their essential natures; we can only seek to love whomever God has given into our care.

Affirmation or Approval

On the other hand, to approve of someone else's nature and behavior patterns is to validate them, to sanction them, to take a favorable view of them. To affirm a person is to say, in essence, "You're a valuable addition to the human race. I'm glad you exist. I'm glad you are exactly the way you are." A serious heterosexual Christian must work through all scriptural and traditional objections to homosexual behavior before being able to give wholehearted approval to gay Christian individuals. So, for that matter, must a serious Christian who is gay!

It is no more possible to "approve of homosexuality" in general than it is to "approve of heterosexuality" in general. Some heterosexuals rape other people, or commit incest or child abuse, or make sexual use of other people randomly and without commitment. And a small minority of homosexual persons sometimes commit similar misdeeds. It is impossible for any Christian in her right mind to extend approval to such activities.

But a majority of Christian gay people live lives of great decency, caring, and responsible commitment. To withhold approval (validation) from such people is a function either of heterosexism or homophobia. The point is that approval can never be given to an orientation or a category, but only to an individual life in an individual situation.

Strictly speaking, there is no such thing as a "gay lifestyle," just as there is no such thing as a "heterosexual lifestyle." Attempting to discuss approval of a "gay lifestyle" makes about as much sense as trying to decide whether it is Christianly proper to approve of everything all Italians or Jewish or Irish people do. It is as ridiculous as holding every woman responsible for what every other woman may or may not do.

We dehumanize ourselves and others when we reject or accept people on the basis of stereotyped mental categories. We are not fully defined when we are categorized as black, or as blind, or as gay. We all remain people, and must be respected or otherwise evaluated as the complex individuals we are.

It must be emphasized that supporting someone's civil and human rights has absolutely nothing to do with approval of their ideas and behavior patterns. I disapprove of some of Jerry Falwell's ideas and actions, but I would oppose any attempt to jeopardize his rights as an American citizen. I did not approve of Jim Bakker's irresponsible sexual behavior, but if it ever came to a vote, without hesitation I would vote to protect his civil and human rights. Unless gay people have grossly harmed other people, in which case ordinary laws will apply, surely they as a group deserve the protection extended to other citizens of the United States.

Interaction between Approval and Acceptance

On a more personal basis, I'd like to illustrate some interactions between acceptance and approval. I deeply love and support my brother Bob, but our ideas differ drastically. He feels called to minister primarily to men "because according to the Bible, men are the heads of the home, the church, and society."

This view is repellent and unscriptural to me, for I see Christ as the head of the Christian home and church and as the hope of society. Yet my brother and I are able to recognize each other's sincerity, spiritual commitment, and respect for Scripture. There is no way we can approve of each other's views, but we can tolerate them.

On an affectional level, then, we approve of each other, while on a cognitive level we accept each other by tolerating what to both of us is intellectually intolerable apart from respecting the otherness of the other.

I do not need my brother's approval of my concepts any more than he needs my approval of his. Each of us feels that God has called us to our different ministries, and God's approval is sufficient. Nevertheless, it does feel wonderful to know that we accept each other's differences and approve of each other's sincerity and commitment.

In a democratic, pluralistic society, explicit civil and human rights protection should be provided for every citizen without regard for approval or disapproval of a minority category to which they belong. And in the Christian community, there is no excuse for denying first-class citizenship to gay people who insist on the integrity of a public image that matches their private behavior.

Being one in Christ Jesus does not require that we be all one color or one sex or one class or one sexual orientation. If God created more than one sexual orientation—and how else could people have discovered these differences that they did not choose and cannot change—then it is the church's duty to accept the diversity and individuality of its members.

Affirmation or approval is lovely, but it is in most situations at this time still a luxury. By contrast, acceptance is an urgent necessity. This is not even so much for the benefit of gay Christians themselves as for the health and grace of the church and the peace of the world community.

—— ◆ ——

Fear of Aging: The Beginning of Wisdom

by Kristin Johnson Ingram

Daughters of Sarah, January/February 1991 issue on aging. At that time Kristin Johnson Ingram was from Springfield, Oregon, had published eight books and many articles.

This morning I stood in front of the mirror, trying to comprehend the fact that on the nineteenth of January I will be sixty years old. Immediately, an evil creature thrusts itself in to harass me. This Demon is also a Fool: he trembles before my elder wisdom, hoping to reduce me to babyhood. He invented magazines with "Golden" in their titles, and he calls old women "Sweetie."

The Demon is dangerous because he invites me to see my aging not as a process of lost beauty, discovered wisdom, aching, infirmity, death, dust, and finally resurrection, but as an opportunity to become attractively childlike. The Demon, this dumb spirit that loudly kids and flirts with his elders, would rather rock a baby than try to manage a wise old woman.

In some societies at some times I would have been highly honored for my age. Lamentably, my young friends think the greatest compliment they can offer is denial; the Demon is already activated in them. They try to reassure me: *We would never guess you were **sixty**, Kris. You're the youngest woman we know.*...They don't know how patronizing that sounds. Is sixty something ugly, that I should disguise it?

This isn't the worst of it. The Fool Demon's most destructive activity is Cute.

Give me a few years and the Demon possessed will no longer say of me, *activist or outspoken or high-principled;* instead, they'll say I'm spry and peppery and cute. (In fact, if I live long enough, I'll even be called cantankerous.)

The Demon effected Cute in my own family. My mother had been a widow for some years when someone put her in touch with her high-school sweetheart, a man she'd loved sixty years earlier, and whose wife had died. They married several months after their reunion, and the otherwise-sensible people around them began to coo and hum like idiots.

"Isn't that cute!" they crooned, in a tone one might use while leaning over a bassinet. "Aren't they adorable?"

It wasn't cute, and they weren't adorable. They were deeply in love, a couple who chose in their late seventies to give themselves to that love. Like all married people, they experience physical pleasure and humor and companionship—along with jealousy and inconvenience and fighting over housekeeping or politics. These are dignified humans whose skills and wisdom should be recognized; but the Demon, perhaps unable to stand the very thought of old bodies making love or of white-haired folks quarreling like newlyweds, reduces them to Cute.

Even the people who run our local Senior Center are so chillingly patient and feloniously hearty that I avoid the place. Actually, I try to avoid any place that calls me a Senior or any events with euphemistic names like Golden Opportunities. I don't need to be cheered up or cajoled or kidded; nor do I need some Thirtysomething with a fresh M.S.W. to devise time-killing education or entertainment for me.

These years, this seventh decade and beyond, aren't Senior or Golden or Adorable. They are simply the time that leads toward my end. And the physical process is hard.

Once I could run long distances like the wind, I could almost fly, I could press my bosom against the tape and hear the crowd cheer. Now my bones are brittling, and when I jogged around our neighborhood loop, I chipped my heel. My doctor shook her head and reminded me that at my age I need lower-impact exercise.

Once I could play the piano better than anyone in town. Now my wrists ache and my fingers protest when they try to leap from octave to octave of Schumann or ornament Bach with an inverted trill.

Once I could read until dawn and still make it through the day, I could dance or talk all night, I could easily lift a laughing, twenty-pound infant over my head. Once I was straight as a birch tree, thin as a winter fox, blond as dawn. Now I go to bed earlier and still sleep less; my strength is subsiding. I have begun to bend in the wind of time, to fatten and slump with gravity, and my blondness relies on artifice.

I hate all these aging symptoms: must I wear out before I die? Must I die before I see God?

Wisdom whispers, yes, that as I get closer to the end, yes, I must become more infirm, more dependent on other people, more wakeful in the middle of the night, and more scared. Scared of senility, incontinence, pain—and most of all, scared of seeing God face to face, even though that has been what I have longed for all my fife. The concept of being in the Presence is glorious, the longing for it unassuageable, and the reality terrifying. *What if God doesn't like me? What if I don't like God?*

Yet these fears of aging and death are the beginnings of power and glory and a new kind of humility. Once I danced heedless of time to the altar on Sunday mornings to receive Communion; now I kneel with some terror as I take the Elements, because—at last—I realize what I am doing. Once I was smart; now I am wise as an ancient stone.

My teenage grandson, with his straight teeth and unscathed eyes is not afraid of death: he flies over curbs and curves on his skateboard, helmetless, daring injury, believing he will be young and immune to serious pain forever. Neither is he yet wise.

I was like that once. But somewhere in the past ten years I began to see the terminus of the journey, and my bones shrank with fear of it; my marrow is drying and my eyes have lost focus for fear of it. The picture of myself as a crazed old woman with loose skin on my neck and arms, with raddled face and rheumy eye, lying in my own pee, finally having to experience that terrifying moment that means the end of mortality—this is scary stuff. So if I want to experience aging neither by becoming Cute, nor with neurotic existential despair, the only thing left for me is to let fear lead me to wisdom.

Begone, Demon Fool. For the fears of old age are preparation, teaching me finally to hate this body until I am willing to depart from it, the way pubescent daughters despise their mothers for a while, to dull the pain of leaving and starting their own adult lives. This fear is the shaping of my spirit for death and resurrection; and as I begin to lean toward God with age, I cast out the Demon of Cute and offer my earned wisdom to the world.

A few come to me already: my grandchildren, asking what is a runcible spoon, or how do you find gold, or what are Fibonacci numbers; young writers, burgeoning with talent and energy, begging to know how to calm that raw ability into strings of words that people want to read; friends whose spouses drink too much, or neglect the children, and long to know what to do; neighbors who inquire about how to rid the cat of hairballs or find a wall stud to hang a picture; everyone I know in their forties, wanting to know when I finally made myself happy, and how they can do it, too.

And the more active my fear of dying ugly and insane and the harder I quake at the thought of seeing God, face to face, the wiser I get. Wisdom is a stop on the journey, an opportunity to share my knowledge and anyone's hunger for it.

My friends might be right; maybe I don't look like a sixty-year-old woman. I still wear sneakers and jeans, my ears are double-pierced, and I like some wild music. But time has brought me to the brink of old age, and pushed me in, and I must swim madly toward death and then God, urged on by fear and the other voices of wisdom that went before me.

———◆———

Our Spirituality Is Not for Sale

by Andi Smith

Daughters of Sarah, Summer 1995 issue on racism. Andi Smith is a member of Women of All Red Nations.

The New Age movement has sparked an interest in Native American traditional spirituality among European-American women who claim to be feminists. Indian spirituality, with its respect for nature and the interconnectedness of all things, is often presented as the panacea for all individual and global problems. Not surprisingly, many white "feminists" see the opportunity to make a great profit from this movement. They sell sweat lodges or sacred pipe ceremonies, which promise to bring individual and global healing. Or they sell books and records that supposedly describe Indian traditional practices so that you too can be Indian.

On the surface, it may appear that this new craze is based on a respect for Indian spirituality. In fact, however, the New Age movement is part of a very old story of white racism and genocide of the Indian people. The "Indian" ways that these white, New Age "feminists" are practicing have little grounding in reality.

True spiritual leaders do not make a profit from their teachings, whether it's through selling books, workshops, sweat lodges, or otherwise. Spiritual leaders teach the people because it is their responsibility to pass what they have learned from their elders to the younger generations. They do not charge for their services.

Furthermore, the idea that an Indian medicine woman would instruct a white woman to preach the "true path" of Indian spirituality sounds more reminiscent of evangelical Christianity than traditional Indian spirituality. Indian religions are community-based, not proselytizing religions. There is not one Indian religion. Indian spiritual practices reflect the needs of a particular community. Indians do not generally believe that their way is "the" way and, consequently, they have no desire to tell outsiders about their practices. Also, considering how many Indians there are who do not know the traditions, why would a medicine woman spend so much time teaching a white woman? A medicine woman would be more likely to advise a white woman to look into her own culture and find what is liberating in it.

However, some white women seem determined not to look into their own cultures for sources of strength. This is puzzling since pre-Christian European cultures are also earth-based and contain many of the same elements that white women are ostensibly looking for in Native American cultures. This phenomenon leads me to suspect that there is a more insidious motive for latching onto Indian spirituality.

When white "feminists" see how white people have historically oppressed others and how they are coming very close to destroying the earth, they often want to disassociate themselves from their whiteness. They do this by opting to "become Indian." In this way, they can escape responsibility and accountability for white racism.

Of course, white "feminists" want to become only partly Indian. They do not want to be part of our struggles for survival against genocide, and they do not want to fight for treaty rights or an end to substance abuse or sterilization abuse. They do not want to do anything that would tarnish their romanticized notions of what it means to be an Indian.

Moreover, they want to become Indian without holding themselves accountable to Indian communities. If they did, they would have to listen to Indians telling them to stop carrying around sacred pipes, stop doing their own sweat lodges, and stop appropriating our spiritual practices. Rather, these New Agers see Indians as romanticized gurus who exist only to meet their consumerist needs. Consequently, they do not understand our struggles for survival, and thus they can have no genuine understanding of Indian spiritual practices.

While New Agers may think that they are escaping white racism by becoming "Indian," they are in fact continuing the same genocidal practices of their forebears. The one thing that has maintained the survival of Indian people through five hundred years of colonialism has been the spiritual bonds that keep us together. When the colonizers saw the strength of our spirituality, they tried to destroy Indian religions by making them illegal. They forced Indian children into white, missionary schools and cut their tongues if they spoke their Native languages. Sun dances were made illegal and Indian participation in the Ghost Dance precipitated the Wounded Knee massacre. The colonizers recognized that it was our spirituality that maintained our spirit of resistance and sense of community.

Many white New Agers continue this practice of destroying Indian spirituality. They trivialize Native American practices so that these practices lose their spiritual force, and they have the white privilege and power to make themselves heard at the expense of Native Americans. Our voices are silenced, and consequently the younger generation of Indians who are trying to find their way back to the Old Ways become hopelessly lost in this morass of consumerist spirituality.

These practices also promote the subordination of Indian women to European-American women. We are told that we are greedy if we do not choose to share our spirituality. Apparently, it is our burden to service white women's needs rather than to spend time organizing within our own communities. Their perceived need for warm and fuzzy mysticism takes precedence over our need to survive.

The New Age movement trivializes the oppression we as Indian women face. Indian women are suddenly no longer the women who are forcibly sterilized and tested with unsafe drugs such as Depo Vera; we are no longer the women who have a life expectancy of forty-seven years; and we are no longer the women who generally live below the poverty level and face a seventy-five percent unemployment rate. No, we're too busy being cool and spiritual.

This trivialization of our oppression is compounded by the fact that today anyone can be Indian if s/he wants. All that is required is that one be Indian in a former life, or take part in a sweat lodge, or be mentored by a "medicine woman," or read a how-to book.

The most disturbing aspect of these racist practices is that they are promoted in the name of feminism. Sometimes it seems I can't open a feminist periodical without seeing ads promoting white "feminist" practices with little medicine wheel designs. It seems I can't go to a feminist conference without the only Indian presenter being the woman who begins the conference with a ceremony. Participants then feel so "spiritual" after this opening that they fail to notice the absence of Indian women in the rest of the conference or the fact that there will be nobody discussing any pressing issues in Native American communities. And I certainly can't go to a feminist bookstore without seeing books that exploit Indian spirituality.

Promotion of this material is destroying freedom of speech for Native Americans by ensuring that our voices will never be heard. Feminists have already made choices about what they will promote (I haven't seen many books by right-wing, fundamentalist women sold in feminist bookstores since feminists recognize that these books are oppressive.) The issue is not censorship; the issue is racism. Feminists must make a choice between respecting Indian political and spiritual autonomy or promoting materials that are fundamentally racist under the guise of "freedom of speech."

As long as they take part in Indian spiritual abuse, either by being consumers of it or by refusing to take a stand on it, Indian women will consider white "feminists" to be nothing more than agents in the genocide of their people.

Our spirituality is not for sale.

———— ◆ ————

Chapter 9

Women, Society, & Social Justice

"T"he personal is political." This insight from second-wave feminism enabled women to see their own personal and family lives as part of the web of larger society governed by issues of power and authority.

The first writer in this chapter (page 210) is a linguist who exposed the misguided efforts of the Christian right not only to keep wives under their husbands' authority, but to show them how to enjoy it! Though "chain-of-command" language was more popular in Christian right circles during the 1970s and 1980s, the concept is alive and well. Recently the Southern Baptists, the largest church body in the country, issued a strong statement to wives to "graciously submit" to their husbands' authority. And Laura Doyle propounds a secularized version in *The Surrendered Wife: A Practical Guide to Finding Intimacy, Passion, and Peace with Your Man* (Fireside, 2001).

If indeed the personal is political, then it is not such a far cry from "chains of command" to the plight of growing numbers of women in prison and the resulting fracturing of family life and devaluing of the children, both born and unborn, of these women. See "Choosing Life: For Rich Mothers Only" (page 218).

If the personal is political, then the decision of one young military woman to become a conscientious objector to war at the outset of the Gulf War ripples far beyond her own struggle (page 221). Dorothy Samuel's "Women and Nonviolence" binds the larger concept of women's equality to Jesus' model of proactive peacemaking (page 224).

If the personal is political, then a woman's concern for wholeness and well-being extends to the whole creation. Carolyn Raffensperger notes that men have been making major ecological messes for generations, and "ecofeminists have much to teach men about planet housekeeping" (page 228).

In this chapter, in these women's words, the personal is indeed political.

— ◆ —

Forging Chains of Command

by Linda Coleman

Daughters of Sarah, May/June 1980. At that time Linda Coleman was working on her Ph.D. in Linguistics at the University of California at Berkeley.

Many conservative Christians provide a large market for books and seminars that deal with Christian living on a day-to-day basis. Merging some principles of psychology with traditional interpretations of scripture, these resources make claims about what Christian men and women are like, and how they should relate to each other within family, church, and society.

Everyone is familiar with the Total Woman *phenomenon, both the book which has sold over three million copies, and the seminar which has reached thousands of women.* Fascinating Womanhood *by Helen Andelin, Larry Christenson's* The Christian Family, *Judith Miles'* The Feminine Principle, *and books by Tim and/or Beverly LaHaye can be found in most Christian book stores, along with many similar volumes. Bill Gothard's thirty-two hours of lecture in his Institute of Basic Youth Conflicts often attracts 20,000 people at one time. Seminars for married or soon-to-be-married women abound.*

In the following article, Linda Coleman points out that the presumptions which undergird such materials may not be as theologically or biblically sound as one may assume.

Growing numbers of people are turning to seminars and books like those mentioned above for help and information on living the Christian life. They want to know how to be a Christian woman (or man), how to establish a Christian marriage, and how to raise children by Christian principles. In the process they are absorbing a view of women as exceedingly limited and restrictive.

Why do almost all of the materials on Christian living take such a harsh stance on women?

It is my contention that there are underlying assumptions woven into the fabric of contemporary culture which lead to conclusions about the "chain of command" and woman's submissive role in it. These assumptions are not primarily theological. Instead, they show how biblical interpretations have unconsciously been affected by secular culture.

Illustration by Anna Trimiew, published in *Daughters of Sarah*, May/June 1980.

The Mind as Computer

First of all, Christian living materials, both books and seminars, tend to make broad statements about what certain categories of people are like—men, women, teenagers, etc. Once it is ascertained how each group thinks and responds, sets of rules are given for how to behave toward these categories in order to get the results one wants.

This attitude of over-generalizing was strengthened as computer terminology developed and gave us a new model: the human mind as computer. Clear and concise input results in clear and concise output. If the output is wrong, it can be blamed on improper input.

If so, then it stands to reason that most of our problems are just a matter of a slip in the programming. Since we are still in touch with reality and leading fairly normal lives, this slip may be minor enough that we could even correct it ourselves, if we only knew how. This factor contributed to the growth of more casual forms of therapy. No longer were the only problems worth worrying about those which seriously disrupted one's ability to carry on a normal life, and needed a highly trained psychoanalyst. Rather, people became concerned about minor adjustments in their mental and emotional behavior, easily made if programming was all there was to it.

These assumptions about the predictability of human behavior were rejected by evangelical Christians when first proposed. They sounded too manipulative, too deterministic; not enough room was allowed for free will. However, these very assumptions now form the basis of the teachings of the Christian living seminars and books that are eagerly accepted by many Christians. Fairly simple rules that are said to lead to predictable results are attractive.

Thus, biblical interpretation amounts to little more than a list of the proper inputs and their expected outputs, like the list of answers at the end of a math textbook. Slight concern is shown for differences in individuals, situations and abilities. Everything is translated into "do X and Y will result;" "honor your parents and you will have a long life."

I would suggest that the Bible is much more like the mathematical principles and examples of their use in the body of the textbook, rather than the answers at the back. Given a set of general principles and an example or two, we can see how a problem can be solved. This enhances Paul's words in II Timothy 3:16 about the profitableness of all scripture. A principle is more useful and wide-ranging than a set answer. (Most of the Christian living materials purport to give sets of "principles," however, if we look at these principles, we see that most of them are actually simple rules—more like mathematical equations than general principles.)

The problem with going beyond using the Bible as a book of rules is that it requires a lot of work. One needs some knowledge of the culture in which it was written, a willingness to spend time looking for the intent of the writer, attention to recognized biblical scholarship, and the guidance of the Holy Spirit. It may mean conceding more than one acceptable solution to a problem. How much easier to condense biblical material into a set of simple rules including only those that fit one's presuppositions.

Peace with God

Second, these materials share the goal of secular therapies: tranquility, good relationships, and freedom from interpersonal conflict. The difference is that the secular view holds these outcomes as ends in themselves. The Christian view sees them as a sign of a Christ-controlled life. Conflicts or difficulties mean one is out of touch with the Lord. The inner life of a successful Christian should flow smoothly.

These Christian living materials make a conflict-free and peaceful life a test of success. On the secular scene, this is no problem, since the test is the same as the outcome one was looking for anyway. If you have fewer conflicts, then the therapy intended to give you fewer conflicts has worked. For the Christian, however, this method confuses the test (fewer conflicts, better relationships) with the desired outcome (closeness to God). One needs only to ponder the miseries of Job or Jeremiah or observe Jesus' bad relationships with certain authority figures to question this assumption.

Majority Wins

This leads to the third presupposition I want to challenge. If one is setting up a lot of simple rules, and if the goal is conflict-free family life, then the easiest way to reach it is to have everyone do what they were trained to do—hence, what they do best.

From early childhood, most women, especially Christians, have been conditioned to submit, to attend to others' desires and repress their own. Boys, on the other hand, tend to be taught decision-making, independence and assertiveness. Therefore, if you can encourage people to do what the majority already does best, your success rate will be high, and the majority of women and men will be functioning efficiently. If the minority are discontented, they are viewed as less spiritual than the others.

Add to this the tremendous internal resistance to changing one's ingrained behavior. Women may know that they need to be more independent and assertive, but have never learned to do so. This teaching gets them off the hook. Men know they need to practice submission but resist the painful process of learning. Many people say they were never really happy and fulfilled until they got into "God's chain of command." What has happened, of course, is that they have simply received permission to avoid learning some foreign, and thus difficult, aspects of discipleship.

The easiest way to avoid conflicts and keep relationships running smoothly is to make one person entirely responsible for giving in, in this case the woman. If each partner has some responsibility to submit, more conflicts will naturally arise.

In the above section, I have pointed out three basic assumptions made by the proponents of male-dominance, female-submission. The first is the assumption that it is possible for the human mind and interpersonal relationships to be simple and predictable. The second is that good relationships and lack of conflict are a sign of being close to God. The third is the notion that if there are two or more ways of doing something, the easiest way is always the best.

"Sayin' So Don't Make It So"

The fourth fallacy is basically a problem of semantics. It asserts that a change in the way you refer to something necessarily denotes a change in the thing itself. For example: women are "lower in position" but not "inferior in fact." Women are worth as much as men, but their function and role is different. Men must lead because they are rational, while women are emotional and therefore must not be allowed to be in control, but that does not necessarily put a higher premium on either rationality or men.

Carrying the same logic further: women are to be submissive, but not doormats. They are to be totally obedient to their husbands, but this does not say that they have no will of their own or that they never get to exercise it.

The Christian living materials are full of such statements. I have read the explanations carefully. I am grateful to the many people loyal to the seminars who have tried to explain the distinctions to me. But I have also had many years studying language and communication, and if there is a distinction there, I fail to see it.

These statements are doubletalk, pure and simple. In her gut, any woman knows that a submissive position is viewed as inferior, both in the church and in the world. The teaching of male leadership and female submission subtly but effectively erodes the true equality of worth which men and women have before God and should have in the church. That is why so many women struggle with a poor self-concept.

These semantic shifts keep the Christian living materials ostensibly on biblical ground. But by keeping the letter of the law, the spirit of liberation in Christ is squelched. I doubt, however, that the producers of these materials consciously intend to deceive. They probably figured out that to have women submit was an expedient way to arrive at good relationships and fewer conflicts—and then found scripture passages to confirm these conclusions.

We all want simple answers and predictable responses, and it is a pleasant thought that Christian growth might be so easy. A seminar run with any other presuppositions would fizzle at once. People will not pay good money to be told to make their own decisions, or that things are more complicated than they seem.

Martyrdom and Magic

These simplistic rules also appeal to two other concepts, one typically Christian, one universally human. The Christian idea is that you should expect to have to give in a lot, to have your rights violated, to be somewhat martyred; and that there is a reward for all this. Hence, women come to believe that the behavior required of them is good for them.

The other concept is the instinctive belief in magic. Although we have a society in which magic is not officially accepted, the idea of precise manipulation of people and events by certain specific forms of behavior is still with us. If a particular procedure doesn't work, you have merely omitted the proper gesture or magical phrase. (People who grew up in Christian homes may recall their vague feeling in childhood that if a prayer wasn't answered, the form wasn't correct. One had not been specific enough, or had forgotten to say "in Jesus' name" before the amen.)

The same holds true for the seminars and books. It is a comforting thought that if you followed all the rules and your children still rebelled, it's not that the world works differently from what you had thought. Rather, you probably just didn't apply the rules quite right. This creates guilt. But it's better than feeling absolutely helpless.

The attempt to reduce human behavior to a simple set of rules is based on an unbiblical worldview. The same can be said for the attitudes towards women which accompany the rules. Predictability is vital to this worldview, and predictability can only be achieved if people do only what they have been doing all their lives. This alone severely restricts women, and the restrictions are increased by making the woman primarily responsible—overtly or otherwise—for the success of relationships, as well as for maintaining her own status as a subordinate human being.

———— ◆ ————

Church Custodian:
Practicing What I Preach

by Jo Ellen Heil

Daughters of Sarah, September/October 1989. At that time Jo Ellen Heil lectured in Women's History. She is now a newspaper columnist, children's bookseller, and works in a public library. This article was reprinted from *Tradeswoman,* a magazine for women in blue-collar, nontraditional work.

Illustration by Kari Sandhaas, published in *Daughters of Sarah,* September/October 1989.

"**W**ell, here we are...." His cheerful words trailed off as we stood facing the nemesis of cleaning folk everywhere—the men's urinal. "It helps to do the bathrooms first, get the yucky part over with," he explained. My new boss vigorously grabbed the scrub brush and thrust it into the stained porcelain. I nodded in what I hoped was an experienced manner. He stood aside to let me try my hand. I smiled confidently, told myself, "she who hesitates is lost," and scrubbed away. The custodian of Camarillo Covenant Church had begun her official duties.

In Southern California, custodians are "supposed" to be Hispanic men with limited English skills, not petite, blue-eyed women with M.A.'s in History. Exactly how had I landed this job, anyway?

Our church had been born two years earlier. Since we recognized that God was "an equal opportunity employer," we chose to be too. In my other position with the Superintendent of Schools I enthusiastically worked to promote women in nontraditional occupations. Then the church needed a part-time custodian. It was a perfect time to practice what I preached.

Our custodians, like every other member of the church, had been distinctive individuals. They'd run the gamut from a 69-year-old retired man and a young husband/wife team to a disabled person. And now me—a single woman who'd never seen a urinal before in her life (except for that one wrong turn in the theater...).

Announcing my unique new position to my friends was an experience. My excitement was often met with blank looks of incomprehension or polite pity. One former co-worker, genuinely concerned for my well-being, looked quickly around to see if anyone had overheard our conversation and then asked in hushed tones, "Just how many people have you told?" I was doing physical, semi-skilled labor! They might not have considered themselves mechanically minded, but it was clear they thought they knew just where a screw was loose.

There were advantages, I reassured myself. I could pretty much set my own hours, wear comfortable clothing, and do my tasks in any order I chose. I was not required to answer the phone, nor was the work stressful. The pay per hour was higher than for many of the clerical positions I'd had in the past. When it came right down to it, where else could I exchange an enthusiastic hug from the secretary or play with her good-natured, giggling toddler before beginning work?

Yet I quickly realized that cleaning the church was changing my outlook on life. Potlucks and receptions, the lifeblood of any church's social life, became measured by how many trash bags I filled and lugged to the nearby dumpster. I suppressed a neurotic tendency to follow after people who held half-empty cake plates in their hands. I began to empathize with Hansel and Gretel's wicked stepmother as toddlers left their own little trails of cookie crumbs and mashed Cheerios through the foyer.

Physical hazards, too, were part of my job. But banged ankles and pinched fingers paled in comparison to my twice-weekly battle with The Tree. Sitting by the piano, this oversized shrub added a homey touch to the front of our sanctuary. Duty dictated I carry it to and from the foyer, some distance away, where it received sunlight and warmth. (Unfortunately, it was not trained in the fine art of self-mobility.)

The Tree resisted my every effort. It was as tall as I was, and certainly wider. I refused to be intimidated. Didn't all my plants at home love me? Didn't I have two green thumbs? I talked, cajoled, bullied, and even sang to The Tree, but to no avail. It flipped its branches into my eyes, dropped leaves onto my freshly vacuumed carpet, and dribbled water along my arms and down into my clothes. The Tree even refused to grow in any direction except one, despite a careful rotation in the sunlight. It became side-heavy and a real hazard to the pianist. I could just imagine the workers' compensation report—"Cause of injury: attack by tree."

Yet such hazards did not diminish my satisfaction as I learned new skills. After a thorough cleaning one afternoon, only one task remained before I was finished for the day. Ironically, it was that most feminized chore—making coffee. A brand-new can of coffee sat on my storage shelf, just waiting to be opened and enjoyed after the morning service.

I struggled with the five-pound can and small metal opener. It was unlike my manual one at home. I twisted and turned it in ways its inventor never dreamed of. But no amount of shaking and manipulation was going to unlock its secrets...or the can of coffee.

As I struggled, I attempted to encourage myself. Hadn't I built my home with my father, a union carpenter? And hadn't I just finished using the power saw on the new doghouse that weekend? I was the one who always boasted of women's self-sufficiency; surely I'd be able to open a simple can of coffee. I wondered if Susan B. Anthony was watching.

I heard the scratch of the pastor's pen coming from the office. Sunday's sermon was being prepared. No one else was there; the coffee had to be made. Did I dare interrupt and ask for help? With such a domestic chore? I struggled a bit longer, got more desperate, and realized that asking for help was the better part of valor in this adventure.

"Pastor, would you mind terribly coming to help for a minute?" Together, two pairs of hands attacked the resistant can opener.

"We used to use these when we went camping, " muttered the pastor, peering at the can opener as if to do spiritual battle. "Wait, wait...I think I've got it!"

The can opener connected with the edge of the can, pierced the gleaming metal, and released the aromatic fragrance of fresh coffee with a whoosh. We cheered; I expressed my gratitude.

"Glad to help," she said, walking back to her office. "You know what they say—the best man for the job may be a woman!"

———◆———

Choosing Life: For Rich Mothers Only

by Sr. Margaret Ellen Traxler

Daughters of Sarah, January/February 1988 issue. Sr. Margaret Ellen Traxler is the founder and was, at that time, director of the Institute of Women Today, an organization sponsored by church-related Protestant, Catholic, and Jewish women. One of their major activities is sending teams of skilled professionals to women's prisons on weekend workshops to sponsor self-help groups and provide legal, educational, and medical aid. For more information, contact Institute of Women Today, 1307 S. Wabash Avenue, Chicago, IL 60605; 312-341-9159 or 312-374-3199. The address for the Women's Health and Learning Center of Boston is 20 West St., 4th Floor, Boston, AM 02111; 617-350-5099.

The guards held her legs together in order to forestall the birth of the baby until the ambulance arrived. The expectant mother was a prisoner and her baby was overdue. Typically, there had been no prenatal care for the mother or preparation for the birth of her baby.

This incident underscores the inadequate attention given to pregnancies of women in jails and prisons. Studies funded by the California State Department of Health Services involving 464 incarcerated women in three women's correctional sites in 1985 revealed this chilling statistic: forty-five percent of pregnancies of women in prison resulted in miscarriages or stillbirths.

The same year this study was done Senator Jesse Helms introduced an amendment to an appropriation bill prohibiting federal funds to be used for abortion for prison women. It would seem that Helms could have better used his energies to safe-guard medical assistance to prison mothers who want safe delivery of their babies, rather than address the issue of abortion.

In fourteen years of serving women in jails and prisons, I have never seen a situation where incarcerated women felt they were given adequate medical help for any health need, much less perinatal care. In all instances, I have felt their grievances were justified.

What causes such a high incidence of infant mortality in babies born to prison mothers? The California Prison Match research showed a clear correlation between pregnancy complications and women not having prenatal care and/or being on public assistance. The conclusions drawn by the study, though given with caution, were as follows: "We suspect the following chain of events: low socioeconomic status leads to prenatal complications. Incarceration increases the chances of these complications." In other words, infant mortality is highest when mothers are poor.

Stress and tension appear to be major reasons why pregnant women lose their babies before birth. Teams of specialists from our Institute of Women Today spend weekends with women in many prisons. Nurses take the women's blood pressure, and on any given weekend we find that not one prisoner tested has a normal rate. The blood pressure levels of pregnant women seem especially high. Says Arlene Specht, one of the nurse volunteers, "If anyone in the 'free world' had blood pressure as high as we see in prison, she would be hospitalized at once." In one prison the Institute of Women Today visits regularly, pregnant women must walk up and down six flights of stairs four to five times daily. No vitamin supplements are added to their diet.

Above all, the personal histories of women in prison do not predict healthy pregnancy because most of these women have been early victims of sexual abuse. At one of our recent workshops in a state prison, Shirley showed me a picture of her ten-year-old daughter, Jane. Questioning revealed that Shirley was just turning nineteen and that her father had impregnated her at the age of eight. When I asked who was taking care of Jane while she was in prison, Shirley replied, "My mother and father."

Although stress, poor health, and childhood sexual abuse plague most women in prison, some long-range programs have been designed to redress these unfortunate predictors of failure. One program worthy of national coverage and trial is proposed by the Women's Health and Learning Center of Boston. An Expectant Mothers' Task Force offers comprehensive medical and human services to pregnant prisoners. In a community-based residence, the Task Force provides structure and a supportive environment. A mother is assisted for up to one year, and treatment is offered to her entire family.

In the New York State Bedford Hills Prison program, a baby remains for one year with its mother. The mothers' prison work includes taking parenting classes in aerobics, nutrition, and health care. This is a far cry from prison laws in most states that require a newborn infant to be removed from its natural mother within two days of birth. This prevents adequate bonding and causes trauma to both mother and baby.

Why are women in prison? In Massachusetts, as in most states, it has been documented that the vast majority of women are convicted for property-related crimes. The rise in women's prison population in the past six years is in direct relation to the increasing pauperization of women. According to figures from the U.S. Justice

Department, the number of women in state and federal prisons has increased from 13,200 in 1980 to 26,600 in 1986. (The total state and federal prison population—men and women—increased 66 percent from 1980 to 1986-from nearly 330,000 to over 547,000.) The female population in the New York City Jail increased from 300 in 1983 to 1,200 in 1987; in the Cook County Jail of Chicago it grew from 150 in 1983 to 350 in 1987.* Poverty leads to desperate measures that would not be considered in better times.

The obsession with women's wombs suffered by some men in Congress and by some in organized religions could be expressed more productively by working to protect poor women, especially those who are pregnant. Fanatics such as Helms, Hyde, and the clinic bombers do not serve life constructively. Were congressional leaders to direct help toward programs like those of the Women's Health and Learning Center in Boston, the infant mortality rates in the prison population could improve one hundred percent within one year.

At present our society is telling women, in effect, to choose life—but only if you can afford it.

---

*Female prisoner population has more than doubled from 1990 to 1999. At year end, 1999, 90,688 women and 1,276,053 men were in state and federal prisons. Overall, the U.S. incarcerated 2,026,596 persons at year end 1999—this includes every kind of jail and correction facility in all jurisdictions. The number of women in the United States "under correctional supervision"—meaning either in prison or on parole under all jurisdictions—doubled between 1986 to 1997 from 410,300 to 895,300. (Source: Institute of Women Today)

———◆———

The Phone Call That Changed My Life

by Stephanie R. Atkinson

Daughters of Sarah, Spring 1992 issue on war and peace. At that time Stephanie R. Atkinson was the first female to resist service in the Persian Gulf War. She was hoping to study sexism and its link to militarism at the University of California, Santa Cruz.

On October 10, 1990, at 11:30 p.m., my life was irrevocably changed by an unexpected phone call. My first sergeant from the U.S. Army Reserve unit I had served six years with was notifying me of the unit's activation to Saudi Arabia in Operation Desert Shield. I put down the phone in disbelief. My worst fears were coming true.

I had enlisted in the U.S. Army Reserves in the delayed-entry program at the age of seventeen. I was a successful senior in high school. Although I was active in Beta club, the National Honor Society, and other academic clubs, I had no plans for the future.

In early September I went with a friend to a recruiting station. My friend was interested in joining the Naval Reserve, and I had merely gone along for the ride. When he was refused because of health reasons, the recruiter turned to me.

"And how about you, young lady?"

I was the perfect recruit: good grades, good scores on the military entrance examination—and political naïveté. I was sold on the promise of economic independence and funds for a college education. This was especially appealing to me, since it would release my working-class single mother from financial hardship. I was also motivated to enlist by the idea of protecting American ideals and becoming a productive citizen.

Upon graduation from high school, I went to basic training at Fort Jackson, South Carolina. During the five-and-a-half months of my active duty, the military myth became clear to me and my ideals were shattered. I and other young women were demoralized and berated on the basis of our gender. We were put through grueling mental and physical "exercises" in order to make us "lean, green fighting machines." Physical injury through heat exhaustion and attempted suicides were common fare. I was beginning to feel I had sold my soul.

One of the promises made to me in the recruiter's office was overseas travel. That promise was actualized, but not in the way I had expected. I was not a welcome visitor in these countries. I was a member of an occupying force which destroyed the land in "war games" and adversely affected the people by making them accoutrements to American demands. In South Korea I was especially disturbed by my country's attitude to the people there. An overall disdain and disrespect, especially towards women who were prostitutes, left me with a sense of remorse and shame.

I began attending Southern Illinois University in Carbondale in the spring of 1986, with an interest in English and liberal arts. During my four years at the university, my mind reawakened from its slumber under military dogma. I was exposed to new ideas. I read great works of literature and had philosophy classes in which I examined existential questions like, "Am I responsible for my actions? What is my responsibility to other human beings?"

As I pondered some of these questions, I also began attending protests against Strategic Defense Initiative (Star Wars) research on my campus and against U.S. intervention in Central America. At the time I felt that my activities while not in uniform had nothing to do with my military status. However, it became increasingly difficult for me to set aside my inquisitive student self to meet the demands of the military, even for two or three days a month. I did not realize then that I was beginning to experience a change in feelings known as conscientious objection to war.

After six years of active reserve service, September 24, 1990, had come, and I was celebrating what I believed to be my transfer to inactive reserves. As a member of the inactive reserves, my name would be on a list and I would only be activated if all the active duty and active reserve forces were depleted. What I was not aware of, however, was that a "stop loss order" authorizing the Secretary of Defense to withhold all separation actions of military personnel—retirements, end of enlistment discharges, and transfers to inactive reserves—had been signed on August 22, 1990. Thus, when the call came on October 10, I was not prepared for my order to activation.

I couldn't sleep that night. I began to review six years of my personal history. Had I been sincere in my actions at campus protests? When I refused to qualify with my M-16 rifle on the firing range earlier that year, had I made a stand for my conscience? Did I have enough knowledge and political awareness of the situation in the Middle East to be part of the effort to make war? The memories of people I had helped to exploit merely by my presence on their soil came to mind. This time it would be for real.

After days of preparing myself to go—making a will, packing my gear, notifying friends and family—I came to the decision that I had a moral responsibility to refuse, no matter what the consequences. I thought of the writings of Rev. Martin Luther King, Jr. I remember being taught in Sunday school to ask, "What would Jesus do?" if I ever had any doubt about what was right.

I came to the conclusion that my days as a closet peace-seeker were over. Peace is not a reward that one waits to receive. Peace is a pro-active stance, something we are to take responsibility for and work toward. As King said, peace is not merely "the absence of violence."

I contacted a G.I. civil rights advocacy group in New York. In a decision about my immediate plans, we agreed that I would begin to prepare an application for discharge on the grounds of conscientious objection and that I would not report for active duty. It was also suggested that I take a highly public stand on my case. I began speaking out boldly in New York City, on national television, and in my own small rural community. After a week and a half I was arrested and taken to the personnel confinement facility at Fort Knox, Kentucky. While there I received many letters and phone calls of support from members of the religious community, veterans, and other conscientious objectors around the country. I also received calls from the press about my status, but I was under orders not to speak to the media, or my situation could become "very difficult." After a week and a half I was released with an "other than honorable" discharge in lieu of court martials for desertion and missing troop movement. I have no doubt that without the avid support of the peace community, I would be in the stockade now.

After my release I began to think about how I could wage peace. It was mid-November and the war had not yet begun. I became even more outspoken and seized every opportunity to protest the military build-up, to support the growing mass of other conscientious objectors, and reciprocate the love and support of those who had helped me.

I have just completed an internship with the American Friends Service Committee Youth and Militarism program. While there I learned to become a military counselor and provide support to others still in the military who want to get out. I have worked on the National Campaign to Demilitarize Our Schools, a broad coalition of both national and grass-roots organizations to get to youth before recruiters do. Veterans for Peace has provided me with a touchstone for healing. The group consists of veterans of all eras who seek to abolish war. My life has been changed for the better.

One of the military slogans I remember is "Lead by Example." I no longer attribute that call to action to the military, but rather to the great leaders who have by their examples led toward peace: Martin Luther King, Gandhi, and Jesus. I now attempt to follow in the path of those who bear witness against militarism and violence. I thank these peacekeepers for my new understanding of peace, responsibility, and humanity.

— ◆ —

Women and Nonviolence: A Her-etical Feminist View

by Dorothy Samuel

Daughters of Sarah, Spring 1992 issue on war and peace. Dorothy Samuel, from St. Cloud, Minnesota, was an active worker for peace and sexual equality long before the modern feminist movement organized. She looks back now with no diminution of conviction, but with a new sadness at the equality of temptation for women and for men.

Just as the gospel of Jesus Christ calls men to turn from violence as their automatic response to insult, injury, or threat, so women have come to see that the gospel calls them to turn from subservience as their automatic response to insult, injury, or threat. Christian feminism rediscovered the universality of Jesus' message and example, which made no distinction between Jew and Greek, slave and free, male and female (Gal. 3:28). We are "all one," not only *in* Christ Jesus but equally responsible to Christ Jesus. Both his requirements and his power fall upon us all alike in every facet of our daily living.

The above distinction I have made between men and women in relation to violence is a broad generalization, but I believe few will quarrel with it. There is neither need nor space to quote statistics of criminal participation, enthusiasm for contact sports, purchase and use of guns, and willingness to go to war. Whether by nature or nurture, violence is not instinctive to women in the same way it is to men.

The thesis I wish to examine follows from this assumption of some overall difference between women and men as it relates to violence. For women, the way to full stature in the peaceable realm of Christ is not to imitate the tendencies of men toward threat and violence. Neither, I believe, is it the way of sanitized violence: massed protest, name calling, verbal abuse, bodily interference which counts upon the reluctance of others to do physical harm. The way for women to grow to full maturity is not to become like "natural" men.

The pacifism of Jesus was not the pacifism of "L.B.J. How Many Babies Did You Kill Today?" or even "Bush's War." It is not the pacifism of the little boy Milton Mayer tells about in *Biodegradable Man* (University of Georgia Press, 1990) who explained that he was beating up on another boy because "he does not love like I love." The pacifism of Jesus was of an entirely different order. It was a pacifism that loved the other too much to want to harm, humiliate, or cast out.

Clarence Jordan of Koinonia Farms, Georgia, a man who suffered much under the abuse of neighbors and government, redefined that much abused word "love." Clarence insisted that Jesus saw "love" as all-encompassing good will. It was not silly sentimentalism, not enabling doormatism, not an impossible striving to force ourselves to feel as warmly toward the stranger or intruder as we feel about our intimate family and friends. This all-encompassing good will wants the best for everyone, never rejoices in the harm that comes to anyone, and prays for God's love to surround everyone we meet or touch or read about.

The pacifism Jesus lived and taught was not a separate gospel. It was the result of accepting the one gospel, the good news about Jesus and the coming of a new order. It was not an ethic to be pushed upon those who had not yet entered this new order, this reign of God. It was a flame in those who had been transformed by it.

In John 8 we have an account of Jesus' pacifism in action—in the story of the woman taken in adultery. Here he encounters both oppressed and oppressor, the woman who appears to have been "caught in the very act" and the men who want to keep the law of God by stoning her. Three qualities which are absent in most present day pacifism mark this little story. First, Jesus devoted no time to proving her innocent or guilty. Second, he did not attack the men with fury, physical or verbal. Third, he did not vindicate or excuse her, but gave her the same charge he gave the men: to examine herself, to come into the love of God, to "go and sin no more" (KJV).

Though there is not space here for further exegesis or reference to other thinkers, I want to offer a series of generalizations about the pacifism of Jesus.

First, the renunciation of violence preached by Jesus began on the foundation of the sixth commandment, "You shall not kill." He broadened it to include resentment and rancor against another, and even calling another "You fool." But Jesus was never satisfied with negatives. To him, pacifism was a positive: go the second mile, forgive over and over, actively seek the other's good.

Second, though Jesus lived in a time of great unrest and under military occupation by a foreign power, he supported military violence neither by the Romans nor by Jewish guerrilla resistance groups. He neither threatened nor protested Roman occupancy, nor did he call his followers to resist a violent government. He assumed his followers would not themselves be soldiering—as indeed they did not for two hundred fifty years after his death. As a citizen of Palestine, Jesus refused to challenge armed authority. He told those who used Caesar's currency to pay their taxes with the coin of Caesar's kingdom (Mt. 17:24f). Ultimately, he refused to be defended against the

Jewish police in the garden of Gethsemane. According to Luke 22:51, he even restored the ear of the soldier whom Peter impetuously attacked.

Third, in personal interactions with people, he treated all alike, whether they were Jews, Samaritans, or Romans, including the Roman centurion who begged him to heal his slave (Matt. 8:5f; Luke 7:1f). He gave to all whatever they could receive—healing, food, answers to sincere questions. He called all to faith in God and praised faith no matter where he found it. He did not wait until men had given up soldiering or tax collecting or slaveholding or stoning women before he would recognize them as objects of his love.

Those loving, pacifist behaviors, he seemed to expect, would result from embracing the good news of God's love. Without that repentance and rebirth into God's love, people were naturally involved in violence, greed, and self-interest. That was why he pitied them; they could not understand.

Though Jesus refused to allow his followers to fight the soldiers in Gethsemane, he never preached subservience. They were not to hang around while others cursed them. All-encompassing goodwill is not to invite abuse. Where their invitation to God's love was refused, they were to depart and "shake off the dust of that house or city...." (Matt. 10:14), just as Jesus repeatedly removed himself from mobs who would harm him (Luke 4:29, 30; Matt. 12:14,15).

Nor were they to hang around arguing about the wrongness of others. Jesus did not preach pacifism and nonviolence to mobs who turned against him nor to the soldiers who attacked him in the garden. He did not preach pacifism to authority, to Caiaphas the high priest, nor to Pilate the Roman procurator. These people (like our own government leaders) were still "of the world." They were doing what they could be expected to do, what Jesus himself would do were his allegiance and authority "of this world" (see John 18:36). It was the same with individuals. Jesus did not rail back at the thief on the cross who reviled him, but he did reach out instantly to the thief who called upon him for forgiveness (Luke 23:39-43).

This is the pacifism and nonviolence to which women are called from their history of subservience just as men are called from their history of aggression. We are none of us called to force other people to stop using force. We are called upon to love them where they are, to include them in our all-encompassing good will. This is the pacifism against which we must measure the pacifism of our present Christian feminism.

Has our "Christian love" for the people far away (most recently in Iran and Kuwait) squeezed out any love or compassion for the people in our own government? True, we have not sought to assassinate them, but we have gone no second miles—or even first miles. We have not forgiven them nor prayed for them in love. We have called them far worse names than "fool." We have judged them—oh, how we have judged them!

And in all of this judging, we have held them to standards which have not yet come alive in them—to standards of the gospel whereby it is better to suffer and even to die than to cause suffering and death. "Then they will hand you over to be tortured and will put you to death, and you will be hated by all nations...." (Matt. 24:9 *NRSV*, see also John 15:18-16:4 and John 16:33). Jesus' followers were adjured always to "be not like them" (pagans, Gentiles, those in the world). He did not tell those in the world to be like himself.

In our personal lives as Christian women, we face a degree of violence unrivaled in recent history and different in kind from the pervasive violence to which women were subjected in early centuries. The number of women in the United States who are assaulted, raped, abused, mugged, harassed, humiliated, and discriminated against in public and in the home, whether doing paid work or burdened with unpaid work, has exploded over the last fifty years. Few women today live a lifetime without experiencing some form of violence from some man.

As the Jews of Jesus' day were at the mercy of the Romans, so women today are at the mercy of men. Not every Roman abused individual Jews, and not every man abuses individual women. But the threat, the opportunity, and the institutional protection of those men who do pervades the streets and businesses and homes of our land.

Can Christian pacifists walk these streets and live under this government with the same all-encompassing good will that Jesus manifested? Can we model a pacifism that does not simply do no physical violence but that radiates positive goodwill? Are we ready for a nonviolent pacifism that precludes both the ingrained male response of attack and the ingrained female response of subservience?

Walking among people in an atmosphere of all-encompassing good will often brings us a certain protection, as I documented in my book, *Safe Passage on City Streets* (Liberty Literary Works, 1991). We may touch the man under the stereotypic image of criminal or abuser; we may at least de-escalate violent responses.

But all-encompassing good will eventually brought Jesus to the cross. It was not unexpected by him in the violent world in which he lived. Nor was it unexpected for those numerous executed Christians, male and female, who followed him.

— ◆ —

"All God's Critters Got a Place in the Choir"

by Carolyn Raffensperger

Daughters of Sarah May/June 1990 issue on ecofeminism. At that time Carolyn Raffensperger was an environmentalist working for the Sierra Club in Chicago, Illinois. Her church, Oak Park Mennonite, never uses styrofoam cups.

I discovered the relationship between environmentalism and feminism when I read a single question in a book review that asked, "Would we rape the earth if we called it he?" Several years later I discovered that other women had been thinking about these questions since the 1970s. The women who had been working on this relationship called themselves *ecofeminists.*

Ecofeminism is a philosophy that opposes patriarchy in all its guises. According to Patricia Hynes in *The Recurring Silent Spring* (Pergamon Press, 1989), ecofeminism declares that we live in a world "in which nature and women are presumed to exist for the use and convenience of men, so that the destruction of nature and violence against women are interconnected [and] increasingly technologized." Essentially, ecofeminists have allied themselves with nature in their fight for equality and justice. But forging an identity as a Christian ecofeminist has seemed troublesome for three reasons. The first is that it is hard to get Christians to believe in the urgency of environmental issues—and more importantly, to act on them. I spend endless hours talking to congregations about why they should stop using styrofoam and why they should give a diaper service to new parents at baby showers rather than disposable diapers. Getting them to understand the connections of ecology and Christianity seems like a monumental task, even though the connections are rather apparent.

The second difficulty is that the professional environmental community doesn't spend much time talking about philosophy. The world is careening toward ecological disaster and most environmentalists would rather lobby a politician or plant another tree than discuss philosophical grounds for action.

Third, many ecofeminists believe that Christianity has perpetrated the abuse of women and nature and thus violated the basic tenets of feminism and environmentalism. In spite of their rejection of Christianity, most ecofeminists seek a religious grounding because they believe that life has intrinsic, spiritual value. They have looked for spiritual connections in religious traditions such as the Goddess cult, Native

American spirituality, and Wicca.

Ecofeminists have raised valid concerns about Christianity. And yet I believe that wonderful ideas can arise from the melding of ecology, feminism, and Christianity.

In the Beginning God Created

Creation stories of any culture are often the key to ethical systems. Unfortunately the Judeo-Christian tradition, beginning with our creation story, has been viewed as one of the major philosophical underpinnings for patriarchy. Hence it appears to add insult to injury when it comes to exploitation of women and the environment. Man, so the traditional interpretation goes, was given dominion over the earth. And woman was created as a helper to man. A neat pyramid of importance was worked out where men are right next to God and women are a distant second, ranked just above whales and trees in the totem pole of value. Too often women have tried to use this hierarchical system rather than devise a new, more functional, system. By using the old hierarchy, women and nature end up competing with men.

Women are discovering that if we compete with men, using their ground rules, we lose. We must formulate a new understanding that destroys the hierarchy and forges an egalitarian, cooperative community of connectedness. We all have a place in creation. Elie Wiesel says that our place is one of being guests of God. We are guests— not owners—in our creation home.

I Will Dwell in the House of the Lord

The word ecology is based on the Greek root meaning home. (In current scientific usage it refers to the study of communities of plants and animals.) Home is something women understand pretty well. The communities of plants and animals on this planet comprise our true home. Home requires tending and care, something that, feminists have argued, men often don't really understand. Many studies show women working two shifts, one outside the home and the second at home cleaning up after husbands and children. Few men spend as much time running households as women do.

Our planet home has suffered from the patriarchal mentality that someone else will clean up after men make the messes of doing business. After interviewing the CEO of Exxon following the oil spill in Alaska, one reporter noted that the CEO probably didn't have to pick up his socks at home either. Men have spent generations making messes: witness Bhopal, Chernobyl, and Prince William Sound in Alaska. These men demonstrate that they have little idea about cleaning up, much less what actually constitutes "clean." Ecofeminists have much to teach men about planet housekeeping.

He That Hath Ears Let Him Hear

Traditional language has always reflected the singular importance of human men, while at the same time it tacitly assumes the irrelevance of creatures and creatureliness. It is no accident that we have referred to ourselves (male and female) as mankind and not humankind or, God forbid, animalkind.

In *Buffalo Gals and Other Animal Presences,* (New American Library, 1987), Ursula LeGuin notes that "in literature as in 'real life,' women, children, and animals are the obscure matter upon which Civilization erects itself phallologically." She goes on to say, "Civilized Man has gone deaf. He can't hear the wolf calling him brother—not Master, but brother. He can't hear the earth calling him child—not Father, but son. He hears only his own words making up the world."

The Christian feminist agenda emphasizes nonsexist language, and rightly so. However, we may still be leaving out other creatures, to our own detriment. In order to sing a holy song, the language of the choir must be composed not just of basses and sopranos singing in English. It needs an extravagant cacophony of chirps, squeaks, trills, trumpets, and growls in order to fully sing God's praise. As the wise folk song goes, "All God's critters got a place in the choir." Some biblical passages take this argument even further. Habakkuk 2:11 speaks of rocks and woodwork crying out from the houses of those who through their greed have plundered nations, destroyed lands, and shed blood.

Reconciling Creation

In spite of exploitation done in the name of Christianity, I believe that at its core, the Christian faith can make a unique contribution to ecofeminism. While Christianity and ecofeminism are both philosophies of hope, the Christian gospel also proclaims a theology of reconciliation. For Christian ecofeminists, our hope is to be reconciled to the natural world—both to the earth and to our bodies—through Christ. On the practical level, I struggle to understand what that reconciliation will look like. What does Colossians 1:20 mean that Christ will reconcile to himself all things whether on earth or in heaven?

Specific issues where reconciliation is needed are difficult indeed. Take, for example, technology's role in food production and human reproduction. The production of food, which lies at the heart of nurturance, is often twisted into a declaration of war on the land and its creatures. Each year massive amounts of soil are forever lost through erosion; pesticides are dumped on trees and plants; animals suffer as we cage, cramp, and experiment upon them. Today genetic engineering upon both plants and animals seems an inevitable result of our domination of nature. In the area of food production, how do we Christian ecofeminists look to Christ to reconcile all things to himself?

In human reproduction, biotechnology has reduced our sense of the miraculous in conception and birth. When it comes to abortion, Christian feminists have been wary of a battle where men have made decisions about women's bodies. At the same time we have a gut feeling that life is sacred. By our silence, we have allowed men to make decisions about in vitro fertilization, amniocentesis, and other procedures which violate our bodies and our dignity. In the area of human reproduction there is great need for Christian ecofeminists to work toward reconciliation.

As a Christian ecofeminist, a second and very specific area of concern I have is how we demonstrate lack of ecological awareness in our congregational life by using styrofoam cups and nonrecycled paper. Church congregations could be taking the lead in recycling efforts. Using ceramic or paper cups for social functions can be a small but significant step toward reverent care of God's creation.

A third area where reconciliation is needed is more theological. Word-oriented theologies which now exist in many of our churches are now being challenged by more Creation-oriented theologies. Is there hope for reconciliation of these theologies through Christ who was both called the Word of God and the Source of Creation, and who lived fully within our created world and shared our bread and wine?

There is much I do not understand. What I do know is how greatly our theology is enriched when we learn from the earth itself. This is because creation is the other Word of God, just as significant as the written Word. The poet Seamus Heaney said that landscape is sacramental, to be read as text. It is Word as image, designed for right-brain interpreters. I believe that what creation tells us about God and our own creatureliness is as important as Paul's letter to the Romans or the Sermon on the Mount.

But for now the creation groans in travail and pain because of our blatant disregard for its wellbeing and our attitude that we can use it up. Can we hear this cry of the earth? Can we let its lament join our feminist song for survival and equality? Do we believe that Christ can indeed heal the grievous wounds of all creation?

——◆——

Chapter 10

Herstory

Herstory is powerful and transformative. Since the early days of second wave feminism, the liberation movement that began in the 1960s, women (and some men) have devoted energy to the recovery of women's contributions within history and culture. What they found was a wealth of activism by women throughout history.

Tragically, much recorded history had failed women. Women's stories were for the most part unknown and missing, but with the emergence of *herstory*, recovery began. Conscious-raising became the process for connecting the dots between concepts of equality and personal experience. From such grassroots gatherings emerged the women's liberation slogan, *the personal is political.*

The rich heritage of herstory became the seeds that enabled a small group of Chicago women to see possibilities for change within biblically-centered evangelical and Anabaptist churches. Thus *Daughters of Sarah* was born. I vividly recall the exciting possibilities biographical accounts of nineteenth-century women like Catherine Booth or Katherine Bushnell or biblical women like Phoebe of Romans 16 or the unnamed disciple of Mark 14 brought to my own sense of self.

Members of that early *Daughters of Sarah* group helped shape the agendas of Evangelicals for Social Action, the Evangelical and Ecumenical Women's Caucus, and Christians for Biblical Equality. May the following herstories inspire others to continue to put women's experiences in the center and to remember that conversion to Christian feminism is both personal and social.

—Introduction by Sue Horner, former editorial board member, book review editor, and resource development director for *Daughters of Sarah* magazine. Currently a Visiting Associate Professor of Women's Studies at North Park University, Chicago, Sue is now completing a book on evangelical feminism and pondering fictional renderings of feminist frailties.

— ◆ —

Hooked on Herstory

by Mary Ann Millhone

Daughters of Sarah Fall 1991 issue on herstory. At that time Mary Ann Millhone had recently graduated from McCormick Theological Seminary in Chicago. She has taught church history in Egypt and Iowa. Her research on Julian of Norwich was conducted under a grant from the American Association of University Women. She is now on staff at Face to Face with Diversity.

On my desk is a photo reproduction of a medieval wax seal showing a woman celebrating mass. This enigmatic medieval women symbolizes for me the buried information that women were there—we were *there*—throughout the history of our faith. I keep it to remind myself to continue struggling for the acceptance of women's ordination and leadership in the contemporary church.

Christian women are paying attention to their history. Attend a regional gathering of your denomination and you're likely to find a workshop on the history of the women's missionary movement or a dance performance interpreting the religious experience of colonial, Native American, or slave women. Books on the history of women in Christianity, such as those by Eleanor McLaughlin or Barbara MacHaffie, have made it onto church library shelves. And actors like Roberta Nobleman and Rev. Linda Loving attract crowds that fill sanctuaries and auditoriums as they portray Simon Peter's wife, Augustine's mistress, or Dame Julian of Norwich.

Why do we women need to pay attention to our herstory? I can think of three important reasons.

First, to set the record straight.

Women were there, you know. From Sarah of Genesis to Sarah Edwards of colonial America, we were there. Making visible the shapes of our foremothers helps heal our own personal experiences of being treated as invisible.

It was a full twenty years after acquiring an M.A. in history that I first heard about the fourteenth century Dame Julian of Norwich, one of John Wycliffe's contemporaries. As my research on her proceeded, I found with joy that Sr. Ritamary Bradley and others had made substantial advances in scholarship, not only about Julian, but about other medieval women mystics as well. (Similar strides have been taken for other periods and locations.) We've also learned how much we don't know. Elizabeth Petroff noted in a lecture on women's spirituality at Nebraska Wesleyan University that there are still over two thousand untranslated Latin manuscripts by medieval women literally buried in European monasteries!

Setting the record straight involves dealing not only with the omission of women, but also with the distortion and trivialization of their experience. When I was a graduate student in history, students could infer from what was said about the Puritan Anne Hutchinson that she was "an irrational, menopausal woman." A more feminist assessment sees her as well-educated with theological and rhetorical skills, but a woman who became a threat to established male authority.

Writing women back into history has forced historians toward different lines of inquiry. Rather than emphasizing official church records and treatises of famous theologians, they are searching diaries and archaeological records for clues to domestic and popular religious rituals and art. They are raising new questions. All histories are inevitably a matter of selection and interpretation, and specialists in women's history have called all historians to watch for and state their biases, modeling this themselves.

Second, women need to pay attention to history in order to see more clearly where we are now.

For example, the so-called "traditional" view of "women's place is in the home" is still used to limit women's roles in church and society. Moving out of the domestic sphere, women are told, is unnatural and a reversal of a centuries-old practice.

In reality, the relationship of home and workplace is very different depending on the era, class, and geographical location. And "woman's place" in each of these eras, classes, and locations is also very different. Recent research suggests, for instance, that European women in the Middle Ages had a somewhat wider range of occupations than their Protestant daughters after the Reformation. There is more evidence of medieval women in trades, such as blacksmith, or as merchants—as well as the option of being a nun with its possibilities for a measure of autonomy and power. Calvin and Luther may have increased respect for woman as wife and mother, but this respect also prescribed her activities.

"The Cult of Domesticity" emerged during the nineteenth century, when the Industrial Revolution had separated workplace from home. The home, created by a godly wife, was meant to be an escape from the materialistic world of the factory and marketplace. Ladies' magazines (edited by men) and sermons (preached by men) helped shape these expectations, which were aimed at middle-class white women while ignoring the experience of black women and lower-class factory and domestic workers.

Knowing that such expectations are not necessarily God-given but rather served a particular political function at a particular time and place can have a powerful effect on our understanding of the present. Women and men can better understand that rigid gender roles do not help us exercise our gifts as children of God and only waste individual and group resources.

Third, women need to pay attention to history in order to know where we are going.

Learning our history helps women create new visions for the future. What, for example, can we learn from finding out that women in the church largely withdrew their energies from the suffrage/feminist movement of the late nineteenth century? What did they gain or lose when this happened? Will it happen again in the 1990s? Or will we build coalitions with secular feminists on public issues like the Family and Medical Leave Act? Will we continue to act as if white middle-class Christian women's experience is normative for Christian women of all races and classes?

In an interview at McCormick Seminary in Chicago, church historian David Daniels pointed out two reasons why people with little power are energized by learning about their own history: identity and subversion. When we women recover our herstory, we find out who we really have been—apart from men's definitions—and therefore who we are now and who we can become. And since what we learn is different from the official written record, it has potential to subvert (turn upside down) prevailing practices. Judy Chicago said it even more succinctly: "Our heritage is our power."

—◆—

Our Foremothers: Anna Howard Shaw

by Bonnie R. Borgeson

Daughters of Sarah March/April 1975. Bonnie R. Borgeson was one of the original members of *Daughters of Sarah*. She did the layout for the newsletter for the first several years while she worked with publications at North Park College (now North Park University) in Chicago, Illinois.

"The golden-tongued orator of the women's suffrage movement" reads one description of the Reverend Dr. Anna Howard Shaw. That's one side, certainly the most well-known, of a multi-faceted woman who was, all in one lifetime, a pioneer in America's wilderness, an ordained minister, a medical doctor, a lecturer on temperance, and a tireless co-worker with Susan B. Anthony for "The Cause"— women's suffrage.

Born in England in 1847, Anna emigrated with her family to Massachusetts at the age of four. She received from her idealistic father an education and a freedom unusual for a girl in those Victorian times. He even gave her a hammer and nails as a birthday gift!

Her love of the out-of-doors and physical work enabled her family to survive as homesteaders in the untamed north woods of Michigan. While he stayed behind in Massachusetts and sent money, Anna's father sent his family to live in a crude log cabin he had built. At the age of thirteen Anna dug a well, chopped down trees, and farmed the land she had cleared.

It was in the wilderness that she felt the call to become a preacher. As a girl she stood on a stump and preached to the trees. Her determination to follow her call led her to enter high school at the age of twenty-four, and then move on to Albion College. While at Albion she was licensed as a "local preacher" in the Big Rapids, Michigan, circuit of the Methodist Episcopal Church, where she preached for three years.

In 1875 she entered Boston University School of Theology and emerged in 1878 as its second woman graduate. It was not an easy three years. She was denied many privileges, including cheap food and lodging, because she was a woman. Not only was she always poor and often hungry, she had almost no moral support along the path she had chosen. Her family and friends were strongly against her becoming a preacher. For her fellow-students, she wrote in her autobiography, "…Throughout my entire course I rarely entered my classroom without the abysmal conviction that I was not really wanted there."

Still she persevered. As she once wrote, "Men have no right to define for us our limitations. Who shall interpret to a woman the divine element in her being?"

After graduation she was called to a church on Cape Cod, later taking on a second congregation, ministering to them both from 1878–1884. Not busy enough as pastor to two churches, she entered Boston University again in 1882, this time the School of Medicine. While in medical school she worked in Boston's slums. Her contacts there, especially with prostitutes, convinced her that the only way to improve women's condition was to change the social structure through making laws. From this time in her life stems her interest in women's suffrage.

In 1880 Dr. Shaw sought ordination in her denomination, the Methodist Episcopal Church. After being denied it by several lower authorities, she and another woman, Anna Oliver, took their cases to the General Conference. Again, after heated debate, they were turned down. Dr. Shaw decided to switch allegiance to the Methodist Protestant Church, where a group was anxious to see her ordained. As she explained, "I do not intend to fight my church. I am called to preach the gospel; and if I cannot preach it in my own church, I will certainly preach it in some other church!" And in October of 1880 she became the first woman ordained in the Methodist Protestant Church.

Dr. Shaw left the pastorate in 1885, spending the rest of her life lecturing, traveling, organizing, and working for women's suffrage. The constant companion of Susan B. Anthony for eighteen years, she took over from her the presidency of the National Women's Suffrage Association, which she held for twelve years, almost up to her death in 1919. She died knowing that the nineteenth Amendment was in the process of being ratified.

Although not a pastor after 1885, Anna Howard Shaw saw her whole life as a ministry, living out God's orders, part of his plan and purpose. Her life could be summed up in her own words: "To be a Christian is not merely to be a member of a church, to believe a creed. It is not merely to be born in a Christian land. It is not to believe, it is not an action, it is not an emotion. It is a life."

———◆———

"Try Me!"
Edna Griffin: The Story of a Foremother

by Gracia Fay Ellwood

Daughters of Sarah, November/December 1989. At that time Gracia Fay Ellwood was a poet and writer living in Pasadena, California. She now resides in Ojai, California.

It happened about 1925, when people of a certain range of skin color were either Negroes or niggers, depending on the speaker's outlook. The setting was a passenger train traveling into the southern United States. Black people and white occupied the same coach cars until the Mason-Dixon line was reached. At this point a uniformed Black porter came through the cars calling instructions to all Negroes to move forward.

They knew what this was all about. In the South, Negroes traveled in the Jim Crow car, the one just behind the engine, where passengers either sweltered behind closed windows or choked on the cinders. Separate but equal.

The Blacks in one particular car got up unenthusiastically and began to move forward with what dignity they could salvage. All except one. This one was by no means the most formidable-looking to a quick glance. Twenty years old, small, light-skinned, her features more like those associated with Native Americans than with Blacks, Edna Griffin had the sort of delicate beauty that has long signaled the Weaker Sex.....

The porter stopped by her seat and reiterated his commands. Edna gazed levelly and very un-weakly at him. "I'm very well satisfied with this seat, thank you."

After a moment's uncertainty the porter disappeared, and soon the white conductor bore down on the uppity nigger. "Didn't you hear the order? All Negroes move forward."

With impeccable politeness Edna reiterated, "I'm very well satisfied with this seat, thank you."

This was intolerable. "If you don't move forward we'll stop the train and have you put in jail!" the conductor blustered. Edna's steady look dared him to do it. Of course he wasn't going to let this nigger get away with this...he would.... The conductor too disappeared; the train continued on its way.

Nothing more happened. The early-day Rosa Parks did not get put in jail; the Civil Rights movement still lay thirty years in the future.

I first heard of Edna Griffin from a member of my Quaker meeting. She was described as a retired physician who had cared for Japanese internees during World War II. But when I actually met her, I was literally on my knees apologizing for having failed to give her a promised ride home from Meeting for Worship! From this unlikely beginning came one of the most heartening friendships I've ever had.

Edna was born in Fort Smith, Arkansas, in 1905, to parents both life-giving and able. Her father, born to a slave and her white master, had gained an education and become a Methodist minister. Her mother, powerful alike in prayer and practical matters, continued her leadership of the household when her father was away on circuit and after his death in the 1918 flu epidemic when Edna was twelve.

Edna graduated from Philander Smith College with honors, taught school for a time, and was at work on a master's degree in math at the University of Chicago when she was chosen to be the recipient of a medical scholarship. Denied entrance to the University of Southern California, University of California Berkeley, and other universities by outright bigotry or a tight quota system, she chose Meharry Medical School and was accepted.

An incident near the end of her studies is revealing. It was the last Sunday in May 1932, and Edna had been studying so long and arduously for the comprehensive finals that she decided to relax at a baseball game between the Homestead Grays and the Kansas City Monarchs. She had barely sat down when someone tapped her on the shoulder. It was "Pops" Talbot, her professor of anatomy. "Well, Edna, you must be sure of yourself!" he teased.

Edna sat up straight and looked him in the eye. "Try me!" The following day she scored a ninety-five in his exam.

Not long after becoming Dr. Griffin, Edna married Dr. Albert Heard, whom she had met at Meharry. It was a passionate love match, but was entered upon with trepidations because of early storm warnings. They worked at their marriage during her internship at Tuskegee Institute (where she knew George Washington Carver) and her residency in Evansville, Indiana. But Heard was too badly damaged by his past to be able or willing to deal with his pathological jealousy and violent rages. Edna did not have the benefit of contemporary feminist analysis to tell her that battering behavior is addictive and tends to worsen. But she had a sense of justice. The first time he became physically violent, knocking her against a bathtub and breaking several ribs, was the last and only time. She walked out.

For a time she maintained a separate practice in Evansville, cherishing a hope that the marriage might be repaired. But something intervened—perhaps her own unconscious insight, perhaps evidence of a paranormal gift. One night Edna suddenly heard her mother's voice address her (her mother was in Fort Smith): "You have to get out of this city. Either he will kill you, or you will kill him."

She had no doubts at all. The next morning she went to the courthouse and finalized the divorce. Then she packed her things and set out for Pasadena, California.

Dr. Griffin expected good things from the Pasadena of the 1930s. It was reputed to be the noblest city of the land; there were no Jim Crow laws; Black physicians were much needed. But it did not take her long to discover that Pasadena's corporate sins differed little from those of Arkansas or Indiana. As her biographer Helen Kitchen Branson recounts the story (*Let There Be Life*, 1948), it was only a few weeks after arriving that Edna telephoned a local hospital to make arrangements for an emergency appendectomy, and was assured that a ward bed would be ready within an hour. She drove the patient, a frightened middle-aged Black woman, to the hospital herself.

When the receptionist saw that both physician and patient were the Wrong Color, she began making polite rejecting noises. "I'm sure you understand...." The upshot was that the patient, on the point of rupture, had to be sent to Los Angeles County Hospital twenty miles away. She died before she ever got to surgery.

There were other deaths, many due to childbirth complications, when proper hospital facilities would have made all the difference. Dr. Griffin made innumerable house calls to crowded shacks, often bringing hope and renewed health, and learning to deal with her grief on occasions when her best could not save a life.

For years she worked together with other Black persons in Pasadena to realize the dream of an adequate hospital that would turn no one away. Legal injustices and sometimes opposition from other Blacks made the struggle long and painful. Eventually, thanks to these pioneers and the support garnered by Helen Branson's book, Edna was to see all Pasadena hospitals racially integrated.

She also found time to work for racial justice in other areas. One day while making a house call on a Mexican-American family, she saw a small boy on the front porch, sobbing. To her kindly questions he replied that his brothers and sisters were swimming in the city pool at Brookside Park, but he had been kept out because he was darker-skinned. The feelings of one small boy became the catalyst for a lawsuit. At that time Edna was president of the Pasadena NAACP, which at her urging brought the suit against the city, lost, appealed, and finally won.

Edna also worked toward the integration of churches and restaurants, the latter with the help of a Caucasian friend, Quaker Elizabeth Paige. Each Sunday the two women would make reservations at a restaurant in the name of Dr. Edna Griffin. Each time the restaurant personnel would address Elizabeth Paige as "Dr. Griffin." If any of them failed to seat the two, Edna sued. She won each time.

About 1971 Edna reluctantly retired from her practice, with hearing and vision impaired, though with her skills and her extraordinary mind still keen and vital. Together with a long-time friend and former patient, Olga Boyd, a woman of great spiritual and physical beauty, she bought a duplex. They had planned to each take one of the apartments, but found themselves so compatible they settled down in one and rented out the other.

Doc came to depend heavily on Olga as her sight and hearing deteriorated further, and two strokes greatly limited her movements. Six years Edna's junior, Olga was strong and competent, and Edna cherished both her care and companionship. Occasionally Edna would make remarks to the effect that, "When I go you are to have…" and each time Olga would say, "It isn't written in heaven that you will go first."

In the summer of 1985 Olga was diagnosed with terminal cancer. Her choice was to die at home and it was Edna's choice to provide the essential care that made that possible. By this time Edna's own movements were slow and labored, and even her close relatives were not given to see the heroic proportions of her gift to Olga. Olga died on May 1, 1986. Doc tells me this ordeal, coupled with the death of her faithful doggy companion a few months later, was the hardest thing she has ever had to bear.

I have learned much from Dr. Edna Griffin since my *felix culpa* that launched our friendship, and I keep going back to learn more. What is it like to face the closed ranks of the hostile white male establishment of the 1930s, and not only get in but excel? What is it like to be a professional doctor who, because of color, is sent to the basement to treat her patients or to the baggage car to ride? To move from pioneering and leadership experiences to a state of dependency on one's friends and family? What is the cost to affirm life in all these circumstances?

Each week if possible I go to Doc with some article or book I'm excited about, or that I think will interest her—to share it, hear her often-surprising reactions, and discuss. Most of all, however, I am hoping for the opening of a window into the deeps of her being through which her indomitable spirit will flash out and strengthen mine.

To say "Try me!" to the universe is risky. But in the case of Edna Griffin, the result for the rest of us has been fine gold.

— ◆ —

Decision

by Irene Zimmerman

Daughters of Sarah, July/August 1991. At that time Irene Zimmerman, a School Sister of St. Francis, lived in Milwaukee, Wisconsin, and worked in the International Office of her community. Her most recent book of poetry is *Woman Un-Bent* (Saint Mary's Press, 1999).

We sit inside myself:

I: afraid, unsure,
perching at an inner river edge,
burst out to you at last,
"I know it sounds so grandiose—
I want to write poems
to help save the world."

I: practical, experienced, wise,
look at you with empathetic face.
(How to tell you that the urgency
and pain will go away?
that the world's too large a place
to fill with your small words?
that your hopeful poems will soon deflate—
balloons sticking to themselves?)

I read the writing on my older face.
"That may be right," I nod, jumping in.

Despite it all, I know I have to take
the risk of sending up inflated words.
I have to tell our truth while I have breath.

—— ◆ ——

"And I Was a Man"
The Power and Problem of Perpetua

by David M. Scholer

Daughters of Sarah, September/October 1989 issue on gender roles. At that time David M. Scholer taught New Testament at North Park Theological Seminary in Chicago. He now teaches at Fuller Theological Seminary in Pasadena, California.

On the day of Pentecost, Peter quoted the promise from the book of Joel that in these last days the Spirit would be poured out on both women and men, and both sons and daughters would prophesy. Ever since then the church has struggled to understand how such apparent equality should actually be expressed. In a patriarchal, male-oriented society, how can a woman be empowered for leadership by the Spirit? How does gender affect a Christian's calling and behavior? The story of two martyrs from the early third century provides insight into how the male-dominated Greco-Roman culture of that time interpreted the actions of courageous Christian women.

Perpetua was a young woman of the early church, born around A.D.180. She lived in Carthage in North Africa, where by this time there was a strong Christian community. She was one of the earliest, although not the first, female Christian martyr, dying in A.D. 203 at age twenty-two. Her servant Felicitas was martyred with her.

Our source for this story is *The Martyrdom of Perpetua and Felicitas*, an historically significant document containing Perpetua's prison diary, which describes her four visions. It is the first diary we have from any person, man or woman, from the early church. Some unknown editor, very possibly a woman, edited and published this text.

Given its historical context, many scholars agree that the editor, besides wanting to honor martyrs, is arguing the cause of the Montanist movement. This movement arose in the church around A.D. 175, called itself The New Prophecy, and emphasized the continuing work of the Holy Spirit. The editor's introduction stresses how this document proves that

Saints Perpetua and Felicitas, by Ade Bethune

the present activity of the Holy Spirit—especially as seen through Perpetua's visions—is just as significant as it was in the New Testament period.

The Crisis of Perpetua's Sexuality

The editor tells us that Perpetua had been recently married and shortly before her arrest had given birth to a boy. Her parents are still living, as is one brother, the other having died earlier. Perpetua and her brother are new Christians, as yet unbaptized, though their parents are pagan. The family is wealthy and of high social status.

The diary begins with Perpetua's overwhelming anxiety about caring for her baby in prison and how he will fare. At one point she asks her mother to come and take her son. But she was still breastfeeding him, and later she requests permission from the authorities to get the baby back. They allow her to keep him in prison, and she nurses him again. She is so happy "the prison becomes a palace."

At this point she is rejoicing in her motherhood. But the tension mounts as her father twice visits her to get her to renounce her faith for the sake of her family and son. In chapter six she is taken out of prison for a hearing, after which she records in her diary, "My father appeared with my son, dragged me from the step, and said, 'Perform the sacrifice! Have pity on your baby!'"

Perpetua refuses to do that, so her father then keeps the child against her will. At first she is upset, but then records in her diary, "As God wills, the baby had no more desire for the breast, and so I was relieved of any anxiety for my child and of any discomfort in my breasts." This is the last time the baby is mentioned.

What has happened in Perpetua's pilgrimage from great anxiety about her baby to feeling totally confident that her baby is fine without her? She has transcended her traditional female sexual role and can now play the role of an empowered martyred leader in the church. Her visions, especially the fourth one, further clarify this.

In the first vision, Perpetua receives assurance from God that she will die as a martyr. The second vision shows her dead younger brother suffering in hell. She prays for him, and in the third vision he is drinking the water of life in heaven. This is one of the earliest texts we have about someone's prayers for the dead affecting another's destiny in eternity. Although these second and third visions do not deal with her sexuality, they are further indications of her empowerment as a spiritual leader.

In the fourth vision, Perpetua is in gladitorial combat in the arena as a martyr. Her opponent is an Egyptian gladiator, who represents Satan. She wins, meaning that she defeats Satan and is faithful unto death. A curious line occurs during her account of this combat: Perpetua says, "And I was a man" (10:7). I see this statement as very significant. It represents Perpetua's new identity in that context—by which she transcends her own sexuality to become an empowered leader in the church.

That Perpetua has indeed become a woman of great authority is clear from the editor's praise of her and the care with which the diary was edited, published, and preserved. There is a second diary in this text, written by a man named Saturus (chapters 11-13), which records his vision of heaven. A bishop and an elder are having a dispute that no one can settle, and it is rending the church apart. Then Perpetua comes and settles the dispute. This can be interpreted not only on the level that martyrs were sometimes considered to have greater power than those in church office, but that in this case it is a woman martyr who has power over male leaders.

The Significance of Women Becoming Men

In the ancient world, women were generally considered inferior to men and were put in a subordinate place. Because of the patriarchalism and androcentrism in those cultures, often when women are described as empowered persons, especially in Jewish or Christian traditions, they are described as taking on the characteristics of a man. Was this a put-down, or was it one of the few ways in that context that empowered women could be described? I endorse the latter explanation.

There are two slightly older Jewish texts which pick up on the same motif of a woman becoming a man. Fourth Maccabbees, written in the second half of the first century B.C., depicts a gruesome scene of a mother and her seven sons who were martyred during the Maccabbean War. The mother is forced to watch each son in turn being brutally murdered, and then she is also martyred. The mother is discussed in IV Maccabbees 14:11–17:1. The text points out that mothers are the weaker sex, but then states: "But devout reason, giving her heart a man's courage in the very midst of her emotions, strengthened her to disregard her temporal love for her children" (15:23).

This statement presupposes that a woman is basically a person of emotions, and that her prime role in life is to be devoted to her children. But this mother transcends that by having a man's courage and disregards her mother's love for her children, in order to be a faithful servant of God and the Law. Chapter 15:30 continues, "O, more noble than males in steadfastness and more manly than men in endurance!" In 16:14 the author says, "In word and deed you have proved more powerful than a man," and concludes in 18:23 with "the sons of Abraham, with their victorious mother, are gathered together in the chorus of the fathers. " The only way that male-centered culture knew how to express ultimate courage was to call it manly. In this woman's case, she was seen to be even more manly than a man.

The second example is the first century Jewish text, *Joseph and Asenath*—the story of Joseph's Egyptian wife and her conversion to the true God Yahweh. An archangel appears to her to tell her she can marry Joseph since she believes in the true God. She is wearing a veil as any woman would in those days. The angel says to her, "'Remove the veil from your head, and for what purpose do you do this? For you are a chaste virgin today, and your head is like that of a young man.' And Asenath removed the veil from her head."

This woman has received empowerment from God, since a special emissary from God has come to speak to her. Her sexuality is transcended, symbolized in the text by her virginity and by the fact that she takes off her veil. Like a man, she is receiving the direct message of God through the archangel.

Examples from Christian Texts

It is not clear whether the Coptic *Gospel of Thomas* came from the first or second century. It contains one-hundred-fourteen sayings of Jesus. The very last one depicts Mary (Magdalene?) coming to Jesus and the male disciples. Peter tries to keep her away and says there is no place for a woman in the kingdom. Jesus rebukes Peter and invites Mary to become a disciple if she would become like a man. Again, I believe this text does not mean to put down Mary. This is her empowerment to be a disciple.

A popular story in the second century was *The Acts of Paul and Thecla*. Thecla converts to the Christian faith and follows Paul and wants to preach like him. He tells her she's not ready yet. Eventually she is baptized, cuts her hair short like a man, and wears a man's clothing. Then Paul allows her to join him, and later she goes on her own successful preaching mission.

Thecla becomes very prominent in the ancient church. People make pilgrimages to visit holy places where she had been, and churches are built in her honor.

That this document was written not to put down women, but rather to empower them can be seen in the reaction of one contemporary church father, Tertullian. He did not think women had the right to teach, and he explicitly condemns this document on the grounds that it does support the right of women to teach and preach.

In his four sermons on Perpetua, St. Augustine did not miss the significance of Perpetua's declaration that she became "like a man." In his first sermon, he says, "They [Perpetua and Felicitas] are indeed according to the inward man neither male nor female, so that even in them that are women in body, the manliness of their soul hides the sex of their flesh."

From the second sermon: "For where the sex was more frail, there is the crown more glorious. Truly toward these women a manly courage did work a marvel, when beneath so great a burden their womanly weakness failed not…. [Christ] made these women to die in manly and faithful fashion who for their sakes did mercifully vouchsafe to be born of a woman." Though Augustine's view of women was fairly misogynous, he is expressing very well this understanding of the early church that women were women on the outside but could become men on the inside.

Significance of These Texts for Feminist Reflection

Some scholars have interpreted Perpetua's story—as well as other material about women being like men in antiquity—in a very negative way. One example is Sue Maitland, from her essay, "Women's Experience" (*Sex and God: Some Varieties of Women's Religious Experience*, [ed. L. Hurcombe; Routledge and Kegan Paul, 1987]). Maitland sees this as capitulation, and that these women have ultimately given in to sexism and misogyny and cannot be heroes for twentieth century feminist women.

However, a number of feminist scholars, such as Rosemary Reuther, Ross Kraemer, and Virginia Burrus, have spoken of Perpetua as a hero. I would agree with them that Perpetua is a positive example of women's empowerment in the early church. This empowerment was usually expressed, in the Jewish and Christian tradition, in terms of these women becoming "like a man."

I might add, though, that because the ascetic tradition was so strong at that time, men also were often perceived as empowered when they renounced sexuality. In the case of a man, this was due not to androcentrism, but to a general negative view of sexuality, sometimes taking extreme forms in Gnostic and ascetic movements. In the New Testament, however, such sexual renunciation is not pursued vigorously at all.

Perpetua illustrates how empowered women were often described in the ancient church, which was very patriarchal and androcentric. From our twentieth-century perspective, such descriptions violate our sense of the integrity of one's sexuality. The question we face is, what is the relationship between empowerment and sexuality for us? My vision would be true to Paul as stated in Galatians 3:28 and elsewhere: the Spirit can empower both women and men without the need to deny one's human sexuality.

—◆—

Catherine Booth: Co-Founder of the Salvation Army

by Lucille Sider Dayton

Daughters of Sarah, July/August 1978. Lucille Sider Dayton was the founder of *Daughters of Sarah*. Biographer citations in this article are from *The Life of Catherine Booth*, by Frederick St. George de Lautour Booth-Tucker, (NY: Revell, 1892).

"Woman has a fibre more in the heart and a cell less in the brain," argued William Booth in a letter to his fiancee, Catherine Mumford. Catherine denied this. She insisted that lack of training and opportunity were solely responsible for woman's secondary place in society. If given a chance, woman would be found equal to man on *every* level. Unless William would change his mind, Catherine threatened, the engagement would have to be broken. Gradually William began to acquiesce. It was the clear logic and wit of Catherine herself that changed him. Although he had been called "the most talented and brilliant Methodist of the day" and is today considered *sole* founder of the Salvation Army, in Catherine Mumford he met his equal.

Born January 17, 1829, in Derbyshire, England, Catherine began to read at three. Before she reached twelve she had read the Bible from cover to cover eight times. Her biographers laud her precocious moral development and early identification with the oppressed. One day at age nine she was skipping down the road when an appalling scene caught her eye: "A prisoner [was] being dragged to the lock-up by a constable. A jeering mob was hooting the unfortunate culprit.... Quick as lightening Catherine sprang to his side, and marched down the street with him, determined that he should feel that there was at least one heart that sympathised with him."

At twelve she defended the Temperance Movement in letters to editors of journals disguising her name lest they learn she was a child. And in her father's parlor she debated with intellectuals of the day the pros and cons of the Movement. She entered school at twelve, devouring every book she could find. Illness, which kept her in pain most of her life, stopped her formal education two years later, but Catherine continued to study. She loved theology and her notes reveal she had grappled with the deepest theological problems by the time she reached sixteen.

Five years later she met William Booth, a Methodist minister. In their first meeting they debated the temperance issue and clashed sharply. Their friendship developed but their difference continued to cause problems. Only after William was persuaded to become a teetotaler would Catherine consider marrying him. The other problem, of course, was William's view of the inferiority of women. On both points he capitulated, and three years later, in 1855, they were married.

Meanwhile Catherine encountered opposition to her views about women on other fronts. At age twenty-four, she wrote to her pastor protesting his statement that Satan found woman "the most assailable of our race." Inferior training, not inferior nature, was woman's problem: "Her training from babyhood…has hitherto been such as to cramp and paralyse, rather than to develop and strengthen her energies." Catherine insisted that while the Fall subjected woman, the New Testament restored her to her original position of equality: "In Christ Jesus there is neither male nor female, and the promise of the outpouring of the Spirit is no less to the handmaidens than to the servants of the Lord."

A year later, in her first published article, she took up the question again: "Let the female converts be not only allowed to use their newly awakened faculties, but positively encouraged to exercise them. Let them be taught their obligations to work in the vineyard of the Lord, and made to feel that the plea of bashfulness, or custom, will not excuse them from Him Who put such honor on them." Women were "last at the Cross and first at the Sepulchre" and testified first to His resurrection, though few dared to believe them. "Oh that the Church would excite its female members to emulate their zeal and remove all undue restraint to its development." Catherine reminded her readers of the degeneration of the Methodist Church since its beginning, for Wesley, the founder had encouraged women to be leaders and ministers.

At this time Catherine had no aspirations to lecture or preach. But only three years later on December 7, 1857, she wrote to her father: "I went to hear a popular female lecturer, and felt much encouraged to make an attempt. I only wish I had begun years ago. Had I been brought up amongst the Primitives, I believe I should have been preaching now." Soon after this Catherine began to lecture, though she still hesitated to preach. On December 23 of the same year having given her first lecture, she wrote: "Indeed, I felt quite at home on the platform, far more so than I do in the kitchen!"

In the next three years Catherine gave birth to two of her eight children. Starting while they were still very young, she tried to break the stereotypes that forced them into certain moulds. "I have tried to grind it into my boys that their sisters were just as intelligent and capable as themselves. Jesus Christ's principle was to put woman on the same platform as men, although I am sorry to say His apostles did not always act upon it." She instilled into her daughters pride in their family name and when married they retained it, hyphenated it with their husband's and thus became Booth-Tucker,

Booth-Clibborn, etc.

During this time, Catherine was influenced by a woman lay evangelist from America, Phoebe Palmer, who had just written *The Promise of the Father*, which argued the right of women to preach. A leading minister was appalled to hear Palmer and responded with a pamphlet which violently attacked on scriptural grounds the right of women to preach. Catherine was enraged and within the week produced a thirty-two page response. She described Jesus' humane and liberating attitude toward women and unfolded the work of the prophetesses in the New Testament. She argued that at Pentecost "The Spirit was given to the female as to the male disciples and this is cited by Peter...as the peculiar speciality of the later dispensation. What a remarkable device of the devil that he has so long succeeded in hiding this...but the time of her deliverance draweth nigh."

The principles laid down in this pamphlet became the foundation on which the Salvation Army was built. From the beginning it insisted on the equality of men and women. It emphatically declared that "no laws can be good in effect that profess to care for and guard the interests of one sex at the expense of the other." Women in the Salvation Army were admitted to all ranks including those which had authority over men. In 1934 Evangeline Booth, daughter of Catherine and William, was elected to the highest office in the Army, that of General.

Soon after the pamphlet was written, Catherine, in a religious experience during an illness, promised to obey God whatever that might mean. She found what that meant a few Sundays later, when, after her husband's sermon, she felt God telling her to go to the pulpit and confess her call to preach. She went and preached, and after that moment, her biographer declares, "It became impossible for her to turn back. She had scarcely resumed her seat when, true to his nature, Mr. Booth pounced upon her to preach at night. She could not refuse. The people were delighted. They overwhelmed her with congratulations. Her servant, who was at the meeting, went home and danced around the kitchen table with delight, calling out to the nurse, 'The mistress has spoken! The mistress has spoken!'" That evening the chapel was packed to the doors and the people sat on the window sills. News spread quickly about Catherine's preaching and she soon received more invitations to preach than she could possibly answer.

William became sick soon after this and Catherine took his place in the pulpit. She wrote to her mother: "William is of course very pleased and says he feels quite comfortable at home minding the bairns knowing who was supplying his place." When William did not get better for some time, Catherine not only preached but she also carried out all of his duties as Superintendent of the circuit of Gateshead.

Catherine and William grew increasingly dissatisfied with the Methodist Church for its insistence that they remain pastors rather than evangelists. When the church conference in 1861 suggested a compromise, Catherine, recounts her biographer, was overcome with indignation: "Rising from her seat, Mrs. Booth's clear voice rang through the Conference as she said to her husband, 'Never.' There was a pause of bewilderment and dismay. Every eye was turned toward the speaker in the gallery. The idea of a woman daring to utter her protest in the Conference produced little short of consternation.... Her 'Never' seemed to penetrate like an electric flash through every heart.... Mr. Booth sprang to his feet and waved his hat in the direction of the door. Heedless of the ministerial cries of 'Order, order' and not pausing for another word, they hurried forth, met and embraced each other at the foot of the gallery stairs, and turned their backs upon the Conference, resolved to trust God for the future...."

Catherine and William travelled all around England after their break with the Methodist Church, with Catherine conducting special meetings for women. During their Cornish campaign she entreated 2,500 women: "Resolve that you will be original, natural human beings, as God would have you, resolve that you won't be squozen into this mould, or into that, to please anybody; that you will be an independent woman, educated and refined by intercourse with God; but be yourself, and do not aim to be anybody else."

For several years Catherine worked with her husband, but then she decided to strike out on her own, thereby "doubling their power for good." Crowds of men and women thronged to her meetings. At Hastings 2,500 attended nightly. In Portsmouth, London, the crowd averaged 1,000 for 17 consecutive weeks. Some attended just to hear a woman, for her advertisements read, "Come and hear a woman preach." But it was more than curiosity that sustained the interest of her listeners. "Mrs. Booth possesses remarkable powers as a preacher," the Chatham newspaper in 1873 reported. "With a pleasing voice, distinct in all its tones, now colloquial, now persuasive, she can rise to the height of a great argument with an impassioned force and fervour that thrills her hearers. Quiet in her demeanour, her looks, her words, her actions are peculiarly emphatic. She can, indeed, 'suit the action to the word, the word to the action.' And yet there is no ranting—nothing to offend the most fastidious taste—but much to enchain attention. The matter is full, the manner excellent."

Catherine was at ease with the rich as well as the poor. William had been reluctant to tackle the intellectuals of London until her success there convinced them in 1865 to open a mission which became the Salvation Army in 1878. Catherine preached to royalty and did not hesitate to lobby with Queen Victoria for changes in oppressive laws. She fearlessly castigated the wealthy for their irresponsibility to the poor: "Mr. Moneymaker may keep scores of employees standing wearily 16 hours per day...and on salaries so small that all hope of marriage or home is denied to them."

At a time in England when the poor were without allies, Catherine and William Booth joined them. They opened inexpensive clothing and food stores; they started programs for prisoners, giving them the option of prison or a Salvation Army agency; they built orphanages for the homeless children, homes for unwed mothers, food and shelter depots for transients, labor bureaus for the unemployed; and they fought to change oppressive laws. Through mass meetings and a petition with 343,000 signatures, the Salvation Army was responsible for the Criminal Law Amendment which raised the age of consent in the white slave traffic from thirteen to sixteen.

Catherine continued to preach and write (authoring half a dozen books) for the rest of her life. When she died with cancer at age sixty one, all of England mourned. Fifty thousand people filed past her coffin. William reflected at her death that she was indeed the Army Mother. Other religious organizations had Fathers as guides and authorities but God, in his wisdom and mercy, gave the Salvation Army a Mother as well as a Father. While William was the creative organizer, Catherine had the critical and analytical intellect. To the end of her life he had embarked on no important enterprise without her advice. Today Catherine Booth's place in the founding of the Salvation Army is usually ignored. But at her death her co-founder husband recognized the place that was rightfully hers.

Catherine Booth not only gained for herself a position hitherto unknown to women but she fought for the freedom of all women. "She was to the end of her days an unfailing, unflinching, uncompromising champion of woman's rights," declared her son-in-law biographer, Booth-Tucker (*The Life of Catherine Booth*, Revell, 1892). "One half of her mission consisted in resurrecting the buried talents of her sex, the other half in humanizing...the spiritual, in bringing religion out of the vague...into the area of practical politics." And though much too idealist, he claimed: "When an unprejudiced posterity distributes its award, surely no secondary place will be allotted to her who fought and won the Waterloo of woman's equal right to serve and save, cancelling the absurd monopoly of man, and banishing the perpetual and inglorious exile, the dicta of prejudice and pride."

— ◆ —

Gospel Music Mothers

by M. J Rinderer

Daughters of Sarah, Fall 1991 issue on herstory. M. J. (Nikki) Rinderer is president of Writing Technologies, Inc., a Chicago-based firm providing writing workshops and services to business, professional, and non-profit organizations.

Thomas A. Dorsey, composer of the well-known gospel hymn "Precious Lord, Take My Hand" is considered the father of gospel music. But in looking back at the history of gospel, it is apparent that without the mothers of gospel there would be no gospel music child.

And what a child it is—a child with an uncommon ability to communicate the power and joy and vitality of the gospel of our God. For me, there is no music that communicates the passion of God nearly as well as gospel. My white, middle-class evangelical background acquaints me all too well with sappy anemic ditties mincing around "The joy of the Lord is my strength." But the gospel singers shout it out: "The JOY! JOY! JOY! of the L O R D is MY STRENGTH!!!" In the words of James Baldwin in *The Fire Next Time*:

> *There is no music like that music, no drama like the drama of the saints rejoicing, the sinners moaning, the tambourines racing, and all those voices coming together and crying holy unto the Lord. There is still, for me, no pathos quite like the pathos of those multi-coloured, worn, somehow triumphant and transfigured faces, speaking from the depths of a visible, tangible, continuing despair of the goodness of the Lord. I have never seen anything to equal the fire and excitement that sometimes, without warning, fills a church, causing the church, as Leadbelly and so many others have testified, to rock.*

We owe the existence of this glorious child to the gospel mothers. Patti LaBelle, in her Public Broadcasting System special called "Going Home to Gospel with Patti LaBelle" (which aired Sunday, March 31, 1991 at 8 p.m. on WTTW Channel 11 in Chicago), suggested the following women as gospel mothers: Sallie Martin, Willie Mae

Ford Smith, Mahalia Jackson, Roberta Martin, Sister Rosetta Tharpe, and Clara Ward. They are a few of the important women that gave voice to this music and brought it into the world for all to hear.

In this article I'd like to introduce you to these women, magnificent communicators to whom we owe the glory of gospel music. But I'd also like to do something else. For me, gospel music has been one of the avenues by which I've become aware of my own lack of understanding of Afro-American history and culture. Bell Hooks has suggested that it is less than optimum for Euro-American people to write about Afro-American history, and there are many reasons why this is so. However, writing about something is one of the best ways to learn about it, and if racism is ever to be truly undone in this world, white people are going to have to learn more about black history and the need that the white person has for people of color. The study of black female gospel singers is a tiny and sometimes stereotyped piece of that history, but these women have carried an important message to me that I think is worth sharing with you.

In Chicago in 1932, Thomas A. Dorsey was trying unsuccessfully to peddle some new sheet music he had written that he called gospel. It was an integration of the blues styles he had learned from women such as Ma Rainey, Ethel Waters, and Bessie Smith, with the spirituals that had been popularized across the nation by pioneering groups such as The Fisk Jubilee Singers, The Tuskegee Institute Singers, and The Pace Jubilee Singers in the late 1800s and early 1900s. Dorsey's new music was not easily accepted. Many people considered it the voice of Satan that came out of the lives of the blues "sinners" and not enough from the lives of the spirituals saints. But Sallie Martin, a young Christian woman in the Holiness Church, saw the possibilities of this music, and in 1932 she teamed up with Dorsey and they began to get gospel music out. They were a good team. In the words of Viv Broughton,

> *If Dorsey was the creative inspiration, Sallie Martin was the promotional genius. She was no great shakes as a singer's singer, she never could hit the sweet high notes nor could she seduce with the low resonating moans of a gospel blues, but she knew that rare art of charging up an audience out of her own strength of conviction and very little else.*

The two of them appealed to the youth who were quick to get in on this joyous, vital music, and they organized the first National Convention of Gospel Choirs and

Choruses. Gospel music was on its way.

The second female pioneer to team up with Dorsey was Willie Mae Ford Smith. Willie Mae was one of a family of thirteen children born in Mississippi and raised in Memphis, Tennessee, as a devout Baptist. Unlike Sallie Martin, Willie Mae could sing. Dorsey thought she had the vocal power to surpass even Bessie Smith, and in 1932 she also joined Dorsey and began to give voice to his music. Her job with Dorsey was to organize the Soloists Bureau for the National Convention, and in that role she became the mentor and inspiration for many of the great female gospel singers that were to follow.

Among these disciples of Willie Mae was a twenty-one-year-old singer in Chicago's Greater Salem Baptist Church Choir named Mahalia Jackson. Mahalia had left her home town of New Orleans at the age of sixteen and came to Chicago determined to find an outlet for her already powerful voice. Willie Mae recognized Mahalia's genius and encouraged her to leave her work in a small beauty shop and establish herself as a singer. By May of 1937 Mahalia had cut her first album and was well on her way to becoming the world's best known and favorite gospel singer of all time. Mahalia also partnered with Dorsey for awhile after Sallie Martin stopped working with him in 1940, but by 1946 she was back doing her own albums and establishing herself as the first superstar of gospel. She was also the first gospel singer to take her music to the white audience, a move which earned her considerable criticism among some of her black colleagues.

Another woman who joined the leading edge of gospel in the thirties was Roberta Martin (not related to Sallie). Roberta was as popular as Mahalia Jackson in the black community and was responsible for forming one of the first popular gospel groups, The Roberta Martin Singers. Roberta was especially popular in Chicago, considered to be the seat of black gospel music in America.

In many ways, these four women are truly the mothers of gospel music. But the picture of early female gospel would not be complete without a look at two of their important descendants. Sister Rosetta Tharpe (born Rosetta Nubin in Cotton Plant, Arkansas) first sang before an audience at the age of six, and she quickly became one of the most popular women in gospel. She was one of the few gospel singers to be successful both in the nightclub circuit (with the Cab Calloway Orchestra) and in church. By gospel's golden age in the 1950s, Rosetta was drawing crowds to her gospel concerts of as many as 25,000 people. She was one of the more individualistic of the early gospel singers and was known for having her own style as well as for her ever-present guitar.

The other popular prodigy of gospel's golden age was Clara Ward. In 1943, when Clara was fourteen, her mother Gertrude introduced her at the National Baptist Convention in Philadelphia, and Clara was an instant hit. Clara's group, The Ward Singers, was the most successful female group in gospel for over twenty years. The gospel preacher and singer James Cleveland said about Clara Ward,

I watched her carry gospel into many, many places where it hadn't been before and it hasn't been since.... Many young persons who were inspired by her as I was will pick up and carry on like Clara would have wanted them to.

One of the places Clara carried gospel to where it hadn't been before was the middle-class suburban high school I attended in California. Clara and the Ward Singers rolled up the drive to my high school to perform in an all-school assembly, and I was assigned the duty of escorting them to the room that would serve as their dressing room, then to the gym and back again afterwards.

What I remember most about being with these women was a sense of astonishment at their power, their presence, and their raucous and teasing good humor. I had previously had very little contact with black people, and they scared me to death. But I couldn't forget them, and I later skipped school and found a way to get to Disneyland because I knew they were performing on stage there. I remember Clara spotting me in the front row and waving to me—a skinny little naïve white girl who she had no cause to remember, but she did. Clara Ward stirred something in me and I have never forgotten it. But what was it, and what did it mean?

Brenda Salter McNeil, in a talk at LaSalle Street Church in Chicago on "Biblical Models for Racial Reconciliation" (October 14, 1990) spoke of the fact that when confronted with issues of racism, many white people ask the question, "What can I (we) do to help?" Her response to that question is that "we need to need, not help." Similarly, *The Other Side* magazine has a T-shirt for sale with the words of an aboriginal woman printed on it, "If you have come to help me, you are wasting your time. But if you have come because your liberation is bound up with mine, then let us work together."

We need to ask ourselves what we need this person of another race or color or ethnic background for? How is our liberation bound up with theirs? Clara Ward and the mothers of gospel music have shown me that I need them for many things. I need them because they broaden my sense of God's power and release me from my sometimes pale and constricted forms of worship. I need them because they show me what Dr. Toinette Eugene meant when she said, "I had such a good time in church, it was a sin" (Evangelical Women's Conference, July 1990). I need them because they show me what it means to have joy in the face of sorrow and oppression and to have personal strength because of my relationship with God. They have made me aware that, in fact, "my God is too small. " Sister Thea Bowman, F.S.P.A., Ph.D., in her introduction to the African American Catholic Hymnal, *Lead Me, Guide Me*, "The Gift of African American Sacred Song," says, "Black sacred song is soulful song—holistic, participatory, real, spirit-filled, life-giving." And a holistic, participatory, real, spiritfilled, life-giving approach to God is something I need.

The six women we briefly looked at in this article spread the gospel of Jesus Christ through their powerful music referred to simply as "the gospel sound." And they paved the way for other black female singers of many musical genres: Aretha Franklin, Ruth Davis, Dinah Washington, Albertina Walker, Bessie Griffin, Marion Williams, Shirly Caesar, Dionne Warwick, Vanessa Bell Armstrong, and Patti LaBelle, to name just a few.

Alice Walker once commented that it was through singing that Black women's creativity was kept alive through all the years when reading and writing were punishable crimes for black people, and the possibility of painting or sculpting did not exist. What if singing too had been forbidden? Walker remembers the voices of Bessie Smith, Billie Holiday, Nina Simone, Roberta Flack, Aretha Franklin, and others, and cannot imagine what would have become of her heritage in the dreadful silence and loss. I'm thankful too that these voices have not been muzzled. I'm thankful for the richness of their spirituality and what they have taught and continue to teach me about God.

—◆—

Illustration by Kari Sandhaas, cover art for "Prophecy" issue, *Daughters of Sarah*, Summer 1992.

Benedicte

by Mary Zimmer

Daughters of Sarah, November/December 1990. At that time Mary Zimmer lived in Louisville, Kentucky, and wrote guided imagery meditations on women in the Bible for use in public worship or private reflection.

May the God of Eve
 teach you to dance.

May the God of Hagar
 bring you comfort in the desert.

May the God of Miriam
 bring companions to you when you struggle.

May the God of Deborah
 teach you courage for your battles.

May the Christ who knew Mary and Martha
 show you the way of balance.

May the Christ who healed the bent-over woman
 heal your pain.

May the Christ of Mary Magdala
 send you out to proclaim your story.

In the name of Christ
 who is the memory, hope, and authority of the future. Amen.

———◆———

Editors' Biographies

RETA HALTEMAN FINGER lived in Chicago and participated in the *Daughters of Sarah* collective from 1976 to 1994, serving as editor from 1979 to 1994. During that time she also studied New Testament and received her doctorate in theological studies from the Joint Program of Garrett-Evangelical Theological Seminary and Northwestern University, in Evanston, Illinois, in 1997. Since 1995 she has been teaching New Testament at Messiah College, Grantham, Pennsylvania.

Reta has two sons and two grandsons and is a member of the Mennonite Church, USA. Besides her family and friends, her passions are reading, travel, swimming, and understanding the Bible through the lens of women's experience.

KARI SANDHAAS' lifework has been an interweaving of art, theology, education, and social justice. She was *Daughters of Sarah's* art director, illustrator, and editorial board member from 1987 through 1994. Inspired by *Daughters* and other feminist writers to dive deeper into the study of feminist theology and ethics, she earned her MTS at Garrett-Evangelical Theological Seminary in Evanston, Illinois. During that time she juggled a three-hour commute to Evanston from her home in central Illinois, two Chicago-area jobs, parenting her daughter Loretta, as well as graduate school. Through her work as director of the women's center at Garrett, she received the Myrtle Saylor Speer Award for outstanding contributions to women in ministry.

She is currently creative director for The Laurasian Institution, a non-profit international education organization, and the Teleologic Learning Company in Atlanta, Illinois.

Back Issues of Daughters of Sarah Magazine

Some back issues of the magazine are still available. Below is a listing of issues containing articles and poetry related to each of the chapters in this book. Back issues are $1.50 each or ten for $10. Send order and check to Reta Finger at Messiah College, One College Avenue, Grantham, PA 17027; or email inquiries to lfinger@messiah.edu.

Chapter 1 WOMEN IN SCRIPTURE — Feminist biblical analysis pervades all issues of *Daughters of Sarah*, with one or more articles devoted to some aspect of it. See especially: Jan/Feb 1984, Jul/Aug 1984, Jan/Feb 1985, Mar/Apr 1985, Jul/Aug 1985, Jul/Aug 1988, Nov/Dec 1988.

Chapter 2 GOD AS SHE — on women's spirituality and images of God:
May/Jun 1981, Nov/Dec 1985, Nov/Dec 1987, Nov/Dec 1988, Jul/Aug 1989, May/Jun 1990, Nov/Dec 1990, Fall 1995.

Chapter 3 WOMEN IN MINISTRY — on women in ministry:
Mar/Apr 1977, Jan/Feb 1979, Jul/Aug 1986, Sept/Oct 1986, Nov/Dec 1989, and Spring 1993.

Chapter 4 WOMEN, THEOLOGY, AND RELIGION — on feminist theology:
Jul/Aug 1984, May/Jun 1987, Jan/Feb 1988, Jan/Feb 1990, Summer, 1992, Fall, 1994.

Chapter 5 "OUR BODIES, OUR SELVES" — on body image and sense of self:
Jul/Aug 1981, all of 1982, May/June 1985, Sept/Oct 1985, Nov/Dec 1985, Sept/Oct 1989, Jan/Feb 1991, Fall 1992, Winter 1993, Fall 1993, Spring 1995, Winter 1996

Chapter 6 WOMEN AND ABUSE — on violence against and abuse of women and children:
May/June 1982, Jul/Aug 1987, Sep/Oct 1987, Jan/Feb 1989, Jan/Feb 1990, Spring 1992, Winter 1993, Summer 1994.

Chapter 7 WOMEN, LOVE, AND FAMILY — on women and family relationships:
May/June 1979, Sept/Oct 1979, Mar/Apr 1981, Nov/Dec 1982, Sep/Oct 1986, Mar/Apr 1988, May/Jun 1988, Sept/Oct 1988, Jan/Feb 189, Winter 1992, Fall 1992, Winter 1994.

CHAPTER 8 WOMEN AND HUMAN RIGHTS — for issues engaging the *isms:*
Jul/Aug 1979, Nov/Dec 1980, Jan/Feb 1981, Jul/Aug 1981, Nov/Dec 1983, Jan/Feb 1984, Mar/Apr 1984, May/Jun 1984, Nov/Dec 1986, Mar/Apr 1989, Mar/Apr 1990, Sep/Oct 1990, Jan/Feb 1991, Mar/Apr 1991, May/Jun 1991, Summer 1993, Spring 1994.

Chapter 9 WOMEN, SOCIETY, AND SOCIAL JUSTICE — for further social issues:
Mar/Apr 1980, May/Jun 1980, Nov/Dec 1981, May/Jun 1986, May/Jun 1990, Spring 1992, Winter 1993.

Chapter 10 WOMEN AND HERSTORY— highlighting herstories
Nov/Dec 1975, Jul/Aug 1976, Nov/Dec 1976, Jul/Aug 1977, May/Jun 1978, Sept/Oct 1978, Nov/Dec 1978, Mar/Apr 1979, Sep/Oct 1980, Sept/Oct 1984, Nov/Dec 1984, Mar/Apr 1986, Jan/Feb 1988, Jul/Aug 1988, Jul/Aug 1989, Mar/Apr 1990, Fall 1991, Winter 1995.

Index

Index to Scripture References

Index of Contributors

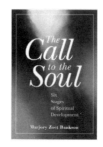